An Introduction to Communications for the AS/400

SECOND EDITION

**JOHN ENCK AND
RUGGERO ADINOLFI**

A Division of
DUKE COMMUNICATIONS
INTERNATIONAL

Loveland, Colorado

Library of Congress Cataloging-in-Publication Data

Enck, John, 1956-
   An introduction to communications for the AS/400 / by John Enck and Ruggero Adinolfi. — 2nd ed.
     p. cm.
   Rev. ed. of: An introduction to communications for the AS/400 / by Ruggero Adinolfi.
   ISBN 1-882419-30-8 (pbk.)
   1. IBM AS/400 (Computer) 2. SNA (Computer network architecture) I. Adinolfi, Ruggero. Introduction to communications for the AS/400. II. Title.
   QA76.8.I25919.A35 1996
   004.6'145—dc20
                                                    96-4518
                                                             CIP

Published by DUKE PRESS
DUKE COMMUNICATIONS INTERNATIONAL
Loveland, Colorado

Copyright © 1993, 1996 by John Enck

All rights reserved. No part of this book may be reproduced in any form by any electronic or mechanical means (including photocopying, recording, or information storage and retrieval) without permission in writing from the publisher.

It is the reader's responsibility to ensure procedures and techniques used from this book are accurate and appropriate for the user's installation. No warranty is implied or expressed.

This book was printed and bound in Canada.

ISBN 1-882419-30-8

2 3 4 5 6 7 WL 0 9 8

In memory of Ruggero Adinolfi

Mr. Adinolfi, the primary author of the first edition of this book, was well known in Italy and Europe for his work in the field of telecommunications and networking.

Table of Contents

PREFACE IX

CHAPTER 1: Introduction to Data Communications 1
Network Components 1
Network Topology 3
Analog Transmission 5
Modems 7
Digital Transmission 8
Transmission Speed 9
Other Network Components 10

CHAPTER 2: Communications Fundamentals 13
Transmission Techniques 13
Peer and Master-Slave Relationships 15
Line Protocols 18
The SDLC Line Protocol 19

CHAPTER 3: Types of Networks 23
Public Networks 23
Private Networks 25
Token-Ring and Ethernet LANs 26
Wireless and FDDI LANs 26
Summary 27

CHAPTER 4: OSI Reference Model Architecture 29
The OSI Model 30
OSI Functional Layers 32
Measuring OSI 35

CHAPTER 5: Systems Network Architecture 37
VTAM 38
Logical Units 41

CHAPTER 6: PU 2.1, LU 6.2, and APPN 45
LU 6.2 46
APPN 46
Connection Services 49
Directory Services 49
Routing Services 49

Differences Between PU 2.1 and APPN 51
SNA-APPN Relationships 51
Future IBM SNA and APPN Direction 52

CHAPTER 7: Networking Roles 59
The AS/400 as Host and Server 62
The AS/400 in Medium-Sized Networks 62
The AS/400 in a Large or Mixed SNA Network 63
The AS/400 in an OSI Network 65
The AS/400 in a TCP/IP Network 66
The AS/400 in a DECnet Network 67

CHAPTER 8: The AS/400 as Host and Server 69
5250 Terminals and Printers 69
ASCII Terminals 70
3270 Terminals 70
Point-of-Sale Terminal Support 71
AS/400 Banking Terminal Support 71
PC Workstations and Client/Server Connections 72
A Problem: AS/400-X.25-PC DOS Connection 74
Fax Services 75

CHAPTER 9: Communications in APPN 77
Execution of Remote Commands 77
Display Station Pass-Through (DSPT) 77
Distributed Data Management (DDM) 79
Distributed Relational Database Architecture (DRDA) 80
File Transfer Support (FTS) 80
Intersystem Communications Function (ICF) 80
SNA Distribution Services/Object Distribution Facility
   (SNADS/ODF) 84
Electronic Mail Distribution 85

CHAPTER 10: Traditional SNA Networks 87
3270 Emulation 88
Communications Between Programs 89
CICS on the AS/400 89
Distributed Data Management (DDM) 89
Remote Job Entry (RJE) 90
Bridge Multiple Virtual Storage/Virtual Machine (MVS/VM) 90
Banking Monitor 91

Host Command Facility/Distributed Host Command Facility
  (HCF/DHCF) 91
NetView/Distribution Manager-Distributed System Node Executive
  (N/DM-DSNX) 92
Network Management 93

CHAPTER 11: OSI 95
OSI Functions 96
IBM OSI Products 96
Electronic Messaging Systems 97
The X.400 Standard 98
UA and MTA Functions 99
Sending the Message 99
X.400 Protocols 100
Directory and Security 100
X.400 Summary 101
Communications Among Incompatible Systems: Standard and Non-
  Standard Solutions 101
OSI vs. SNA 105
The Future of OSI 109

CHAPTER 12: TCP/IP 111
TCP/IP vs. SNA 115
TCP/IP Implementation on the AS/400 115
AnyNet 117
AS/400-RS/6000 Communications 118
AS/400-to-RS/6000 Communications via Third-Party Solutions 119

CHAPTER 13: The AS/400-DEC Connection 121
Digital Network Architecture (DNA) and DECnet Summary 121
The AS/400-DEC Connection: IBM Tools 123
The AS/400-DEC Connection: DEC Tools 123
The AS/400-DEC Connection: Third-Party Solutions 124
Heterogeneous Networks and File Transfer 125

APPENDIX A: AS/400 Network Entities 127
Creating Network Entities 128
Modes and Classes of Service 130
Some Examples of Network Entity Definitions 130

APPENDIX B: Application Synchronization 135

GLOSSARY 139

INDEX 187

Preface

For business enterprises, the importance of communications — and of data communications in particular — is growing steadily. Increased use of online applications on mainframes, midrange systems, and PCs accompanies this expanding business computerization. As the need to access these systems increases, the networks they attach to must expand to meet the need — local-area networks must be interconnected and wide-area networks must reach out into even the most isolated regions of the globe.

The AS/400 is no exception to this trend. The set of communications capabilities designed into the AS/400 is particularly rich, and the system's flexibility and communications software support the AS/400's use as a host in many environments: in a network of dependent downstream terminals, in peer-to-peer relationships with other midrange systems, as a distributed system in traditional IBM SNA networks, in heterogeneous connection with other non-SNA or non-IBM systems, and as a server in a client/server network.

To be able to evaluate the AS/400's system applications capabilities and its potential for expansion, you must understand the communications concepts that lie at the base of all these network environments and how these concepts apply to the AS/400 in particular. Few conceptual guides have existed to help those in data processing prepare for future AS/400 developments and new application potentials. Such a guide is truly needed, because many people — even experts in data processing — stop listening when data communications is discussed.

Part of the problem is the modern communications scene itself. By necessity, it is a broad, wide-ranging area that includes a number of challenging technologies, such as integrated digital networks; optical fibers used in large geographical and local-area networks; client/server relations and products; heterogeneous networks and TCP/IP; various communications standards; the OSI model; proprietary architectures such as IBM SNA; public and private X.25 networks; frame relay; the prospect of new applications made possible by these innovations and by the decreasing costs of the components. When faced with the complex puzzle created by these many options, people often have trouble trying to integrate all the information into a coherent whole.

The idea behind this guide to AS/400 communications is to help you do just that by clarifying general data communications concepts and those concepts that belong specifically to the AS/400. After reading this guide, you should have a clearer understanding of your system's applications possibilities and be better able to plan the use of your AS/400 for online applications.

We have tried to keep the discussion at a high level, both to avoid boring the non-specialist and to highlight the concepts, which are what matter most to the non-experts. Once the concepts are clear, you can find and clarify your understanding of the details in specific manuals (the contrary is not true: Reading some of the many operating manuals does not help much if the basic concepts are not clear).

To meet the goals outlined above, this book discusses the following topics:

- the basics of data communications
- the purpose of line protocols
- types of networks
- the Open Systems Interconnect (OSI) model
- IBM's Systems Network Architecture (SNA)
- IBM's Advanced Peer-to-Peer Network (APPN) architecture
- the roles an AS/400 may play in a network, with particular focus on the AS/400
  — as a central host and server
  — as a peer (APPN) system
  — in a mainframe (SNA) network
  — in an OSI network
  — in a TCP/IP network
  — in a DECnet network

Given the total scope of networking, the AS/400 is a remarkable step forward from the traditional IBM offerings for online communications systems. With the AS/400, IBM communications systems no longer must be managed by a restricted number of highly qualified experts, but instead can be used by a large number of people with less technical expertise. And, thanks to the breadth of its communications functions, this system can be connected easily into a wide variety of network types. In short, the AS/400 combines ease-of-use with powerful network functions to create a unique and highly sophisticated system for today's business enterprises.

CHAPTER 1

Introduction to Data Communications

We live in the age of information. Individual and enterprise productivity and profitability depend on the tools available for accurate, effective information processing and management and the tools available for efficient communication. Computer networks combine these two sets of tools.

A computer network is a set of computers, terminals, and printers connected via a set of transmission lines. The computers can be of any kind, from the most powerful mainframes to the smallest PCs. Furthermore, the transmission lines can be of different types and capabilities, the most common being, even now, standard telephone lines. By means of such networks, which can cover short distances or very large geographic areas, users can gain access, via terminals and via applications, to processing resources and interact with them, regardless of the related distances and the particulars of the sites.

This independence allows an organization to choose the system most suitable for the task at any given location: The network allows any authorized user to access any resource connected to the network. Another advantage of networks is that systems can be specialized: One computer can be used for scientific applications, another one for commercial applications, and so on. Networks also allow for the immediate update of any database in the network. In this way the information made available via the network to users is always current.

Figure 1.1 is an example of a simple network: a line connecting two computers. The computers can be of any kind — a midrange and a PC, for example, or any other couple. The figure shows that there is usually only a single connecting link — a telephone line, for example (there are exceptions to this). This single line can be used for two logical connections (or dialogues or sessions) — a dialogue between the application APA1 on the first computer and the application APB1 on the second computer, and a similar logical connection between APA2 and APB2. The two logical connections use the same physical link. The applications exchange commands and data with each other through specific READ and WRITE instructions.

NETWORK COMPONENTS

The components of the network are often called Data Terminal Equipment (DTE) and Data Communications Equipment (DCE). DTE is the user's equipment (terminal or computer) at the end of the line whose task is to send/receive and process data. DCE is the component between the DTE and the transmission

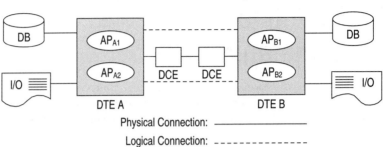

FIGURE 1.1
A Network with Two Computers

line whose task is to receive data from and send data to the DTE. The DCE does this by adapting the data transmission to the characteristics of the line. In the case of a telephone line, the DCE is a modem; for a digital line, the DCE is a Data Service Unit (DSU). On a given line, the connected DTEs can be of different types (a computer and a terminal, for example); but each one uses a DCE, and all DCEs on the line must be of the same type.

Applications only need to know the rules necessary for the correct interaction with each other (e.g., when to transmit, when and for how long to receive, if the interruption of the other is possible). These rules are called protocols. For its part, the application, using the correct application protocol and the READ/WRITE instructions, handles the data transmission and reception over the line. The actual transmission of the data is not, in any case, a direct task of the application. There are, indeed, other components of the system; for example, line adapters, which are responsible for receiving data from the application and for the data transmission on the line. This function is achieved through the use of other transmission protocols.

Several levels of protocols, which are related in a hierarchical structure, include at the lowest level the protocol responsible for transmitting or receiving binary bits to or from the line, and at the highest level the application protocols. In the configuration shown in Figure 1.1, the line connects two DTEs only; in this case, the line is called a point-to-point line. This configuration is the easiest to manage. What is transmitted is always addressed to the other end and, additionally, the line is always ready to transmit what the user has prepared. Sometimes, as in the case of long distances, the cost of these lines is far from insignificant.

Thus, various DTEs usually are connected to the same line to economize; for example, a computer and two, three, or more terminals. This configuration, called multipoint or multidrop, does present a problem: Only one transmission at a time is possible on a standard telephone line; therefore, a rule must be established to determine which terminal can transmit. This is a task of the computer, the "master" on the line. The master allows the terminals to transmit or receive in the two directions only one at a time. The transmission is always from (to) the "slave" terminal to (from) the computer, but never between two terminals. The service to the user is slower than in the case of a point-to-point line because when a message is ready, the terminal generally has to wait some time before receiving the authorization from the computer. The waiting time depends mainly on the traffic present on the line. For this reason, you cannot connect too many terminals to a multidrop line. Furthermore, the computer has the additional task of cyclically offering the terminals the right to transmit and receive.

The transmission flow can be in one direction only (simplex), in both directions simultaneously (full-duplex), or at alternate times (half-duplex). The simplex mode is rarely used in data transmission (it is used with receive-only teletypes, for example, to receive news). Even when data appears to flow in one direction only, as in the case of an application used to record employees' time of arrival at the work site via badge readers, the sending device must always be informed whether the transmission has ended with or without errors, so bidirectional communications are required to provide the positive or negative acknowledgement.

The half-duplex mode is typical of conversational terminals (or stations emulating them). First they send an inquiry, then they receive the answer; then they can send a second inquiry, and so on. In contrast, full-duplex mode is typical of communications between two computers and essentially means communications in two directions of two streams of data that are not directly related to each other. For example, while the first computer is sending a file of collected orders, the second is transmitting a payroll file. But today the full-duplex mode can be very efficient for personal workstations, too; a PC, for example, can have two active conversational sessions and while it is receiving data for the first session it can use the same full-duplex line to send data in the second session.

The physical link also has a bearing on half- and full-duplex transmission. In the case of a normal telephone line made of a single twisted pair (two wires), the transmission can be half- or full-duplex, depending on the distance and the modem used. Furthermore, a full-duplex line using one twisted pair effectively works at a slower speed than a full-duplex line with two twisted pairs (four wires), because the four-wire link can accommodate two distinct simultaneous transmissions, one in each direction.

NETWORK TOPOLOGY

Topology refers to the geometric form of the connections between the network components. The different types of topologies differ in terms of connection reliability, performance, and cost. The most common topologies are shown in Figure 1.2.

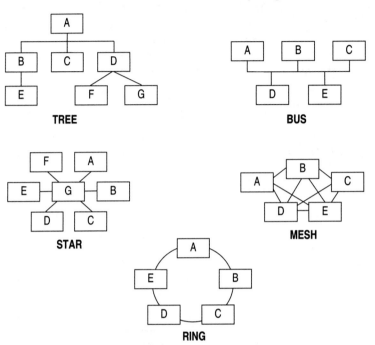

FIGURE 1.2
The Most Common Network Topologies

Tree or Hierarchical Structure. This network structure has a central point, generally the most powerful system in the network, responsible both for the applications most of the connected stations use and for network management. Connected to the central system can be both end-user stations and secondary-level nodes. These nodes run applications at the departmental level and connect other workstations and/or nodes. Traffic flows from the remote station toward the intermediate or top systems. Connections between end users always require the involvement of at least one intermediate system or the primary system. The most important advantage of this topology is the relative ease of operations and management. The most serious drawback is the network exposure: If the system at the top or one of the intermediate systems goes down, all or some of the end users also are cut out.

Star. This configuration is similar to the tree or hierarchical structure. The major difference is that all the processing and network management responsibilities lie with a central system or communications hub, with minimal or no delegation of application and management responsibility to the connected stations.

The star configuration has the same advantages and drawbacks as the tree or hierarchical structure, only each is more pronounced.

Ring. Under a true ring topology, systems are connected to each other to form a physical ring, with traffic flowing in one direction, passing from one system to another. This topology is used by IBM and others' Token-Ring LANs and by FDDI (Fiber Distributed Digital Interface), a 100 Mbps LAN based on optical fiber. A physical ring topology is almost never used for conventional LANs because any break in the ring effectively disables the entire ring. The name notwithstanding, IBM and IEEE 802.5 Token-Ring LANs use a variation of the star topology in which one or more network hubs act as the main ring, and each system attaches to a hub in a star-like fashion.

Bus. The bus is used in traditional Ethernet and IEEE 802.3 LANs, although both can also use a tree or a combined tree/bus structure. A bus is a cable extending into the area where the station to be connected is installed. The transmission of the message on the bus must be bidirectional to reach every other station. You can think of a ring as a bus closed on itself. This means that any station has the possibility of transmitting to any other station even if the transmission is always in one direction.

Mesh. With this topology, network components are connected to each other via multiple routes and redundant facilities. A station can send messages to any other station via one of the possible routes. The flexibility and performance of a mesh network depend on the algorithm used in route selection. The significant advantages are the enhanced network reliability and load balancing, but at the expense of increased line costs. Mesh network management is more difficult and requires more resources than in the other configurations.

ANALOG TRANSMISSION

Subscribers to public telephone services are connected to the local telephone exchange through permanent connections on twisted-pair wiring. The rotary switch or the keypad of the subscribers' telephones enables them to dial the number of any other subscriber. When both individuals are in the same city, the telephone exchange receives the request, sets up a physical circuit of the two subscribers' lines, and rings the called set. The circuit implemented by the exchange enables the two subscribers to communicate; the circuit remains operational until one of the two hangs up and the circuit is broken.

If the subscriber called is located in another city, the circuit is set up through the cooperation of the two local exchanges and of some other intermediate exchanges, depending on the distance. In this case, the circuit between the two subscribers is formed by the permanent lines connecting the subscribers at the two ends, plus any other links between the exchanges that are involved in the route. The conversation requires more resources (more links and more exchanges) than in the previous case, which is why long-distance calls cost more. In any case, the circuit is set up and activated after a specific user's request and remains operative until one of the two hangs up. This kind of connection is called switched, and the exchange has switching responsibility to serve all the requests coming from the subscribers' local community.

Data transmission also can be realized with this approach, and the circuit is set up exactly as described above. In the oldest implementation, the use of a switched connection requires a modem at both ends, each connected to a telephone set. The telephone connected to the modem is used at one end to initiate the call, and the telephone at the other end receives the call. The circuit can then be used for normal voice conversation until a switch on both modems is set to data. At this point, the phones are disconnected, the two DTEs are inserted on the line, and the transmission can start. When receiving remote calls, some modems can switch automatically to data, eliminating the need for any human intervention at the receiving site. This function is called autoanswer.

Another possibility is that of a modem capable of sending the number of the called station directly to the exchange on request of its DTE. The number can be stored in the modem's memory or passed to the modem by the DTE; this function is called autodial or autocall. Autodial is useful when the user has to make many calls, because it eliminates the manual operations to set up the various calls via a telephone set at the calling site. In Europe the function is subject to a specific standard (V.25 bis); in the United States modems commonly follow either the Bell 801 Automatic Calling Unit (ACU) specification or use the Hayes "smart modem" call procedure.

Another advantage of the switched mode is that any other remote station can be called. But the switched approach can also present several drawbacks: The calling phase can last up to 10 or 20 seconds; during network peak hours connections cannot always be made if the public exchanges are overloaded. The quality of the circuit (i.e., the probability of a minimal number of errors in transmission) varies from call to call because the cables used are designed for the human voice. And data transmission speed is generally low.

For low-volume transmissions, the most economical approach is the switched connection. But if transmission over a switched line lasts for a significant period of time, the user will incur high costs. If long transmissions are the norm, leasing a line from the carrier may be a wiser choice. A leased line is set up in exactly the same way as described above and remains operational 24 hours a day and at the complete disposal of the user.

A leased line has a reasonable price if you often transmit a significant amount of data, and it does not have the disadvantages of a switched line. The quality is fixed and generally good; the line is always available to the leasing individual or organization, and the line speed is higher. But the leased connection grants less freedom to the user: The transmission is always directed toward the DTE at the other end. Sending the information to an additional DTE requires either a second line or the capability of the remote end to act as a switcher for some messages.

MODEMS

Telephone lines were originally designed for voice transmission, and their services for that application are generally good. The human voice requires a communications cable capable of accepting a continuous stream of signals (the sounds), normally with no sudden variations, because human conversation has the following characteristics:

- It is a continuous stream of information.
- It uses a range of low frequencies, from 0 to 4,000 Hertz (Hz), which allows voice recognition and understanding of meaning.
- It includes a high tolerance for noise; failing to understand a single word often has no consequences at all, because the word and sentence context enable the listener to understand.
- It includes a tolerance, for the same reason, of micro-interruptions (for example, one tenth of a second).

Data transmission has different characteristics, and therefore different requirements, than voice transmission. The loss of one or more bits cannot be tolerated because the meaning of the received message could be completely changed. Thus, telephone lines are not ideal for data transmission; but they are often used because of the ubiquity of the telephone network.

The modem solves the first problem associated with transmitting data over telephone lines — that of transmitting discrete levels, such as the values 0 and 1, on the telephone line. The message originated by the transmitting DTE is composed of a certain number of characters, or bytes, each of which is formed by a certain number of bits of value 0 or 1 (e.g., 7 bits if the code used is ASCII, 8 bits if it is EBCDIC). The line adapter of the transmitting DTE sends the modem one bit at a time. The modem then takes the bit and translates it into an audible signal appropriate for transmission by the carrier.

As shown by Figure 1.3, the line carries a specific wave form, which is altered to carry voice and data. In the case of the modem, it changes one or more of the characteristics of the carrier (i.e., the height or the frequency or the phase) according to some internal rule and depending on the value of the bit to be transmitted. So the modem can use frequency, phase, or amplitude modulation (modem stands for MOdulator/DEModulator), or a combination of these techniques; and the changes made to the carrier signal are according to the physical parameter selected for modulation and depend on the value to be transmitted.

FIGURE 1.3
The Wave Form of the Carrier

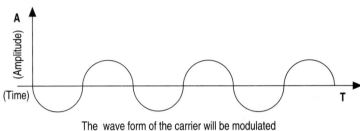

The wave form of the carrier will be modulated
by the modem during the transmission

For example, a modem transmitting the carrier with a frequency of 2,400 Hz (or 2,400 complete cycles of sinusoidal form per second) can alter it to the frequency of 1,800 Hz to transmit a 0, and to 3,000 Hz to transmit a 1. Of course, there must be a modem at the remote end that demodulates the received signal according to the same rule applied by the modulating modem. The changed characteristics must remain constant for a minimum time, depending on the physical properties of the cable used and on the microelectronics used internally in the modem, to be recognized at the receiving end.

Modems must have an internal clock to receive and interpret the signals. The clock is used to determine when the modem should sample the line for the presence of the next bit (based on the agreed-upon bits-per-second rate). The two modems must synchronize their clocks at the beginning of the message transmission, and this synchronization must be maintained for the duration of the transmission. A possible loss of synchronization means a possible loss of bits.

DIGITAL TRANSMISSION

Eventually, analog transmission proved troubling for the switching equipment used with telephone systems. Switches connect the line initiating a call to the line being called — for long distance calls, an end-to-end connection requires the cooperation of many switches working together. As the number of voice lines has dramatically increased, the analog switching equipment required to handle the lines and facilitate the connections has become more complicated and more cumbersome.

After analyzing their telephone switching requirements, the telephone carriers concluded that they could switch more connections faster and more efficiently if they used digital equipment. To implement digital switching, however, the carriers had to convert analog voice information to digital information. In effect, they needed a device that would do the opposite of what a modem does.

The resulting device was termed a *codec* (coder-decoder). Like modems, codecs work in pairs. One codec translates sound from a phone line into digital format before it hits a digital switch. A second codec converts the digital information back into sound before it reaches a human ear. To support the data processing community, the telephone carriers set up links that avoid analog filters and boosters, bypass codecs, and, in short, allow data transmission to occur in native digital format.

Because computer systems can directly transmit digital information over digital lines, no modems are required between the computers and the lines. Instead, a connecting device (normally a Data Set Unit (DSU)) is used to match the computer's physical interface to the phone carrier's physical interface.

TRANSMISSION SPEED

On a circuit made with metallic components, bits travel at a speed approximately equal to two-thirds of the speed of light (200,000 km per second), and in the case of optical transmission, at three-fourths of the speed of light (the true speed of light can only be achieved in a vacuum). This means that, normally, the time taken to arrive at the end of the circuit is insignificant. A bit transmitted in a circuit from New York to Philadelphia arrives in Philadelphia after less than 1/200th of a second. Common sense suggests that, in terms of performance, this time lapse has no influence at all, because it is so short compared to many other parameters, such as the times required to input data online, to process the data, or to analyze the received message. In data transmission over long distances via telephone circuits or similar modes, the number of bits that can travel the distance amounts, at the most, to 38,400 bits per second. So the transmission of a message made of 40,000 bits requires a minimum of slightly more than one second.

Performance is dependent on the number of bits that can travel the line on a per-second basis, which is called the line speed and is measured in bits per second (bps). In this calculation the actual length of the line has no practical impact; a line operating at 2,400 bps that goes from one end of town to the other offers the same performance as a line operating at 2,400 bps that goes from one end of the country to the other. Normal analog telephone lines are used at a speed within the range of 2,400 to 28,800 bps, with exceptions at both ends of the range, and depending upon the modems used.

But there are exceptions when that propagation time can become significant. For example, in satellite communications, the time of transmission in space cannot be ignored because of the long distances involved. And, surprisingly, neither can this time lapse be ignored in the case of short or very short distances, such as in LANs or in the internal circuits used to connect microelectronics chips. As a rule of thumb, when data can be received and processed very quickly (for example, when an adapter can input 10 million bps on the line), then the time data takes to travel the distance becomes quite significant.

Terrestrial digital lines are capable of transmission speeds in the range of 56 Kbps to 1.5 Mbps (64 Kbps to 2 Mbps in Europe); higher speeds (6 Mbps, 34 Mbps, etc.) can be achieved by combining ("bonding") multiple digital lines or using limited distance optical links. Future broadband networks, which will almost certainly be available by the end of this decade, will make available to the user line speeds over long distances in the range of several hundred Mbps. The line speeds over today's LANs lie within a similar range. Although most LANs work with a line speed in the range of 1 to 20 Mbps, 100 Mbps or more are possible in FDDI, 100BaseT Ethernet, or other LANs. The higher the line speed is, the faster the procedure is to transmit a given message on the line, which explains the constant demand for higher speed technologies.

OTHER NETWORK COMPONENTS

In addition to user stations, mainframes, midranges, PCs, printers, or nonprogrammable terminals, a network may include many other components, the most common of which are the following:

Front-end, or communications, controllers. A front-end controller is connected to a mainframe and connects all the lines departing from the mainframe. The controller's task is to transmit and receive messages on behalf of the mainframe. This leaves the mainframe with no direct responsibility over data transmission. By offloading this task to the front end, the mainframe is left with only the logical management and application support responsibilities of data transmission. Midrange systems, which generally connect a small number of lines, have no front end. Instead, they have internal communications processors, each capable of supporting a number of lines, usually in the range from 10 to 12.

Network nodes or Data Switching Equipment (DSE). In mesh networks, network nodes or DSE have the task of receiving the incoming messages, finding the most convenient route for them, and forwarding them along the chosen route.

Cluster controllers. When a location has a significant number of terminals, the terminals can be connected to a cluster controller, whose task is to act as a concentrator for the terminals' inbound and outbound data. Typical in the mainframe world are the 3174 and 3274 controllers of the 3270 display family; in IBM midrange systems networks, similar products for the 5250 display family are the 5294, 5394, and 5494 controller.

Many other types of equipment can be part of a network, such as the following:

Multiplexers. A multiplexer is used to carry the traffic from data terminals working at lower speeds on one or more high-speed lines. Digital multiplexers often are capable of carrying data and voice traffic concurrently on the same high-speed line.

Data enciphering and compression equipment. This equipment transforms the transmitted data to protect it from intrusion along the used circuit or to make the message shorter.

Call-back devices. These devices are used in networks based on switched connections. For protection from intruders, call-back devices intercept incoming calls, require the user's identification, interrupt the connection, and call the telephone number identified as the user's.

CHAPTER 2

Communications Fundamentals

Line protocols have been used since the first implementation of data transmission to allow two DTEs directly connected on a line to communicate with each other. Although many different line protocols have been implemented by a number of vendors, they all share the following general objectives:

- To ensure the synchronization between the two stations and between their modems
- To define the formal structure of the transmitted messages (also called blocks, or packets)
- To enable the transmission not only of data but also of commands, requests, and responses between the two stations communicating on the line (e.g., "Are you ready to receive?" or "Now you are allowed to transmit")
- To supply a control mechanism to determine whether the transmission contains errors and, if necessary, to activate error-recovery procedures and establish how many times these recovery attempts must be repeated before the transmission is aborted

No data transmission can take place without using a given line protocol, so it is important to have a clear understanding of the relevant concepts. One specific concept that underlies all others is the transmission technique used on the line. This technique may be either asynchronous or synchronous, and it plays a major role in determining the line speed limits, the type of modems that can be used, and the specific line protocols that can operate over the link.

TRANSMISSION TECHNIQUES

Transmissions are not always present on the line, thus the connected DTEs (or, more precisely, their line adapters) are normally quiet, or in an "idle" state. Algorithms that ensure synchronization must

- Alert the counterpart when the next transmission is scheduled to occur
- Ensure that synchronization is maintained either at the single-bit level or at the character level (to avoid possible losses)

Let us suppose that a DTE has prepared in its memory a message made of the characters A, B, and C, and that these have to be transmitted in that exact order. The transmission can occur in the two ways shown in Figure 2.1.

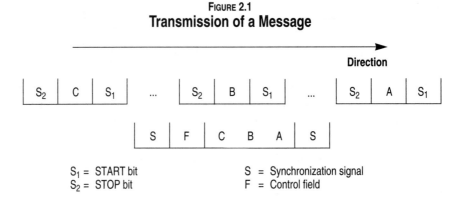

FIGURE 2.1
Transmission of a Message

S_1 = START bit
S_2 = STOP bit

S = Synchronization signal
F = Control field

In the first case, each character travels along the line and is always preceded by one bit called a start bit (generally at level 0), informing the receiver that a character is arriving. Additionally, each character is always followed by one or more stop bits (generally at level 1). This type of transmission is termed asynchronous because each character in a message can be transmitted over the line when it is ready; the start bit alerts the receiver to the arrival of the character and the stop bit confirms the end of the character. Under asynchronous transmission, individual characters can be sent over the line as they are ready for delivery, or groups of characters may be composed and sent as a block. In both cases each character is delimited by a start and a stop bit.

Asynchronous transmission, one of the oldest techniques, was developed to provide communications with unbuffered teletypes when each character typed on the keyboard is immediately sent along the line. In this case, the time gap between two consecutive characters depends on the typist's variable pace. In this book we will use the term start/stop to describe the asynchronous transmission technique.

The second case demonstrates the basic structure of synchronous transmission, which implements synchronization at the block level. With this arrangement, the entire message is sent along the line as usual, character by character and, within every character, bit by bit. This means that the time gap between two bits is fixed, so start and stop bits are not required. Although start and stop bits are not applied to the transmission, a special character is normally inserted at the beginning of the message, at the end of the message, and also may be repeated within the message itself to ensure that synchronization is maintained (in Figure 2.1, the special character is S).

Line protocols that use synchronous transmission are further divided into two families: those that are byte-oriented — typical examples are binary synchronous communications (BSC) and Digital Equipment Corporation's Digital Data Communication Message Protocol (DDCMP) — and, more recently, those that are bit-oriented — such as IBM's Synchronous Data Link Control (SDLC) and the International Standards Organization's (ISO's) High-Level Data Link Control (HDLC). We will discuss the difference between these two sets later.

Line protocols that use start/stop or synchronous transmission must provide a mechanism to identify and control transmission errors (lost bits, a bit transmitted as 0 and received as 1, and the like). The start/stop-oriented protocols generally (but not always) provide this control by adding to each transmitted byte a bit that is used to control parity (or disparity). When parity is in effect, the adapter of the transmitting DTE counts the number of internal "1" bits in each transmitted character. The additional parity bit added assumes the value 0 or 1 to make the total amount of "1" bits always "even" or always "odd" (the use of even or odd parity is normally a configuration option).

With parity checking, a bit transmitted as 0 and received as 1 (or the contrary) will create a failure at the receiving end, and the error will be noted. But what happens if the designated values of two bits within the same byte change during the transmission (a real probability on lines of low or medium quality)? The control at the remote DTE will not reveal the error. So parity and disparity, as used with start/stop transmission, offer rather limited error control.

Another error-control mechanism used by both start/stop and synchronous line protocols is the application of a checksum to a block of characters. Using this method, the bit values in all the characters in the message block are used as variables in a mathematical calculation. The result of this calculation is generally two bytes long and is inserted after the message block by the transmitted equipment; it is recalculated and verified by the receiving equipment. The checksum area of the message is typically assigned a special field name. Older, byte-oriented protocols refer to the checksum field as the Cyclic Redundancy Check (CRC) field, while newer, bit-oriented protocols call it the Frame Check Sequence (FCS). The probability that any transmission error is not revealed with this type of control is in the order of one out of 10 million or more.

PEER AND MASTER-SLAVE RELATIONSHIPS

While the transmission technique determines the structure used to send data over a line, a higher level concept must take into consideration the relationship between the stations connected to the line. The first type of relationship is a peer relation, as represented in Figure 2.2. Under a peer relationship each station on a line has equal access rights to the line and must contend (bid) for access when it has information to transmit. Special control messages are used to convey meanings such as "Are you ready to receive?" "YES," "NO," "Start of data," "End of data," "End of transmission," and so forth. The main characteristic of a peer relationship is that each station can initiate the transmission without permission from the other, simply by asking if the other is ready to receive.

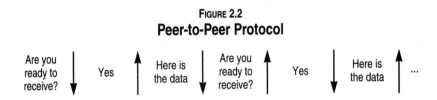

FIGURE 2.2
Peer-to-Peer Protocol

The second type of relationship asserts a master-slave relation among the stations. The master, generally a computer, monitors all the communications and controls the transmission from or to specific slaves, denying transmission to all the others during that time. The transmission is always from the authorized terminal — to the master in one direction and from the master to a terminal in the other direction. Direct transmission between two slave stations on the line is not possible.

The technique used by the master to assign the right to transmit is termed polling. Conversely, the rule followed by the master to send a message to a specific station is called addressing or selection. To understand the process, you must remember that every station is recognized by a specific address. This address is incorporated into the special messages that convey the polling operation (i.e., the invitation to send) and addressing operation (i.e., the question asked by the master to the slave to establish that it is ready to receive).

Now consider Figure 2.3, showing terminals with addresses A, B, and C that are multidropped on the same line. The master must have the address list for these terminals. When the master decides to start the polling, a particular character that means "polling" is transmitted and followed by address A, for example. Every station receives this message, but only A is authorized to answer. Having nothing to send, A will respond with "NO"; the master continues by polling B; B also replies negatively. The process continues with C. C, having a message ready, responds positively and sends a special character meaning "Start of data," followed by the message itself. The master answers "YES" or "NO" to C, according to whether or not it has identified a transmission error. C can still send messages, and each one of them is controlled by the master. When C has no more messages, it sends an "end-of-transmission" character. Now the line is free again in the direction from the master and another polling cycle can start.

Now suppose that at a given time the master has to send a message to B — an answer to a preceding inquiry by B, for example. The master sends the character addressing B along the line, asking if B is ready to receive. If B answers positively, the master sends the message; otherwise, the cycle ends unsuccessfully, because the message is for B and cannot be sent to another terminal. These two examples (based on a BSC-like dialogue) should give you an idea of the concepts of polling and addressing.

FIGURE 2.3
Polling Procedure

The Master Station invites A, then B, and then C, to transmit. In this case only station C has a message ready to be sent.

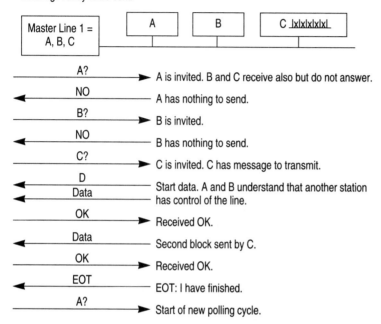

Polling is not a light task for a computer. Imagine a system with 10 lines. First, the system must have 10 polling lists. Second, the polling cycle must be fast enough that terminals with ready messages do not have to wait too long. Third, the cycle must be activated for any connected line. Fourth, a polling cycle that ends with no message has used computing power for nothing. Thus, the pace of polling is always a compromise: If it's too slow, it requires a minimal effort on the part of the computer but forces the terminals to wait too long; if it's too fast, it provides good service to the terminals but puts a heavy load on the computer. As new line protocols have been developed, new techniques have been added to minimize the transmission time and the number of transmission turnarounds.

Turnarounds also have an impact on line performance. On normal telephone lines, the time required for the modem to pass from modulation to demodulation, plus the time required to propagate the message, requires about 20 milliseconds; for comparison, on a satellite link, the time required is about 300 milliseconds.

In Figure 2.3, when terminal C is given the right to transmit, it can transmit any number of blocks. But for every block transmitted, the master must answer "YES" or "NO" to signal whether the block was received correctly. Some protocols use a window concept that provides a way to manage block transmissions in groups. For example, a window value of "three" (or any number agreed upon by the stations), means that the transmitting station has the right to transmit up to three blocks without having to wait for a response; for example:

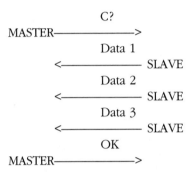

By allowing transmission of a certain number of blocks without having to wait for an answer, the window technique reduces the transfer time of a large file considerably. For this reason, satellite transmissions use very large windows — up to 256 blocks. On the other hand, windows offer no practical advantages in conversational transmissions where each transmitted block elicits a response from the application. Of course, if a block has been received with an error, the necessary information will be provided. In such a case, the "NO" sent after the three blocks will also carry the number of the block containing the error. The transmitting station can choose to retransmit only the block in error, or the block in error plus all the subsequent blocks.

LINE PROTOCOLS

When the transmission technique (start/stop or synchronous) is combined with the relationship (peer or master-slave), a formal line protocol is defined. Figure 2.4 summarizes the most typical and most frequently used line protocols. Note that among those with master-slave relationships are some that do not use polling and addressing, and that some protocols such as BSC and HDLC include options for both peer and master-slave relationships.

Over the years, hundreds of vendors have implemented thousands of line protocols. In the world of IBM, two line protocols that have played a significant role in the development of IBM networking are BSC and SDLC. As noted, BSC is a byte-oriented synchronous protocol supporting both peer and master-slave relationships. BSC was the primary line protocol of choice before the

FIGURE 2.4
Summary of Line Protocols

	Polling	Non-Polling
Master-Slave Relationship	S/S ARQ DDCMP BSC SDLC HDLC	X-on, X-off DTR/CTS TDMA . . .
Peer-To-Peer Relationship	BSC	HDLC (LAP, LAPB, LAPD, LAPX, LLC)

introduction of the Systems Network Architecture (SNA). Although BSC is still in use today, it has been, for the most part, supplanted by SDLC.

SDLC is a bit-oriented synchronous line protocol that was implemented by IBM as the wide-area protocol of choice for SNA networks. IBM submitted the specifications for SDLC to the international standards community. The international standards community then made minor changes to SDLC (including support for peer relationships) and released the altered version as HDLC. Since that time, many other OSI-oriented line protocols have been derived from HDLC: Link Access Procedure (LAP) and Link Access Procedure B (LAPB) for X.25 networks; Link Access Procedure D (LAPD) for the upcoming digital ISDN networks; Link Access Procedure X (LAPX) for teletex; and the Logical Link Control (LLC) protocol for the IEEE LANs. Other derivations of HDLC include many proprietary protocols, such as UDLC of Unisys/Sperry and BDLC of Unisys/Burroughs.

SDLC is virtually the same as HDLC for master-slave relationships. All these protocols are said to be bit-oriented because information control very often requires only a few bits or even only one bit, as shown in the formal structure in Figure 2.5. By contrast, BSC and other protocols that are byte-oriented do not have such a structure, so characters delimiting the block or frame always require at least one byte. Additionally, commands such as polling often require a whole message and cannot travel together with user data, as is possible with bit-oriented protocols.

THE SDLC LINE PROTOCOL

As Figure 2.5 shows, the user data (Information) can be any number of bytes in an SDLC message. At the beginning there are always three bytes — flag, control, and address — which may be followed by the information field and

Figure 2.5
Structure of SDLC and HDLC Frames

FLAG 01111110	FCS	INFORMATION	CONTROL	ADDRESS	FLAG 01111110
1 byte	2 bytes	n bytes	1(or 2) byte	1(or 2) byte	1 byte

Transmission Direction →

by the final three bytes — two for the FCS (checksum) field for error control and the final flag.

The starting and final flags each use the bit configuration 01111110, ensuring synchronization at both byte and bit levels (two inversions are ensured). Such a configuration is impossible to find in the user data, because the SDLC adapter counts the number of consecutive "1s" present in the user data field. Once 5 is reached, the adapter automatically inserts a 0. The receiving station does the reverse operation for incoming bits; having arrived at 5, if the following bit is 0, it is dropped. Otherwise, it must be the ending flag and the two preceding bytes received must be those of the FCS. You should note that the procedure mentioned above, called bit-stuffing, ensures that the user data never has very long sequences of 1 bits, in this way reinforcing the synchronization of the two DTEs.

The address field in the header always contains the line address of the station that has to respond.

The control field is very important. While it can be extended to 2 bytes, normally it is a single byte and for the frames carrying user data has the following format:

```
| N(R) |P/F| N(S) |O|
|_____|___|_____|_|
   876   5   432   1
```

The first bit, set to 0, informs that the frame is also carrying user data. The two subfields N(S) and N(R) carry, respectively, the sequence number of this message, N(S), and of the next message expected from the other station, N(R). A message with N(S)=4 and N(R)=2 means "This is my fourth message and I expect to receive your second message sometime." Implicitly, N(R)=2 means "Your preceding message number 1 was received without errors." By using these two subfields, the control of the sequence is implemented so that no messages are lost. But the two subfields are also used to implement the window concept.

If the window has been set to four, the following transmission sequences can occur:

```
            N(S)=1
MASTER————————————>        SLAVE
            N(S)=2
MASTER————————————>        SLAVE
            N(S)=3
MASTER————————————>        SLAVE
            N(S)=4
MASTER————————————>        SLAVE
             OK
MASTER<————————————        SLAVE
```

When bit P (poll) is set to 1 in the message directed to the secondary or slave station, this means: "You are receiving my data and after that you can send your data" (it implements the polling mechanism). In a response message, the same bit is called F (final) and is set to 1 only in the last block of the message, signaling the end of the transmission. This sequence is shown in the following example:

```
           Data (P=0)
MASTER————————————>        SLAVE
           Data (P=0)
MASTER————————————>        SLAVE
           Data (P=1)
MASTER————————————>        SLAVE
           Data (F=0)
MASTER<————————————        SLAVE
           Data (F=0)
MASTER<————————————        SLAVE
           Data (F=1)
MASTER<————————————        SLAVE
```

SDLC has been a keystone in the development of all other SNA protocols. Variations of SDLC have been implemented to accommodate twinaxial links (TDLC), packet-switching links (QLLC and EHLLC), ISDN links (IDLC), and LAN links. Therefore, although the use of SDLC may actually be decreasing as fewer and fewer telephone lines are used for wide-area connections, the core principles of SDLC live on in all the other SNA protocols.

All the line protocols cover, with different levels of functions and efficiency, the task of allowing transmission between two or more stations directly connected to the same line. They provide synchronization; they accommodate the exchange of commands, requests, answers, and user data; they define the formal structure of the frame; and they also provide for error detection and control during transmission. For appropriate handling of the data once it arrives at the application level, other structures and commands must be inserted in what, for simplicity, we have called user data. We will discuss the principles of these commands and structures in the following chapters.

CHAPTER 3

Types of Networks

The interconnection of workstation, printers, and systems requires one or more types of transmission networks. In the simplest case, the transmission network may be a private, direct-connect network that is totally autonomous and locally controlled. Alternatively, the transmission network may require the services of public carriers — such as the phone company — to facilitate the transmission of data over a broad geographic area. Successful interconnection through both private and public networks, however, depends on the fact that equipment uses the same data-link protocols and conforms to the same network interface guidelines.

A network interface is a series of rules and functions at the physical connection level that pertain to the mechanical, electrical, and transmission characteristics of the cable joining the user's station and the transmission network. Network interfaces are defined and standardized by a number of international standards bodies, including the Electronic Industries Association (EIA), the Institute of Electrical and Electronics Engineers (IEEE), and the International Telegraph and Telephone Consultative Committee (CCITT). All three of these standards bodies are particularly well-known in one respect or another; EIA is best known for its RS-232, RS-422, and other RS-interface standards; IEEE for its 802 series of LAN specifications; and CCITT for its V series of recommendations regarding public (voice/data) networks and for its X series of recommendations regarding public data networks (data only). The actual application of these standards and recommendations, however, is highly dependent on the type of transmission network — public or private — being used. Various factors distinguish public and private networks and, within each category, the types of networks and communications links commonly used. We will discuss these distinctions in the following sections.

PUBLIC NETWORKS

Public networks can be used to carry voice/data, or data only. Dual purpose voice/data networks are termed "public networks," while data-only networks are referred to as "public data networks." Frequently used public and public data networks include the following:

Public telephone networks provide switched or leased analog circuits, with speeds reaching 28,800 bps or, in some cases, up to 38,400 bps when leased lines are used. In general, lower speeds are used (in the range between 1,200 bps and 14,400 bps) depending on the line quality, the modem used, and, in the case of switched connections, the distance. RS-232 and V.24 are the most commonly used physical interfaces. Modem operations in this environment are governed by V.22, V.22 bis, V.33, V.33 bis, V.42, and V.42 bis standards, and every connection requires identical modems at each end of the line. Start/stop and synchronous transmission operations are supported.

Direct digital circuits offer leased (permanent) and switched (virtual) digital circuits for data transmission supporting speeds up to 2 Mbps. In application, the interfaces to digital circuits are normally operated at one of the following rates: 56 Kbps, 64 Kbps, 256 Kbps, 1.44 Mbps (U.S. T1 link) or 2.048 Mbps (European CEPT or E1 link). Higher rates can be achieved by combining ("bonding") multiple digital circuits. Either the V.35 (analog) or the X.21 (digital) interface can be used for device attachment. If V.35 is used, a device called a Data Service Unit (DSU) is used to convert the analog V.35 signals into digital format. If X.21 is used, a device called a junction box facilitates connection to the digital circuit. Synchronous transmission is preferred over digital circuits.

X.25 public packet-switching networks (e.g., Itapac in Italy; Transpac in France; Datapac in Canada; Telenet, Tymnet, and others in the U.S.) are based on intelligent nodes (computers) that connect the users' stations. The functions of the nodes, which are connected to each other in a meshed network via high-speed lines, are to receive the incoming messages or packets (i.e., a message of a maximum length and with a standard format) from the various connected stations, to set the pace of the transmission from the sending stations, to support the service requested by the user, to determine the destination of each packet, and to forward the packet into the network until the destination is reached. Synchronous transmission is used within a native X.25 network.

ISDN (Integrated Services Digital Network) combines the advantages of packet-switching and circuit-switching networks. ISDN has been standardized by a CCITT committee and is being implemented worldwide. ISDN's digital approach supports data, text, voice, fax, and image transmission. To use ISDN, all information must be digitized before transmission, and specific ISDN interfaces are required. The user connection can be (1) narrow-band access (also called "basic" access), which provides the user with two 64-Kbps B channels and a D channel of 16 Kbps for signaling and service requests; and (2) primary access, which provides 30 64-Kbps B channels and a 64-Kbps D channel (in the U.S. and Japan, primary access offers 23 B channels and a D channel). The B channels can be used for data, text, voice, fax, and image transmission. The D channel is used for call set-up and for sideband information.

Frame Relay is similar to ISDN and X.25 in that it lets multiple systems communicate with one another over a wide-area network. Unlike X.25 and ISDN, frame relay was specifically developed to address the unique characteristics of LAN-to-LAN transmission. In particular, Frame Relay switches whole LAN messages through the wide-area mesh network. Frame Relay was designed to accommodate Ethernet frames but has since been adopted for other frame types as well. Frame Relay services are offered by both phone carriers and independent telecommunication companies.

From a global perspective, different countries and locations also offer other types of public networks and public data networks. In Italy, for example, the Rete Fonia e Dati (RFD) is a high-speed, high-quality circuit-switching network for data and voice. V.24 is the interface used for speeds not exceeding 19,200 bps; V.35 and X.21 are used for speeds up to the maximum allowable speed of 64 Kbps. The main characteristic of this network is the good line quality, the fast line switching (all the central exchanges are electronic), facilities such as closed user groups or reverse charging (the payment for the connection is charged on the called system), and tariffs consistent with those of telephone-type networks. Similar networks exist in many countries. You may wonder why, with fast, reliable analog and digital circuit-switching networks, the packet-switching technique is even used. The answer is that packet-switching networks are designed to accommodate data transmission through the network on an on-demand basis. Because the network is operational only when blocks of data are actually being transmitted, circuits can be shared, thereby avoiding the costs and complexities associated with single-use circuits.

PRIVATE NETWORKS

In environments where distance does not dictate the use of public networks, private networks can be constructed using the following types of links:

Twinaxial links permit the connection of 5250 terminals (or PCs and PS/2s with twinaxial interface cards) to integrated and/or standalone 5250 controllers. These controllers connect display terminals of the 5250 series and their printers through twinaxial cables. PS/2s and PCs with an emulation card also can be connected to twinaxial cables. Every controller can support a maximum of 40 local stations, displays, and printers, including PCs and PS/2s. One of the connected terminals can work as the system console. The transmission speed via twinaxial cable is 1 Mbps, and a variation of IBM's SDLC protocol — TDLC — is used for communications.

Direct connections can be made using the RS-232, V.24, or V.35 interfaces. Cross-over connections or modem eliminators are typically required to emulate the functions normally provided by the public network carrier. This type of connection is appropriate for

- System-to-system connections, as in the case of connecting an AS/400 to another AS/400 or a System/38
- System-to-controller connections, as in the case of connecting an AS/400 to a workstation controller
- Connections between ASCII workstations and either an integrated ASCII workstation controller or a 5208 protocol converter. The ASCII

workstation controller and 5208 protocol converter both provide a means of attaching start/stop terminals such as IBM's 3101 and Digital's VT100 to an AS/400.

LAN links are often used when multiple AS/400s need to be interconnected, or when a number of PCs need common connections to one or more AS/400 systems. The two most commonly used LAN types are IBM's Token-Ring (4 or 16 Mbps) and Ethernet (10 Mbps or 100 Mbps). However, the AS/400 also supports LANs based on wireless communication and on the Fiber Distributed Data Interface (FDDI).

TOKEN-RING AND ETHERNET LANs

The Token-Ring uses standard twisted-pair cable (shielded or unshielded) with a star-shaped physical configuration and a logical ring structure. Token-Ring LANs control access to the transmission cable by the passage of a token. Token-Ring is recommended for heavy traffic volumes and high-performance services.

Ethernet LANs operating at 10 Mbps use a variety of structures, including bus, tree, and star. Ethernet cable can be a coaxial cable (standard or thin), or a twisted-pair cable (shielded or unshielded). Ethernet LANs use a casual technique of access while controlling simultaneous accesses. This technique is called carrier sense multiple-access with collision detection (CSMA/CD). CSMA/CD is recommended for easy and immediate access. Operation at 100 Mbps demands the use of unshielded twisted-pair cable and a star topology. Different types of 100 Mbps Ethernet implementations are available; some use the CSMA/CD access methodology, while others use an alternative access methodology that is similar to the Token-Ring access methodology.

Often a business will use two or more LANs of the same or different kinds. Special stations can act as bridge stations between LANs; thanks to these stations, a user's station can communicate with another station on another LAN. For example, IBM's 8209 product can act as a bridge between two Token-Rings or between a Token-Ring and an Ethernet network. The AS/400, and most IBM systems (from 3090 mainframes to PCs and PS/2s), can connect to both types of LANs. The S/38 and a few other systems do not have a direct LAN attachment.

WIRELESS AND FDDI LANs

Wireless and FDDI LANs are emerging as popular alternatives to conventional Ethernet and Token-Ring networks. Each of these two technologies has a unique advantage.

A wireless LAN provides most of the benefits of an Ethernet network, only no cable is required. Instead, transmission between systems in a wireless LAN is handled using radio waves. The use of radio waves allows systems to be interconnected in situations where it is impossible or unreasonable to use physical cabling. Radio waves also allow systems to "roam" around in the network — a portable computer equipped with a wireless LAN adapter can participate in the LAN wherever it happens to be. The one significant drawback associated with wireless LANs is the speed at which they can operate. Most wireless LANs can achieve transmission speeds of no more than 1 Mbps to 2.5 Mbps.

FDDI, on the other hand, offers transmission speeds of 100 Mbps using a token-passing access methodology similar to Token-Ring. Under the original design of FDDI, the LAN is composed of two rings of fiber-optic cable that can range up to 100 kilometers in circumference. The dual-ring nature of FDDI provides a built-in redundancy not available in other LAN technologies. The redundancy and the large geographical area that can be covered by an FDDI LAN are the unique advantages of FDDI.

Although FDDI was designed around fiber-optic cable, support for twisted-pair cable was added later. This type of cable is called Copper Distributed Data Interface (CDDI) or Shielded twisted-pair Distributed Data Interface (SDDI). The twisted-pair variation of FDDI offers the same speed (100 Mbps) and redundancy as FDDI, but is limited to 100 meters per connection. CDDI/SDDI is primarily used as a means of attaching systems to an FDDI backbone.

SUMMARY

The AS/400 system supports a remarkable number of line protocols: SDLC (SNA), BSC, start/stop, HDLC (X.25), IDLC (ISDN), and Frame Relay. The AS/400 also supports a variety of LAN interfaces, including 10 Mbps Ethernet, 100 Mbps Ethernet, wireless Ethernet, Token-Ring, FDDI, and SDDI. This variety of protocols and interfaces allows the AS/400 to be connected to a large set of wide- or local-area networks — analog lines, digital lines, specialized circuit-switching networks (e.g., RFD, X.21, X.25), as well as conventional Token-Ring, Ethernet, and FDDI LANs. These connections support AS/400 connections to mainframes, midrange systems, PCs, and other commercial computers. The AS/400 has a wide set of application functions to be used in one or more of these environments. Most of these functions are integrated within the OS/400 operating system, while a few others require specific software products.

CHAPTER 4

OSI Reference Model Architecture

Achieving interconnection and cooperation between a variety of computer systems using incompatible operating systems is a goal that represents one of the most interesting and most needed computer network possibilities in today's market. Systems capable of such cooperative processing are often called open systems, and usually adhere to Open Systems Interconnection (OSI) standards. These standards were designed by a special committee of the International Standards Organization (ISO), the United Nations agency responsible for defining international communications standards.

These OSI standards came about in response to the widespread need to interconnect incompatible systems on local- and wide-area networks (LANs and WANs). The underlying issue relates to the communications difficulties that exist between two processes that use internally different rules and techniques. These processes can be systems, applications, or users interacting with each other through terminals. In all cases, the relevant issues include defining the structure of the data to be exchanged, the rules that govern the exchange, and the control mechanisms that guard against errors during the exchange.

The ISO committee defined the rules and options available for such interactions by establishing a reference model that divides the necessary logical functions into seven functional strata, or levels. Each level is responsible for a certain number of functions, thus transforming an otherwise complex task into a set of less complex tasks. These tasks are then regulated by rules of symmetry, hierarchical structure, and modularity.

Symmetry means that, according to the standards, the logical functions of both interacting systems must be identical. Symmetry is therefore in contrast to teleprocessing solutions of 20 years ago in which the elaborative and communicative logic was based in one computer only, and the connected stations could only receive and transmit. Symmetry creates a balance in communicative tasks, sharing functions between the counterpart systems, and is the foundation for cooperative application processes.

Hierarchical structure means that the various subsystems (or levels, layers, or strata) form a rigid hierarchy. Each level receives commands from the level above; each level performs certain functions for the superior level and demands services of the inferior level. The highest level is that of the application, or the user. The other six levels, in descending order, are the presentation, session, transport, network, data link control (DLC), and physical levels. This structure is not casual, but rather was developed after a critical analysis of the structure of the first successful transaction processing (TP) monitors, designed and implemented by system engineers.

These layers function according to the following sequence of phases: The application processes the data according to specific user requests and decides what data should be transmitted to the remote terminal and for which purpose (application level). Data is then structured to be comprehensible to the remote user (presentation level). Then the system checks to determine whether the logical connection with the remote counterpart is activated; if not, it must be. If so, data transmission can be defined according to the predefined rules of the interchange (session level). The technical details of cooperation with the remote terminal are then established (the number of message sequences, proceedings in case of an error, and so on) (transport level). The appropriate physical communications route is then selected (network level) based on the available routes (it may be possible, for example, to transmit from Milan to Rome through both Florence and Ancona). Next, the message is structured according to the line protocol chosen (data-link control level). And, finally, the single bits are transmitted according to the physical and transmission characteristics of the line (physical level), in cooperation with the DCE on the line.

The third rule, modularity, means that services are interchangeable within a layer. Because the relationships between the contiguous levels are precisely defined, the internal structure of each level can be modified (for example, to exploit new techniques) with no consequences on the remaining levels. The most obvious example of this modularity is in how it allows the same OSI application data to travel over local- or wide-area networks with no impact on upper-level services.

THE OSI MODEL

The OSI model is shown in Figure 4.1 and works as follows: Each level adds to its received data a heading by which it communicates with the remote counterpart, then executes the requested functions and sends the result on to the next level. The next level adds new headings to the user's data and then functions in the same way as the previous level. The DLC level adds a heading, a tail, and a Frame Check Sequence (FCS) for error control. The message, represented in Figure 4.2, is then transmitted over the line by the physical interface.

The receiving system receives the message at the lowest level. Each level acts according to the contents of the heading, then eliminates the heading and sends the result up to the next level. This level acts in the same way as the previous levels, and, finally, the transmitted data reaches the user or the application. The same process takes place when the second system's application sends new data to the first system, but the roles are reversed.

To further clarify the characteristics of the OSI model, consider the following observations: First, the OSI scheme implies interaction between two, and

FIGURE 4.1
Architectural Model of OSI

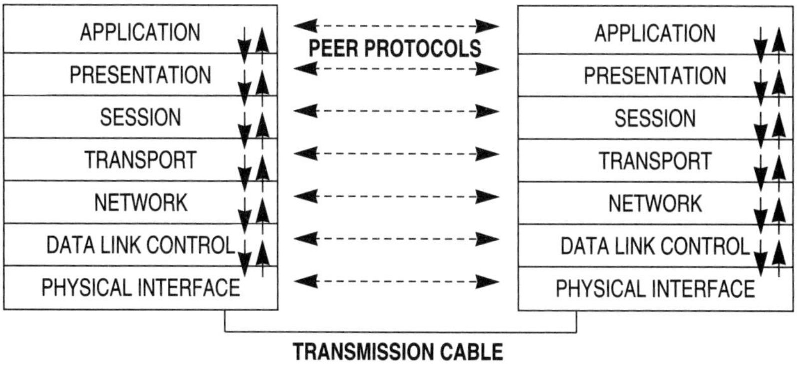

APPLICATION	←----PEER PROTOCOLS----→	APPLICATION
PRESENTATION	←--------------→	PRESENTATION
SESSION	←--------------→	SESSION
TRANSPORT	←--------------→	TRANSPORT
NETWORK	←--------------→	NETWORK
DATA LINK CONTROL	←--------------→	DATA LINK CONTROL
PHYSICAL INTERFACE	←--------------→	PHYSICAL INTERFACE

TRANSMISSION CABLE

FIGURE 4.2
An OSI Message: The Structure

Synch bits	FCS	Data	Head appl.	Head pres.	Head sess.	Head tran.	Head net.	Head DLC	Synch bits

TRANSMISSION DIRECTION →

not more than two, systems — those systems where the final users or applications are located. The OSI model does not take into consideration possible intermediate components, their communications and application functions, or their possible functional relationships with the two end systems. This means, for example, that the interactions between three systems are based on two bilateral interactions.

Second, each level assigns to its subordinate level certain technical tasks it then disregards. The subordinate level cooperates with the corresponding remote level in terms of the received tasks. So we can say that each level "sees" all its subordinates and remote subordinates as an enormous black box where commands and data are entered and from which responses and other data are received. This idea also applies to the application level, which needs to "know" only the rules required to interact with the remote application and how to pass data and commands to its subordinate layer. The application has no need to "know" the techniques used at lower levels. This is, in fact, one of the main advantages of networks based on today's architectures: To use them, the application or the user does not have to understand the sophisticated (and usually complicated) transmission techniques to use them.

OSI FUNCTIONAL LAYERS

The OSI model can be discussed from various points of view. From a summary perspective, the lowest four levels (physical, data-link control, network, and transport) can be said to have few purely application functions, with great importance given to transmission functions. The opposite is true at the three highest levels (session, presentation, and application), which are characterized by dialogue or interactive functions between the two end users or applications.

From yet a different point of view, the three lowest levels have functions related to the intermediate network components (e.g., concentrators and public network nodes, such as those of Itapac in Italy and Accunet or Tymnet in the U.S.), while functions of the four superior levels (transport and the three dialogue levels) disregard the intermediate components and are only interested in the relationships between the two final systems and their respective users. The protocols of the first three levels have box-to-box functions; the protocols of the other levels have end-to-end functions. The resulting logical scheme is shown in Figure 4.3.

The fourth level (transport) is notable because it has pure transmission functions, as do the three lowest levels, but it also has tasks associated with the relationship between the two end systems, as do the upper layers devoted to end-user dialogue. The transport level's main tasks are to control and recover possible errors, to set the transmission pace between the two end users, to

FIGURE 4.3
OSI Model: Layers with Box-to-Box Tasks and Layers with End-to-End Tasks

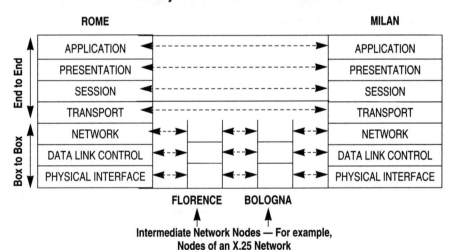

determine whether the end-user data can be segmented during transmission, and to manage the sequencing and related control of user messages.

The rules of these three lower levels relate to the choice of the relative route in the network, the line protocol to be used (e.g., HDLC), and the physical interface; and they apply to the transmission going to the immediately connected box. The box in turn applies the same rules to the next node, and so on, until the final system is reached. The OSI model suggests that in the case of long-distance transmissions, the functions of the three inferior levels must correspond to the functions required to interface a public network defined by the X.25 recommendation of the International Telegraph and Telephone Consultative Committee (CCITT).

Let's suppose that the two systems in Figure 4.3 are ROME and MILAN, that the two nodes are concentrators located in FLORENCE and BOLOGNA, and that outside the picture there is another concentrator located in ANCONA. When the two systems want to enter in session, they must choose whether to use the connection ROME-FLORENCE-BOLOGNA-MILAN or ROME-ANCONA-MILAN. The appointed algorithms, supported at network level, make a decision: They choose to use the route ROME-FLORENCE-BOLOGNA-MILAN for the session between the two systems. (The OSI model for the network layer does not define any routing algorithms, but leaves all that to the X.25 specifications, which at this level define only how to request the service, leaving the maximum freedom of choice for the routing algorithm.)

At the lower levels, the rules of the data-link control and of the physical interface are applied to all transmitted messages and on all lines of the route; in the example, first on the ROME-FLORENCE line, then on the FLORENCE-BOLOGNA line, and finally on the BOLOGNA-MILAN line.

At the upper levels, the rules of the transport level are applied to the direct relationship between the two final systems, disregarding the intermediate nodes, and they manage control functions between the two final systems, such as numbering the sequence of the messages (and the relative sequence control), the procedure to follow in case of error, and others.

Continuing upward through the model, the session level then controls the opening of a session or dialogue between two applications, their modalities (e.g., monodirectional or bidirectional flow), and the synchronization possibilities between the two users.

When the session level passes a message upward, the presentation level must handle the transformation and conversion of the transmitted data's structure to ensure correct interpretation by the remote user.

Finally, the application level defines the communications interfaces and functions according to the user's requirements — a file transfer, sending messages at an interpersonal communications level, access to the database of the

FIGURE 4.4
Summary of the Functions of OSI Layers

APPLICATION	Communications services for applications
PRESENTATION	Presentation services (formats, structures, data code) Conversion Virtual terminal
SESSION	Session handling (opening, use, closing) for the two end users Management of the session dialogue modes (full-duplex or half-duplex conversation, synchronous points, restart, normal or urgent messages)
TRANSPORT	Selection of service quality Communication control end-to-end
NETWORK	Connection requests and modes Network route selection
DATA LINK	To ensure the transmission of data blocks To ensure synchronization To control errors Line Protocol
	| Flag | FCS | Data | Add | Cont | Flag |
PHYSICAL LAYER	To activate and control the bit transmission on the selected circuit Example:

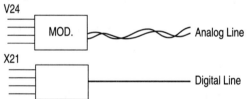

remote system, and others. Figure 4.4 summarizes the main functions of the OSI model.

The standards relating to the OSI reference model are not fixed and rigid structures. The individual standards that constitute the model — and the whole model itself, for that matter — continue to change and evolve in response to the inevitable changes and evolution in the data processing industry. At the present time, many OSI standards have been incorporated into vendor products. These standards include FTAM (for file transfer), X.400 (for electronic messages), X.500 (for directory services), and the IEEE 802 series of LAN protocols (with the most notable of those being the 802.3 Ethernet standard and the 802.5 Token-Ring standard). But work on the OSI model is not complete — indeed, it may never be complete given the constant state of change in the industry.

Because most vendors already provide software that conforms to OSI standards, OSI software can be used today to implement communications between a number of vendor systems (IBM, DEC, HP, and BULL, to name a few) for file transfer and electronic message applications based on OSI application standards such as FTAM and X.400. Alternatively, the two systems could use their OSI stacks for communications between user-written conversational applications. Indeed, at level 7 Application Program Interfaces (APIs) are available in the Application Control Services Element (ACSE) module, which is directly accessible to users.

For information about IBM and AS/400 OSI communications products, as well as a summary comparison of OSI and SNA architecture, please refer to Chapter 11.

MEASURING OSI

OSI presents enormous conceptual benefits, because the model completely and fully defines options for communications between incompatible systems. OSI is a very useful functional guide for anyone designing a proprietary network architecture or for those designing specific products, such as protocol converters. By solving the incompatibility problem, the OSI model facilitates new applications such as electronic data interchange (EDI) between different enterprises. However, some confusion and disagreement still exist regarding actual performance and the excessive number of controls required at some levels of the OSI model, suggesting the possibility of future revision of the standards.

The OSI model must be translated into products, and these products will be judged, as other products are, according to their functionality, application potential, service, performance, system prerequisites, and total cost. Based on these parameters and the specific requirements in a given situation, OSI standards may or may not be preferred over interoperability solutions, including TCP/IP and TCP/IP-related solutions.

CHAPTER 5

Systems Network Architecture

Architecturally, the structures of IBM's Systems Network Architecture (SNA) (Figure 5.1) and ISO's Open Systems Interconnection (OSI) are very similar. Therefore, the advantages presented by each are roughly the same, although there is no exact correspondence between the two structures — some functions found in OSI have no SNA equivalent, some SNA functions have no OSI equivalent, and some functions are present in both but differ in the implementation details. For example, SNA's Synchronous Data Link Control (SDLC) line protocol can be considered equivalent to the High-Level Data Link Control (HDLC) of OSI but lacks the capability for a peer-to-peer relationship over a point-to-point line.

One of the main differences between SNA and OSI is a direct consequence of the overall objectives for the two architectures. The primary function of OSI is to allow application interaction between otherwise incompatible systems; consequently, no provisions or guidelines are included about how to set up the whole network. On the other hand, IBM's intent from the beginning has been to provide users with the necessary components to set up an entire network. Because SNA meets that goal, SNA also defines the roles of the various possible network components and their relationships.

But the most important difference between OSI and SNA is that the SNA structure has been translated into SNA products since the mid-1970s, which means that all IBM systems requiring communications capabilities have assigned SNA functions (this does not exclude other communications options the user may require). IBM has continually added new functions to its SNA products

FIGURE 5.1
SNA Structure and Layers

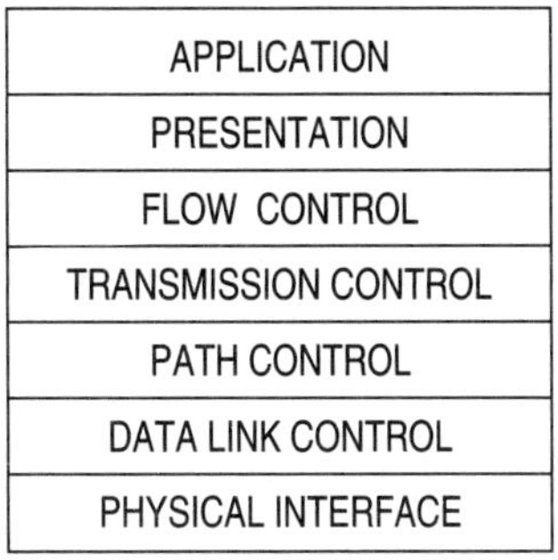

APPLICATION
PRESENTATION
FLOW CONTROL
TRANSMISSION CONTROL
PATH CONTROL
DATA LINK CONTROL
PHYSICAL INTERFACE

according to the market demand; and many SNA networks, including a number of large ones, are installed worldwide.

Figure 5.2 summarizes the most important evolutionary phases of networks based on SNA products. As you can see, the overall SNA network has undergone notable development from the beginning, and now includes highly independent subnetworks (Token-Ring and APPN) that do not depend on the structure formed by components such as the Virtual Telecommunications Access Method (VTAM) and Network Control Program (NCP) products that operate in the mainframe environment. But because midrange systems can be connected to a traditional SNA network (in addition to being connected to one another), the VTAM and NCP functions, which form the basic structure of traditional SNA, need a brief introduction.

VTAM

VTAM functions on central mainframe hosts with the Multiple Virtual Storage (MVS), Virtual Machine (VM), or Disk Operating System/Virtual Storage Extended (DOS/VSE) operating systems. In an SNA network with only one of these hosts, VTAM is responsible for controlling all communications functions on the network, including beginning and ending all operations and maintaining the network configuration. Because of the scope of its duties, VTAM is referred to as a System Services Control Point (SSCP).

VTAM directly supports some components of the network, such as local terminals channel-attached to the host and the host's online applications — Customer Information Control System (CICS), Information Management System (IMS), Time Sharing Option (TSO), to name a few. On a dynamic basis, VTAM enables the conversation ("session") between any terminal and any application of the host. A user of a terminal can therefore ask to be connected to CICS in the morning, then the interaction can be closed and a new session opened with TSO, with VTAM controlling the authorization.

The software functions of VTAM that fulfill these tasks are called "Physical Unit (PU) functions of type 5," or PU 5. If the network has more than one S/370 host, it also has more than one PU 5 and the network is called multidomain. The domain is formed by the components of the network whose activities are controlled by a certain VTAM, or PU 5. Some terminals (or distributed systems) are run by one VTAM, others by a second VTAM, and so forth. A terminal can enter a session with host applications of any domain. The request is always sent to the VTAM controlling the terminal.

If the request for a session relates to an application from another domain, the VTAMs controlling the two domains involved cooperate to establish whether the session is possible and, if so, enable it to take place. In this case, the terminal uses a cross-domain session, even though the mechanism is completely transparent to the user. Working sessions within a multidomain network and

Chapter 5 Systems Network Architecture 39

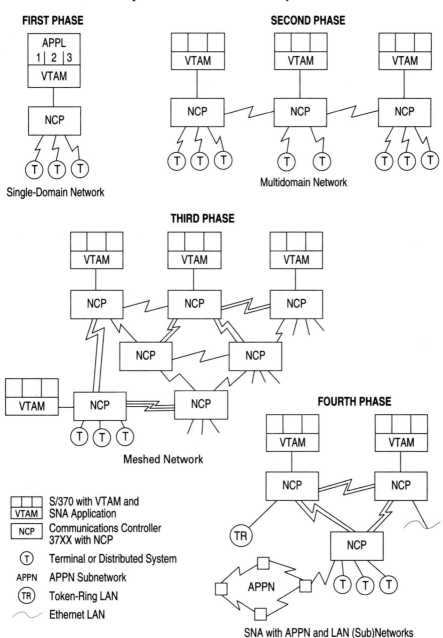

FIGURE 5.2
Major Phases of SNA Developments

under the control of VTAMs are possible when they occur between a terminal or remote system and an application on one of the central systems, or between applications of central systems (for example, between CICS and IMS); but they can never take place between one terminal or distributed system and another terminal or distributed system.

VTAM does not directly control the two-way transmission of messages to remote units; it only controls transmissions to the clusters/terminals that are directly connected to a S/370 channel. For the others, transmission is handled by communications controllers (e.g., 3705, 3720, 3725, 3745). Any host can be connected to one or more communications controllers. Messages arriving on various lines are stored on these units and then sent over a host channel to VTAM, which in turn sends them to their respective central applications.

In output mode, the messages prepared by the applications are sent to the VTAM, which sends them to the communications controller, which transmits the messages to the addressed terminals on the line. The transmission functions to and from the host, and the input and output transmissions, are controlled by the NCP software operating in the communications controller. Additional NCP tasks include cyclical scans ("polls") of the various remote units to establish whether they have data to transmit; control of the fulfillment of transmission operations; when possible, attempts to repeat the operation in case of errors; and informing the VTAM in case of unrecoverable errors. The NCP functions that carry out these tasks are called PU type 4 functions (PU 4) and they are related to transmission only.

A traditional SNA network has at least one PU 5 and one PU 4. The other remote units are PU units of type 1 or 2. The respective SNA software is incorporated in their operating system or, in the case of a non-programmable unit (for example, a cluster controller such as the 3174 or 3274), is located in microcode. IBM no longer produces PU 1 units. Instead, PU 2, which has the capabilities to support more sessions at a time (the number of possible sessions varies from device to device), is used. There are, however, products produced by IBM and others that sometimes emulate the PU 1-type functions; these are characterized by the fact that they can support only one SNA session at a time. It is not unusual, for example, for non-IBM midrange systems to emulate PU 1 during a file-transfer session (or even a job-transfer session) to an IBM host.

All small or intermediate IBM systems are PU 2 units. This includes PCs, PS/2s, S/36s, S/38s, AS/400s, RS/6000s, S/88s, 3684s, and 4700s. Note that although the 9370 is sometimes classified as a "midrange" system, it is, in reality, a PU 5 device.

In terms of communicative autonomy, PU 1 and PU 2 can ask for possible services from the VTAM of the domain that authorizes those services when possible but can decide nothing; PU 1 and PU 2 devices do not determine the "route" (that is, the intermediate nodes involved in the transmission) to be used for the session, and so on. For example, at any given moment two programs on a PS/2 can be in session simultaneously — one with the CICS of host X, and the other with the TSO of host Y. But this happens only after the controlling VTAM has given the authorization.

LOGICAL UNITS

An SNA network can be accessed by the following types of users: applications, terminal operators, and devices such as printers. A working session always occurs between two users. To communicate, the user always needs the services of a Logical Unit (LU), which defines the characteristics of the interaction. A working session between two users therefore occurs through their interaction via the services of their respective Logical Units. The working session in its turn allows the exchange of data between the two users by using a network route determined by the VTAM when the session is requested. Figure 5.3 summarizes how the working session is implemented.

FIGURE 5.3
An SNA Session Between Two End Users (an Application and an Operator)

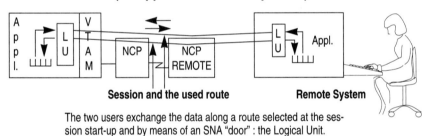

The two users exchange the data along a route selected at the session start-up and by means of an SNA "door" : the Logical Unit.

Logical Units provide the following services: support communications flow inside the session, change that flow according to the requirements of the user, control the modality of data presentation according to the application requirements and functional possibilities of the counterpart, and, finally, ensure exchanges between users at the correct sequence and control the exchange pace. These are "dialogue" functions that exploit the functions of the subordinate transmission level for the actual transfer.

Just as there are different kinds of users, IBM defined various groups of dialogue functions and called them LU 0, LU 1, LU 2, LU 3, LU 4, LU 6 (including LU 6.2), and LU 7. Each LU forms a group of software functions that are incorporated into the operating system of the various network systems (or they can be microcoded). The most important LUs are LU 2, which supports the dialogue between an application and the user of the 3270 workstation; LU 3, which supports the dialogue with a printer in the 3270 family; LU 6, which supports the dialogue between two applications; and LU 7, which supports the dialogue between an application and the user of a terminal or printer in the 5250 family.

Every work session uses two LUs of the same kind, with one LU acting as the primary (controlling) LU and the other LU acting in a secondary role. For example, the dialogue between CICS (and its applications) and a 3270 terminal takes place according to the scheme in Figure 5.4.

FIGURE 5.4
The Logical Units Servicing Two End Users in Session

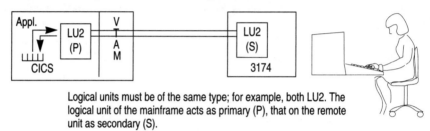

Logical units must be of the same type; for example, both LU2. The logical unit of the mainframe acts as primary (P), that on the remote unit as secondary (S).

Some SNA components support only certain types of LUs. For example, the 3174 cluster controller supports only LU 2 (for displays) and LU 3 (for printers). Others, such as the AS/400, support all kinds of LUs. LU 6.2 is particularly rich in functions relevant to communications from one application to another. For example, while using LU 6.2, any number of sessions can be opened between two applications; as an example, one session could be for priority traffic and another for file transmission or assigning specific tasks according to other criteria. In fact, given two systems, LU 6.2 sessions can be activated even before the application requests it. When a system application needs a session with an application of the second system, it can acquire one of the already activated sessions. Data and commands can be exchanged with the counterpart within one "conversation" that uses the acquired session. When the exchange ends, so does the conversation between the two applications, but the session remains active and eventually can be used by two other applications for further conversation. Figure 5.5 shows the general scheme of LU 6.2-based sessions.

A system having five users in session at a given moment has five activated LUs, each one of them in session with its corresponding remote LU. There is no subordination or relationship between LUs activated by different users of the same system. The respective LUs may or may not be of the same kind, and each one may be in communication with remote applications located on the same or different remote systems. The conceptual scheme for such a session appears in Figure 5.6.

FIGURE 5.5
Two Applications Interacting via LU 6.2

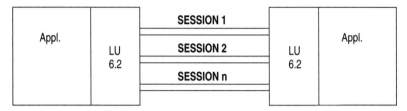

This example shows that two LU 6.2 can support, for the same two applications, multiple parallel sessions

FIGURE 5.6
A Remote System with Multiple Users Using PU 2.0 Functions

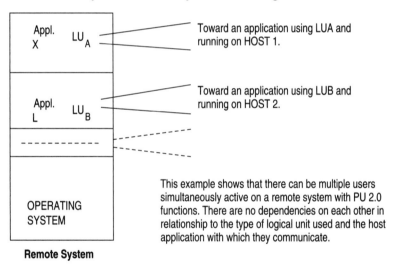

Toward an application using LUA and running on HOST 1.

Toward an application using LUB and running on HOST 2.

This example shows that there can be multiple users simultaneously active on a remote system with PU 2.0 functions. There are no dependencies on each other in relationship to the type of logical unit used and the host application with which they communicate.

Remote System

CHAPTER 6

PU 2.1, LU 6.2, and APPN

As discussed in Chapter 5, a traditional SNA network relies on a S/370 host to direct the communications toward distributed systems (PU 2.0 devices). Unfortunately, this network architecture left those IBM customers using smaller IBM systems (those not part of the S/370 family) out in the cold; they had no SNA-based methodology for interconnecting their systems. This need for direct communications between non-mainframe systems was addressed by the introduction of an SNA PU 2.1 definition, which is included in virtually all distributed systems currently offered by IBM, from PCs and PS/2s to the RS/6000, the S/36, the S/38, and the AS/400.

PU 2.1 allows communications between any two PU 2.1 systems directly connected on the same physical line, such as a connection between a PS/2 and an AS/400. The communicating systems do not need the permission of mainframe-based VTAM software; in fact, PU 2.1 connections can be realized without any reliance on the traditional components of an SNA network.

The key elements that constitute the structure of a PU 2.1 device are

- Control point — can be thought of as a subset of the VTAM function on a mainframe host; responsible for handling both the network addresses and the configuration of communications components and session services
- LU 6.2 support — all communications between the two PU 2.1s are established via this logical unit
- Path control — responsible for the selection of the network route to be used by two LU 6.2s in session. In the case of a PU 2.1 without the additional functions of APPN, this task is very simple, considering that two PU 2.1s and related LU 6.2s can enter in session only when they are at the opposite ends of a single line
- Data link control — supports the various protocols traditionally used in an SNA network: SDLC; the LAPB variant of HDLC for connection to X.25 networks; and the protocols IEEE 802.5 and 802.3 for connections to, respectively, Token-Ring and Ethernet (or Ethernet-compatible) LANs
- Node operator facility — an interface between the control point and the network operator, allowing commands to be entered into the system

The control point maintains a database describing the node resources, contains the descriptions of the physical and logical units and their attributes, and provides for the activation and deactivation of the working sessions between an LU 6.2 on the local system and another LU 6.2 on the remote system.

LU 6.2

LU 6.2 was designed for application-to-application sessions between IBM SNA systems and has been incorporated, for the same purpose, in Systems Application Architecture (SAA). Given that role, LU 6.2 was then chosen for interactive communications between PU 2.1 systems, as shown in Figure 6.1. Some argue that IBM's decision to base all communications between midrange systems on LU 6.2 was wrong because LU 6.2, designed to support interactive application-to-application sessions, is often too sophisticated for the user's requirements.

FIGURE 6.1
LU 6.2 Supported by the Control Point Component

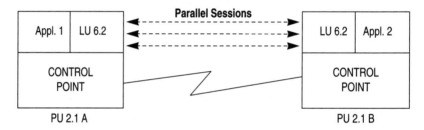

LU 6.2 supported by the control point allows communications between two PU 2.1, i.e., between IBM midrange systems (and also PCs).

On one hand, it is true that LU 6.2 can be used to implement specific, user-defined application-to-application processes using Advanced Program-to-Program Communications (APPC) verbs. APPC is the set of programming functions available to help a programmer handle LU 6.2 functions in an application program. In practical terms, APPC and LU 6.2 are synonymous. The development of programs in this area is, by necessity, complex.

On the other hand, IBM also developed internal utilities for the AS/400 and other midrange systems based on LU 6.2. These utilities provide core networking functions such as remote file access (via the Distributed Data Manager (DDM) facility) and remote terminal access (through the Display Station Passthrough (DSPT) utility). No user programming is required in these cases — the functionality is provided through standard system commands. Figure 6.2 shows the names of the available AS/400 functions based on LU 6.2.

APPN

The real limitation of the PU 2.1/LU 6.2 pair is that they require a direct link between communicating systems. This is because PU 2.1, by itself, does not include a transit node function. So in the case of three systems A, B, and C, the use of PU 2.1 is possible only in the following two configurations:

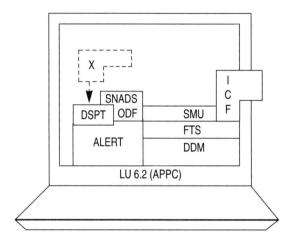

FIGURE 6.2
LU 6.2: The Basis for All Applications and Communications Services Between PU 2.1

NOTE: The outboard part of ICF is a reminder that ICF also can be used in non-SNA connections; X, falling down, means that in the future there will be other LU 6.2-based functions.

- A line between A and B, another between B and C, and a third between C and A. In this way, any user of the three systems can gain access to the resources of the other two systems. The drawback to this solution is that it requires a line — often an expensive resource — between any two systems.
- A line between A and B, and another between B and C. In this way, B's applications talk directly with either A's or C's applications. And if an A application needs to interact with a C application, a trick is necessary: The A application talks with a B application which, in turn, talks, as a relay, with the C application. The drawback to this solution is that it requires an additional application in B, which means an additional load on the system. It is important to limit B's task, in the case of an application session between A and C, to that of simply accepting the data entering from a given line and transmitting it on the other line — without involving applications that are not concerned.

The Advanced Peer-to-Peer Network (APPN) facility is an extension of the PU 2.1 functions (and not of the APPC functions). APPN allows LU 6.2-to-LU 6.2 sessions passing through any number of intermediate nodes as shown in

Figure 6.3. As this figure indicates, there are three kinds of nodes: Network Node (NN), End Node (EN), and Low-Entry Network Node (LENN or LEN).

- Network Node (NN) — Currently, an NN may be an AS/400, a S/36, a PS/2 (OS/2), or even a 3174 cluster controller. The functions of an NN are to serve as a transit node for working sessions; to provide connection and directory services for ENs and LENs (by providing them with services such as searches throughout the network to find out which system contains the required resource); and to provide the route selection service, determining the best network route either for the sessions required by the connected EN and LEN or for the sessions required by applications running in the NN.

- End Node (EN) — At this time, only an AS/400 can be configured as an EN. An EN does not have the transit node and server functions for other nodes. The EN uses the APPN services and functions, available via its NN server. EN functions are very similar to those of an LEN; the basic difference is that an EN can autogenerate the definitions of the entities (devices or LU, controllers or PU) required by the working sessions (the autogeneration function is provided by the OS/400 operating system).

- Low-Entry Network Node (LEN) — An LEN is very similar to an EN. Like an EN, an LEN needs the NN functions to be able to use the resources of the APPN network. Unlike an EN, an LEN cannot autogenerate the communications entities required, as an EN can. For this reason, entities

FIGURE 6.3
Advanced Peer-to-Peer Network (APPN)

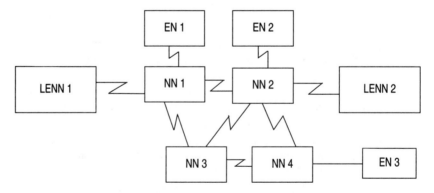

LU 6.2 sessions between two end users can use a path passing through several intermediate nodes (network node).

NN = Network Node   EN = End Node   LENN = Low-Entry Network Node must be predefined as if they were located in the NN server to which they are connected. PCs and PS/2s are commonly configured as LEN devices. Also, an AS/400 with autoconfiguration disabled should be configured as an LEN.

CONNECTION SERVICES

Every NN has a map (topology database) that describes all the active NN nodes in the network and the lines connecting them. The topology database is an extension of the configuration services of a PU 2.1 and is the base for the definition of all the possible routes in the network between any two given systems. When a new NN is connected to the network, specific sessions between its control point (CP) and the CP of neighboring NNs provide them with information about the new NN and its characteristics. Each NN consequently updates its own topology database and passes the same information, for the same purpose, to the other NNs. A similar procedure occurs when an NN is dropped out of the network. As a consequence, the topology database of every NN is continually updated.

DIRECTORY SERVICES

Let us imagine a network configuration like the one in Figure 6.4. Suppose that the application BOB, in EN1, needs a session with the application TOM. The request is sent to server NN1. NN1 searches its local directory, where an updated list is kept of all the resources available on NN1 itself and on the served EN and LEN. TOM is not found on the list. At this point, the system looks up a transit directory called a cache directory, which contains a list of the locations of remote resources previously known. Let's suppose that TOM is not included in the cache directory either. Then NN1 sends a broadcast request to all the other NNs in the network to try to find information about TOM's location. NN2 has TOM listed in its local directory because TOM is an application running on EN2, served by NN2. This information is sent back to NN1. NN1 inserts the new information in its cache directory, thus avoiding future broadcast requests for the same resource. Eventually, via its topology database, NN1 finds out that the possible routes for the BOB-TOM session can be BOB-NN1-NN2-TOM and BOB-NN1-NN3-NN2-TOM.

ROUTING SERVICES

In practice, the routing alternatives concern only the NNs: The EN and LEN are connected only to a given NN and have no alternatives. In our example, the choice is between NN1-NN2 and NN1-NN3-NN2. When multiple routes are available, the selection is narrowed using the class of service associated with the session. A class of service can be explicitly selected by the user or assigned by

Figure 6.4
Network Nodes Search Task

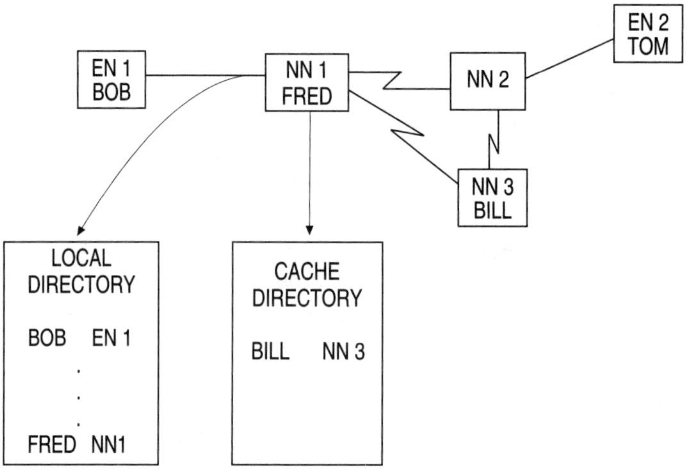

```
                                              EN 2
                                              TOM
   EN 1            NN 1            NN 2
   BOB            FRED
                                    NN 3
                                    BILL

   LOCAL          CACHE
   DIRECTORY      DIRECTORY

   BOB   EN 1     BILL  NN 3
    .
    .
    .
   FRED  NN1
```

Network nodes have the task, on behalf of the users of connected end nodes, to search in the network to identify where other resources are located. In the example, the application BOB in End Node 1, needs to start a session with the application TOM in End Node 2. NN1 has the task to find where Tom is and to select the session route.

default and serves to define the relative importance of the session traffic. In this example, NN1 searches in a specific table assigned to that class of service.

The table is used to assign a given weight to each possible route known by the NN based on the characteristics of the lines and routing nodes. As an example, the parameters to be considered for the lines include the transmission speed, the line reliability, the propagation delay, the level of protection of the line, and so on. The weight assigned to the line grows as these characteristics deteriorate.

A similar categorization exists for the nodes and allows a specific weight to be assigned to them as well. The system takes a variable parameter, the workload, and establishes a parameter with a fixed value called the Route Addition Resistance (higher values are assigned for computers that should not have a heavy load of transit traffic). The NN adds the weight of each line and node for a given route, and the result is the route weight. Among different possible routes, the NN selects the one weighing the least.

In APPN there is no need to predefine all the usable routes, as is necessary in a traditional SNA network. Because the topology database is continually updated, the routes considered are always those in effect and potentially available when the session is requested by the end user.

DIFFERENCES BETWEEN PU 2.1 AND APPN

To stress the difference between the two communications alternatives, PU 2.1 and APPN, we will use System Network Application Distribution Services (SNADS) as an example. SNADS is a communications function for the distribution of objects (files, notes, texts, and so forth) among AS/400s. SNADS uses a mailbox concept for distribution. Mailboxes are files on the system's disks used to send outbound messages and to receive incoming mail. Furthermore, SNADS uses a store-and-forward technique; so in the case of three interconnected systems A, B, and C, as in Figure 6.5, the objects that A users intend to send to C users are, first of all, stored in A's outgoing mailboxes, and later transmitted to C.

FIGURE 6.5
The Advantages of APPN

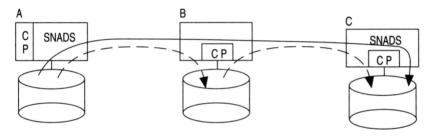

This example shows the advantages of APPN. Without APPN, the transfer of objects (for example, a file) between A and C also requires SNADS in the intermediate node B. The file will be stored in this node for subsequent forwarding. In the case of APPN, the transmission (supposing all systems are active) is directly to C, passing only through B. This means minor transmission time for the applications and minor load for the intermediate node.

If APPN is not used, the B system needs the SNADS function, and all the transmitted objects are stored in B's mailboxes. B will then transmit the objects to C, where they are stored for access in the C users' mailboxes. Alternatively, if APPN is used and all the systems and links are active, the mail outgoing from A is sent directly to C, simply by passing through B. This results in faster transmission, less load on the system, and less disk space utilization on B.

SNA-APPN RELATIONSHIPS

There are significant differences between the services of a traditional SNA network and those of APPN. Characteristics of SNA are that it provides for high traffic, thanks to 1) the processing power of mainframes, 2) the use of dedicated communications controllers, and 3) the lack of the additional load required under APPN for ongoing route information management (because all routes already are predefined in a traditional SNA network).

Moreover, an SNA network requires detailed definitions of all the components, including any modifications as a result of configuration changes. All resources (PU, LU, routes) must be defined and declared when the VTAM and NCP runtime software is generated. Therefore, if a host or communications controller is added to or deleted from the network, one (or more) VTAM and/or NCP modules must be regenerated.

On the other hand, APPN is much easier to define, install, modify, and use. This is a major advantage, especially considering the set of eligible customers — generally companies with small DP staffs. The price for this ease-of-use is a relatively higher processing overhead in an APPN network than in a traditional SNA network. This overhead is required for the dynamic route information management and administration that goes on within the routing nodes; for this reason, APPN is better suited for small networks with a manageable number of routes.

Figure 6.6 summarizes and compares the traditional SNA and AS/400 APPN solutions (the shadowed areas define the respective strong points).

When a PU 2.1 is connected to a traditional SNA network, all the PU 2.1 users can gain access to the resources of both environments. In case this PU 2.1 is an NN of an APPN network, the whole SNA network can be accessed by all the APPN users by defining the 37XX connecting the PU 2.1 as a LEN of the APPN network.

Similarly, when two APPN networks are connected to a common SNA network, the resources of all three networks come together. For example, let us imagine two APPN networks, one being connected to the SNA network via its NN-X and the 37XX-A, the second to the same SNA network via its NN-Y and the 37XX-B. Figure 6.7 explains the configuration.

In this example, all users of the two APPN networks can gain access, via their respective NN-X and NN-Y, to all the resources of the SNA network. In addition (see the dotted line), any user of the first APPN can enter in session with any user of the second APPN. The traffic flows in the SNA network following this pattern: NN-X/37XX-A/a given SNA predefined route/37XX-B/NN-Y. In this case, the SNA network is working as a "backbone" network on behalf of the two APPN communities. Of course, for efficient use of this approach, a company must manage the effect on the response time as a result of all traffic for the interested sessions passing through two APPN networks and the SNA backbone network.

FUTURE IBM SNA AND APPN DIRECTION

IBM statements of direction about networking are significant and deserve comment, as they may influence the future of APPN. IBM has set two guidelines: the extension of APPN Network Node functions to the mainframe environment, and a new strategy based on multivendor and multiprotocol support. These guidelines are based on IBM's acknowledgement that the SNA architecture is

FIGURE 6.6
Hierarchical SNA vs. APPN

	TRADITIONAL SNA	APPN AS/400
NETWORK DEFINITION	• Preliminary definition of all resources	• Minimum definition Autogeneration
ADDITION OF NEW SYSTEMS OR NODES	• Regen of VTAM and of NCP	• Reconfiguration • Automated and adaptive
EASE OF USE	• Normal	• Excellent
ROUTES	• Predefined	• Defined when needed
COMMUNICATIONS	• Distributed system to host	• Any-to-any
NETWORK SOFTWARE	• Many products	• The large majority is integrated in OS/400
LAN SUPPORT	• Token-Ring; Ethernet and token-bus via 3172	• Token-Ring Ethernet
VOICE/DATA APPL.	• No	• Via Callpath
ISDN SUPPORT	• No	• Yes
NETWORK AS BACKBONE	• Yes, for TCP/IP and X.25	• No
TRAFFIC VOLUME SUPPORT	• Very high	• Medium
TRANSMISSION LOAD	• Comm. Controller	• System
LINE SPEED	• Up to 2Mbps	• Max. 64kbps[1]
MAX. NUMBER OF LINES	• Up to thousands	• Hundreds
MAX. NUMBER OF TERM. LS	• Up to tens of thousands per system	• Thousand per system

[1] with some exceptions (ISDN and digital lines)

widely used and therefore must be continuously enhanced for easier implementation and use.

In terms of multivendor support, IBM acknowledges that support must be provided for TCP/IP — the de facto standard for heterogeneous networks and very important in configurations that include UNIX systems — for the standards emerging from the OSI model; and for the most important LAN protocols, such as IBM Netbios and Novell IPX. In addition, there must be support for the new and improved transmission technologies that promise higher transmission bandwidth, such as frame-relay and Asynchronous Transfer Mode (ATM). The latter will become very important in the future, because it is the transmission technology at the foundation of Broadband ISDN (B-ISDN) — the

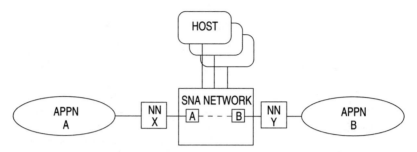

FIGURE 6.7
SNA Backbone Function

Two APPN networks interconnected via an SNA backbone

follow-on of ISDN digital networks — which offers connections at speeds exceeding 100 Mbps.

To satisfy these market requirements, IBM's goal is to implement the communications strategy summarized in Figure 6.8. This strategy is significant — first, because it couples SNA with APPN and second, because SNA is placed at the same level as TCP/IP and OSI. More generally, this development model is multivendor and multiprotocol, making it competitive with other major suppliers' products.

As shown in Figure 6.8, network applications will be able to use three basic sets of network interfaces in IBM networks:

- Common Programming Interface-Communications (CPI-C) — This interface comes from the SAA environment and is based on APPC (LU 6.2) services. The CPI-C is oriented toward peer-to-peer conversations between applications that require synchronization at the application level. This is the traditional SNA and APPN approach to program-to-program communications.

- Remote Procedure Call (RPC) — RPC is from the UNIX environment where it is used in conjunction with TCP/IP. In essence, RPC allows one program to exchange information with a program on a different system using a mechanism very similar to a subroutine call. RPC is also the key underlying communications structure used by the Open Software Foundation (OSF) line of distributed products, such as the Distributed Computing Environment (DCE). In general terms, RPC is well-suited for client-server processing where multiple clients can communicate with a common server.

- Message Queue Interface (MQI) — The MQI approach is common in a number of non-IBM networking environments, with X.400 being the

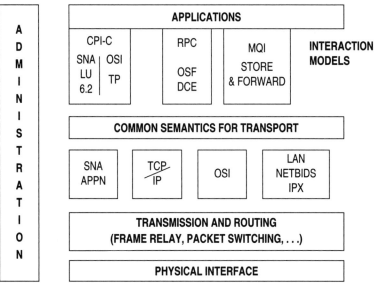

FIGURE 6.8
Summary of IBM's Multiprotocol Strategy

most notable example. Under MQI, programs may send messages to one another in an asynchronous fashion; messages waiting for delivery are held in a queue until the remote program is ready to receive them. The MQI approach allows a program to deliver non-critical information to other distributed programs without having to wait for confirmation of receipt.

Under all these capabilities will be common functions for accessing the session and transport services (those defined in layers 4 and 5 of the OSI reference model discussed in Chapter 3). By means of this common layer's functions, access to the various stacks of layers 4 and 5 of SNA-APPN, TCP/IP, OSI, Netbios, and IPX will be possible.

And thanks to the common semantics layer (shown in Figure 6.8), an application program may combine one of the interfaces mentioned above (CPI-C, RPC, or MQI) with any session and transport. In other words, two applications interacting via LU 6.2 verbs will be able to use the TCP/IP stack or the equivalent SNA-APPN services; alternatively, an application will be able to use the RPC interface over an SNA-APPN network.

The technology is visible, even if only partially, in the multiprotocol IBM 6611 router. This product is capable of transporting and routing frames using TCP/IP or DECnet or X.25 protocols, in addition to those of SNA, allowing the implementation of a wide set of heterogeneous networks. Thanks to the router, both the DEC-to-DEC connection and the SNA IBM-to-IBM connection are possible in a network connecting IBM and DEC systems. The router forwards the various messages to their pertinent destination. With this product, IBM joins the band of router manufacturers — Cisco, Proteon, Vitalink, Wellfleet, and others.

The 6611 is significant in demonstrating the direction IBM intends to follow to support multivendor environments. Equally significant, for the same reasons, is IBM's intent to make available to third parties the source code for APPN NN nodes.

Finally, some comment about the new function, Composite Network Node (CNN), announced for the mainframe environment and shown in Figure 6.9. A CNN consists of a VTAM host and its 37XX controller. While a CNN doesn't change how the VTAM handles its own terminals, it introduces a significant enhancement when used in relationship with a set of distributed AS/400s using APPN. The combination represents an APPN Network Node with the same functions as an AS/400 NN in terms of handling the network topology, finding resources, and selecting the route between two APPN users. With the CNN

FIGURE 6.9
Traditional Multidomain SNA

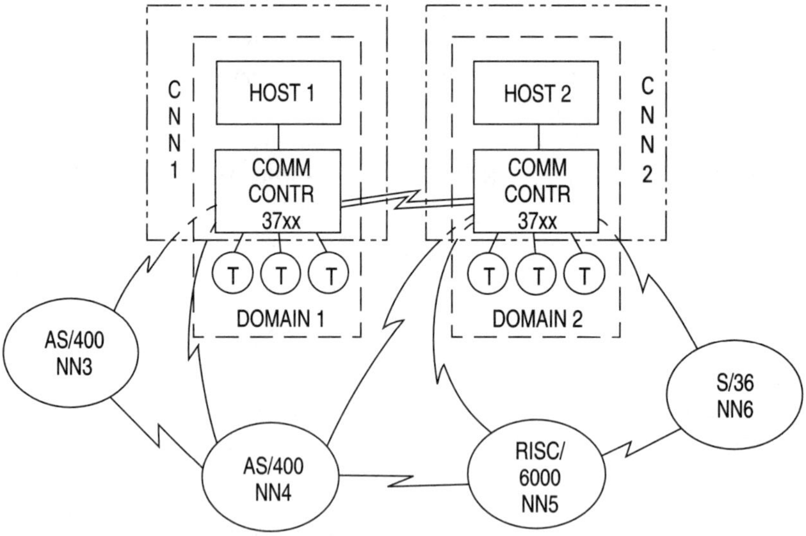

Traditional multidomain SNA maintains its functions in relationship to its PU1 and PU2; in addition, each set of PU5 and PU4 of each domain can be configured as a composed network node (CNN) of an APPN network. The backbone SNA network, thanks to CNN functions, now also has typical adaptive functions to handle APPN traffic.

function, an AS/400 APPN network can be completely integrated into a traditional SNA network. AS/400 users can access not only host resources, but also the SNA host's powerful resources for supporting all the APPN peer-to-peer and adaptive functions already available on the AS/400.

CHAPTER 7

Networking Roles

The AS/400 system's communications capabilities, summarized in Figure 7.1, are possible across all AS/400 models. The variations between AS/400 models are quantitative, representing differences in number of lines and terminals supported and in their performance capabilities. In brief, the AS/400 can assume any of the following networking roles:

- As the host or server within a network of single or clustered terminals and/or systems at a lower level (e.g., PCs, PS/2s, and industry systems)
- In a peer-to-peer network or an APPN network, as a system associated with other systems, such as another AS/400, a S/36, a S/38, and/or an RS/6000
- In a traditional SNA network as a distributed (or peripheral) system
- In connection with an OSI network as a peer system
- In a standard TCP/IP network as both a client and server system
- In a DECnet network as a limited-function peer system

We will discuss each of these environments in subsequent individual chapters in more detail; however, the following sections of this chapter provide a brief summary of each of the above environments.

The necessary AS/400 communications software for PU 2.1/LU 6.2 support and TCP/IP is included in the OS/400 operating system (as of V3R1). Other communications options — such as mainframe RJE and OSI services — require additional licensed products. The usability, general design, and network operating procedures of the AS/400's communications features mirror the overall characteristics of the system: ease of use; access to functions via menu or, for the experts, via the powerful structures of the command language; autoconfiguration of the local workstations; user profiles for resource protection; and related rights. The basic characteristics of the communications software can be summarized as follows:

- In V3R1 (and later), equal priority is given to TCP/IP and peer communications in SNA environments. The communications overhead for other types of networks will not hinder the ability of an AS/400 to perform its routing duties in an APPN network.
- Ease of use: Users can access all the functions and applications via menus. Users can also easily access online help. The typical complexity of the host's network definition and setup under SNA is avoided with

FIGURE 7.1
Summary of AS/400 Communications Capabilities

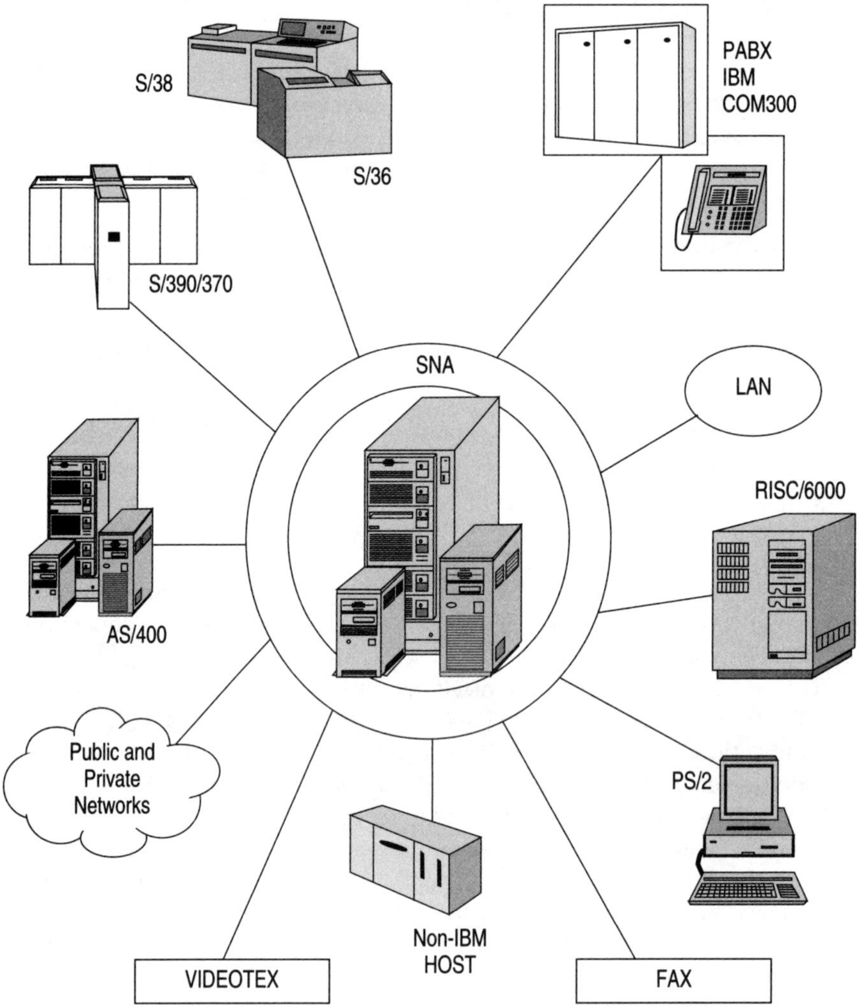

the AS/400's self-configuration capability and adaptive approach under APPN. An AS/400 can automatically generate new network entities such as devices and controller definitions, or it can modify the existing ones, at any time. Once completed, the definition is immediately included within the operating system's internal tables, where it becomes available for further use.

- As Figure 7.2 shows, most of the communications functions on the AS/400 are microcoded; the microcode includes all SNA functions up to the Data Flow Control Layer and all the APPN software.
- Unlike mainframes, AS/400 systems (and most of the other midrange systems) do not support external communications front-ends. Instead, they have integrated communications processors.
- Support exists for various other communications architectures. As stated, IBM's strategy is based on SNA, and the AS/400 system is particularly advanced from this perspective. Nonetheless, connections and applications in start/stop and BSC, and with OSI and TCP/IP architecture and products, are also well founded.

FIGURE 7.2
AS/400 Implementation of SNA and Other Communications Functions

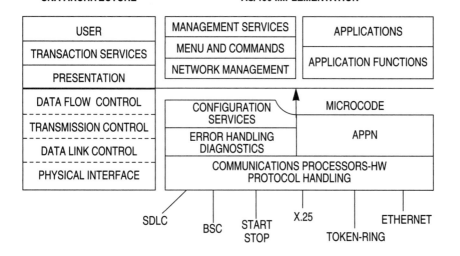

THE AS/400 AS HOST AND SERVER

On its own, the AS/400 can control a significant range of terminals and systems of terminals. Among the most common stations are the 5250 series (display terminals plus optional printers) that are locally connected via twinaxial cable or remotely connected via a 5294, 5394, or 5494 concentration unit. PCs or PS/2s can be connected in various ways — via twinaxial cable (emulating the 5250), connected to a 5X94 unit (again, in 5250 emulation), or downstream connected to a cluster controller 3174 or 3274 that is remotely connected to the system. PCs and PS/2s can also be connected to the AS/400 via a Token-Ring or Ethernet LAN, or they can be connected via a traditional remote line using the SNA/SDLC protocol or start/stop protocol emulating an IBM 3101 terminal. In addition to interfacing the the AS/400 via terminal emulation, PCs and PS/2s can also use underlying AS/400 services to accommodate a variety of client/server solutions.

3270 terminals, connected to 3274 or 3174 cluster controllers on traditional lines, can be supported via 5250 emulation. Terminals for specific uses also can be connected for specialized application environments, such as bank terminals of the IBM 4700 series and Point of Sales (POS) cash terminals through 4650 and 4680 controllers. A wide range of possibilities exists to connect terminals of the start/stop type. The AS/400 can have an integrated ASCII controller that can support ASCII terminals (or PCs emulating ASCII terminals) connected locally or remotely via modems (the ASCII controller provides the terminals with 5250 emulation for access to the system applications). The connection of ASCII terminals (both local and remote) to a 5208 protocol converter attached to the AS/400 via twinaxial cable is equally possible.

THE AS/400 IN MEDIUM-SIZED NETWORKS

Small- and medium-sized enterprises require less processing power than large organizations, so small- to medium-sized system networks (Figure 7.3) meet their requirements. The networks in this kind of environment are called peer-to-peer, because any system of the network may begin and independently run a conversation with any other system on the network to gain access to the remote system's application or data. This approach is particularly useful when it's not possible to accurately predict the need for connections with certain remote resources, as may happen in the case of office applications or with personal computing. A network that supports all possible kinds of connections from any one site to any other is therefore necessary. Thus, these networks must be adaptable to the various needs of the moment in the easiest possible way. (It is no coincidence that the traditional networked solutions of midrange vendors such as DEC and Hewlett Packard included these characteristics.)

In these small- to medium-sized networks, the AS/400 typically uses APPN functions to connect with other AS/400 and/or S/36 and S/38 systems. The

FIGURE 7.3
A Peer-To-Peer Network with AS/400 and Other IBM Midrange Systems

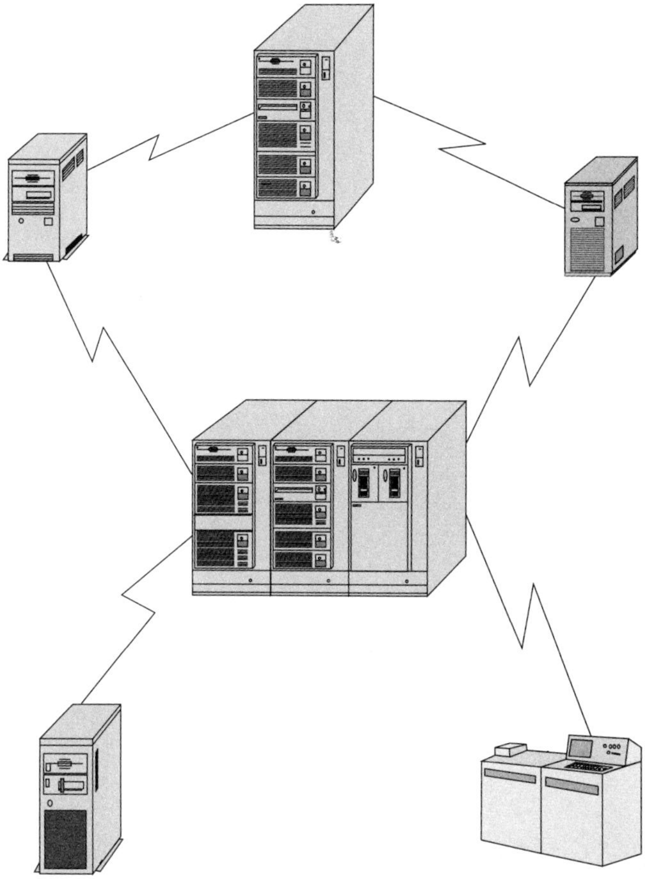

typical profile of this environment is that it includes a limited number of remote units, low to medium traffic volumes, a good balance between predefined procedural processes and contingency processing needs, and a limited number of people and skills to organize the work and help the end users.

THE AS/400 IN A LARGE OR MIXED SNA NETWORK
Many large enterprises have developed an online information system of the hierarchical type illustrated in Figure 7.4. In such a network, the information flow is under the strict control of the central system(s), and the distributed systems fulfill application functions that are typical of peripheral sites — they

FIGURE 7.4
A Centralized Host-Based SNA Network with Distributed AS/400

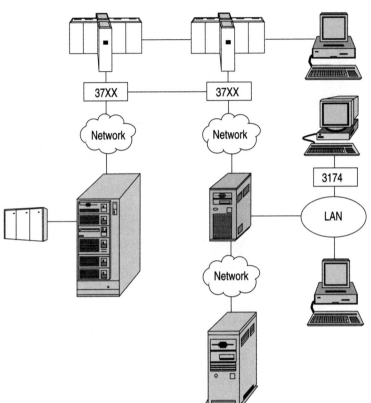

behave as traffic concentrators and connection support between remote terminals and the hosts. The application traffic always flows from the terminal toward the distributed system and from the distributed system toward the central host(s). These networks are characterized by excellent performance.

In most cases the network is SNA-based, and the AS/400 system fulfills PU 2.0 functions (see Chapter 5 for more information about SNA). A few isolated cases still exist where networks of this kind are based on non-SNA software (for example, they use BSC connections and software), but these cases are the minority.

The main characteristics of the large network environments are that they include a large number of remote terminal units, a significant number of central online applications, high-volume traffic, skilled people dedicated to the network at the central site, and a need for software support for network management tasks. The application profile is characterized by a predominance of fixed, procedural, repetitive work with a minimal degree of user freedom, at least when connected to the host.

As described in Chapter 5, the characteristics of peer-to-peer networks are now of interest to those enterprises using a traditional SNA network (Figure 7.5). The availability of APPN communications software allows more freedom in programming distributed and departmental systems' applications and communications functions. On this level, different APPN networks can be planned, each one designed to fulfill a certain number of applications and communications functions for specific departments or remote locations. In the case of a broader SNA network, the various APPN networks can be connected to one another through the "SNA backbone" function. Using PU 2.1 functions, the users of any APPN-connected system can gain access to all the resources of any other system on the APPN network being used, to all host 370 resources of an SNA network, and to the resources of another APPN network.

FIGURE 7.5
Departmental APPN Networks Interconnected with a Traditional SNA Network

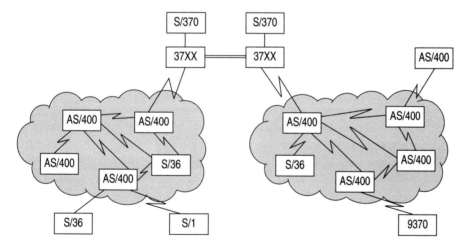

THE AS/400 IN AN OSI NETWORK

The ability to integrate the AS/400 into an OSI network is one of the key areas marked for significant expansion by IBM. This is not to say that the AS/400 has fallen behind the market in this area; the simple truth is that the entire scope of OSI networking continues to be defined and refined. IBM has, in fact, been quick to adapt the AS/400 to new and important standards as they emerge from the standards committees building the OSI model.

The three significant pieces of OSI supported by the AS/400 that enable it to function as a peer system in an OSI network are

- Support for X.500 directory services, which allows the AS/400 to identify users, systems, and global resources in the OSI network
- Support for X.400 message services, which allows the AS/400 to exchange electronic mail with other X.400-compliant systems
- Support for the File Transfer, Access, and Methodology (FTAM) specifications, which allows the AS/400 to participate in file transfer with other OSI systems

THE AS/400 IN A TCP/IP NETWORK

TCP/IP is one of the oldest networking architectures still in widespread use today. TCP/IP is the networking backbone for virtually all UNIX-based systems, and plays an important role in the implementation of the Open Software Foundation's (OSF) and Sun Microsystem's lines of distributed computing products.

The core functions of TCP/IP allow networks to be constructed using LAN and X.25 links; TCP/IP also provides the ability to route messages between networks using dissimilar links. For example, a TCP/IP network can include both LAN and X.25 systems, with certain key systems acting as "gateways" between LAN and X.25 transmission networks.

The TCP/IP architecture also includes "network applications" that facilitate interoperability between systems in a TCP/IP network. The following are those core applications supported by the AS/400:

- The TELNET utility allows AS/400 terminals to access other systems, and vice versa.
- The File Transfer Protocol (FTP) facility permits the exchange of files between TCP/IP systems.
- The Simple Mail Transfer Protocol (SMTP) service enables the flow of electronic mail between systems.
- NFS (Network File System) provides the functions to access shared files.
- Sockets provide a means of developing custom applications that connect to and communicate with other TCP/IP-based programs.

In all these cases, the AS/400 can act as a client and initiate these services or act as a server and receive requests for these services.

THE AS/400 IN A DECNET NETWORK

IBM has provided very few tools to integrate the AS/400 into DECnet or other proprietary LAN-based networks; those tools that are available are oriented toward allowing a Digital terminal to be directly attached to an AS/400 (via an ASCII workstation controller or 5208 protocol converter), and allowing the AS/400 to access the Digital system on a simple asynchronous link.

Fortunately, this area of integration is well addressed by third-party products that allow the AS/400 to operate as a peer system in DECnet networks. These products enable bidirectional terminal services, file transfer, printer sharing, program-to-program communications, and electronic mail distribution.

CHAPTER 8

The AS/400 as Host and Server

The fundamental roles of an AS/400 in a network are that of a host and server system. In either of these capacities, the AS/400 provides central services to a variety of connected devices and remote services, including the following:

- 5250 terminals and printers
- ASCII terminals
- 3270 terminals
- Point-of-Sales (POS) terminals
- Banking terminals
- PC workstations
- Facsimile services

In most cases, the interface to these devices is particularly simple to program on the AS/400, as it is on other 3X systems. A WORKSTATION file must be defined for every terminal to be supported, in the same way as files for traditional I/O are defined. The input instructions are carried out via instructions of the kind READ "name of the file," and output instructions are implemented with WRITE "name of the file" operations. Printers are supported by defining PRINTER files and WRITE operations. Programming interfaces of this kind are available in all programming languages available on the AS/400.

5250 TERMINALS AND PRINTERS

Terminals supported by the AS/400 belong to the 5250 family, whose name derives from the original 5251 model (which continues to be widely used). All the models use block-oriented transmission and can be locally connected via twinaxial cables. The modern line of 5250 terminals is best represented by the 3477 and 3476 terminals, which offer the following features:

The 3477 display terminal can be monochromatic (15-inch screen) or color (7 colors and a 14-inch screen). The monochromatic and color versions both can support one or two simultaneous work sessions between the user and AS/400 applications and can support screen displays up to 132 columns by 27 lines. As an alternative to one of the two user sessions, the 3477 can support a locally connected printer, which can be used as a local or system printer. In comparison, the 3476 monochromatic terminal supports one work session at a time and supports a maximum display size of 80 columns by 24 lines.

The twinaxial cable connects the AS/400 not only to the 5250 displays, but also to various kinds of printers. Printers with a wide range of services are available in many models. Each printer occupies the position of a workstation on the twinaxial cable. The same is true for PCs and PS/2s, which also can be connected to the twinaxial cables.

Remote connections can be implemented for 5250 terminals, printers, and PCs or PS/2s by using cluster controllers of the 5X94 family. For example, a 5394 controller can connect to a maximum of 16 workstations, while the more recent 5494 can connect to a maximum of 32 downstream devices. 5X94s can be connected to the AS/400 through an analog or digital line using the SDLC protocol, or through an X.25 network. The 5494 also can be connected via a LAN and supports downstream PCs and PS/2s on the Token-Ring.

ASCII TERMINALS

IBM 3101 and DEC VT100 terminals using start/stop protocols and ASCII code are supported either locally or remotely via the ASCII terminal controller. The AS/400 automatically converts the terminals' data streams into 5250 data streams; therefore, application programs see these ASCII devices no differently than they see native 5250 devices.

Support for a broader range of ASCII terminals is available through the 5208 protocol converter. The 5208 connects to the AS/400 via a twinaxial link and attaches to the ASCII terminals through direct or remote start/stop links. As in the case of the ASCII terminal controller, the application sees these devices as native 5250 terminals.

3270 TERMINALS

The AS/400 also supports the 3174 and 3274 cluster controllers, which are widely used in traditional SNA networks for the connection of 3270 terminals. The AS/400 connection to the cluster controller is an SDLC link. The terminals, displays, and printers are supported as terminals of the 5250 family; the AS/400 automatically converts their formats and data streams. Small functional differences due to the hardware characteristics of the terminals (the number of lines on the screen, for example) cause some operational constraints. For example, function keys must be remapped; overlapping display attributes are lost (e.g., if bold and blinking text is in effect, only one of those attributes will be visible on a 3270 terminal); and graphics printing is not supported.

AS/400 support of the 3174 and 3274 controllers also allows connection to many IBM and non-IBM systems capable of 3270 emulation. Because so many non-IBM systems offer 3270 emulation (and not 5250 emulation), the AS/400's 3270 support provides a simple and convenient mechanism for small-scale, multivendor integration.

POINT-OF-SALE TERMINAL SUPPORT

The AS/400 can connect downstream systems and terminals such as the 4680, 4684, 3651, and 3684. Connections are always in SNA/SDLC. These systems and terminals were specifically intended as point-of-sale (POS) terminal systems. An OS/400 software component, ICF-retail, allows file exchanges between these systems and the AS/400, and access to terminals for interactive applications. The AS/400 can, therefore, become the central system of a small- or medium-sized distribution enterprise. A further program, the Point-of-Sale Communication Utility, allows the AS/400 to function as a concentrator of these POS devices in SNA connection with S/370 mainframes.

AS/400 BANKING TERMINAL SUPPORT

The AS/400 also can connect 47XX banking systems and PCs or PS/2s equipped as banking workstations via the Financial Branch System Services (FBSS) software (Figure 8.1). Connections are established via an SDLC link or X.25 network and, in the case of PCs and PS/2s with FBSS, via local or remote Token-Ring LANs. The remote Token-Ring connection is established through the use of a PS/2 SNA gateway and connections with the AS/400 via an SDLC line or X.25 network. The 4731 and 4736 (automatic bank dispensers) and 4737 (automatic no-cash self-service) can be connected directly on the line (via SDLC connection or X.25 network) or downstream from a 4701 or 4702 bank controller. Of course, the 4701 and 4702 bank controllers can connect their traditional banking devices (e.g., the 4704 and 4720). The programming support for dialogue between the AS/400 and these units is established by using

- LU 0 for program-to-program communications
- LU 1 for the management of printer data streams
- LU 2 for the management of display terminals in 3270 mode

The application programs using LU 0 on the AS/400 for program-to-program communications can use various software support made available by IBM: Intersystem Communications Function (ICF), Finance I/O Manager and, specifically for PCs and PS/2s with FBSS software, the AS/400 Banking Monitor.

The AS/400 Banking Monitor allows the integration of the AS/400 in a Token-Ring LAN, with communications with PCs and PS/2s having FBSS software and the banking devices connected to them. The AS/400 can be connected directly to the LAN or, in the case of long distances, through an SDLC (or X.25) line plus a PC or PS/2 acting as a Token-Ring SNA gateway. The monitor has the following functions:

- File server, allowing PC and PS/2 access to the AS/400 database
- Application server, allowing application-to-application communications, via LU 0, between the AS/400 and PCs or PS/2s

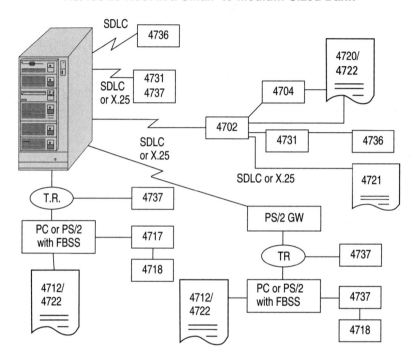

FIGURE 8.1
AS/400 as Host in a Small- to Medium-Sized Bank

4702 is a branch office controller
4736, 4731, 4737 are automatic machines
Other 47xx are branch-office terminals and printers
PCs or PS/2s with FBSS are PCs or PS/2s with banking software

- Communications server, allowing application-to-application communications, via LU 0, between the AS/400 and the DB/DC CICS or IMS monitors on the central mainframes

Thanks to these functions, the AS/400 can be used both as the main bank system, with branch offices using PCs and PS/2s with FBSS, and as a peripheral system at the branch-office level in a large SNA network based on a mainframe.

PC Workstations and Client/Server Connections

IBM's Client Access for OS/400 (CA/400) or its predecessor, PC Support, satisfies the need for data exchange and resource sharing between client systems (PCs or PS/2s) and one or more AS/400 server systems. CA/400 can be used via any physical connection supported by the AS/400: local PCs and PS/2s connected via the twinaxial cable, remote connections on a traditional SDLC line, via the X.25 network, on a LAN, and via a start/stop connection. The following functions are available to the user:

Intelligent Workstation Function. This function allows PCs or PS/2s to emulate a 5250 workstation.

Organizer. The simple choices among the options of the organizer menu allow the activation of applications running on PCs, PS/2s, or on the AS/400 — or, in case of an AS/400 connected to a host S/370, applications on the mainframe. The organizer function also means an easy switch between the local and remote applications. For example, it is possible, using OfficeVision/400, to download a long series of functions from the AS/400 to a PC or PS/2. After the download, these functions are managed directly on the PC processor, resulting in improved service and performance.

Data transfer. This function allows the transfer of data from (to) the AS/400 database files to (from) PC or PS/2 disks, with or without code conversion (ASCII to EBCDIC, or vice versa), and with the option of choosing fields at the record level.

Shared folders. The PC or PS/2 can operate with folders stored on AS/400 disks. These folders contain files, texts, and similar objects and can be shared with other users working on PCs or PS/2s and on normal 5250 terminals using OfficeVision/400.

Printer Sharing. CA/400 allows the PC or PS/2 to use an AS/400 printer as if it were a local printer. Similarly, it can allow a PC-attached printer to serve as an AS/400 printer.

Passthrough. In the case of AS/400 (and/or S/36) systems connected within an APPN network, the PC or PS/2 user can, via CA/400 and the terminal passthrough function, enter in session with applications of any other system on the network.

Messages. The PC or PS/2 user can send messages to the AS/400 system operator for help or explanations.

Data queues. Data queues provide a simple interface to program custom client/server applications. Using this feature, a PC-based application can deposit or retrieve messages from AS/400-based data queues.

Client/server capability. CA/400 establishes a client/server relationship between the PC and the AS/400. But is this relationship functionally comparable to that available on a LAN with Novell NetWare, an IBM LAN Server, or other similar LAN-based servers? Advocates of typical LAN-based servers cite better price/performance in terms of processing files and databases, as well as the LAN-based server's functionally rich offerings of such features as fourth-generation-language development tools.

Advocates of AS/400-based CA/400, on the other hand, cite the flexibility of CA/400 on the AS/400, the large number of applications available, the ease of developing a distributed client/server environment (thanks to APPN), and better overall price/performance if you include the support and management costs.

Because of these differing views, many customers today install both AS/400 and Novell (or similar) servers. Of course, this is one of the reasons IBM introduced the File System I/O Processor (FSIOP), a specialized adapter that allows the AS/400 to function as an IBM LAN server or NetWare server system in a LAN environment. The FSIOP and CA/400 products can be used concurrently to create a client/server environment that offers a broad spectrum of services.

A Problem: AS/400-X.25-PC DOS Connection

A PC DOS connection with an AS/400 via an X.25 network raises a problem not easily solved when using standard IBM hardware and software. This is particularly important given the growing acceptance of remotely installed PCs and the prospect of large numbers of portable IBM and IBM-compatible PCs. In these situations, the daily transmission of small amounts of data, such as collected orders and the like, is necessary. In such cases, X.25 connections are usually the cheapest and most convenient solution.

This type of connection is easily established for PCs or PS/2s running DOS by using an inexpensive asynchronous modem and ASCII terminal emulation software in conjunction with a dialed connection to the nearest standard PAD (Remember, this equipment only supports start/stop devices).

But this solution has two problems. The first and least important one is that communications in start/stop mode to an X.25 network do not optimize the number of packets sent; consequently, transmission costs are not optimized. The second and most important problem is at the remote side, where the AS/400 also must be connected to the X.25 network. The exact nature of this problem can manifest itself in two different ways, depending on the type of connection used between the AS/400 and the X.25 network:

1. If the connection is established via X.25 software to the nearest X.25 node, the AS/400 will expect a synchronous data stream, but will actually receive a start/stop data stream. Therefore, this approach requires a user-written program to manage the connection and interpret the data stream.

2. If the AS/400 uses start/stop lines to connect itself to a PAD network, the AS/400 will need as many start/stop lines to the X.25 PAD as there are remote PCs connected concurrently. This requirement is because the standard PAD supports downstream devices only in point-to-point lines.

To avoid both of these problems, some companies connect the AS/400 via modem or twinaxial cable to a PC that emulates a remote 5X94 cluster controller and supports the X.25 permanent and switched virtual circuits needed for connection to the remote PCs. Thus, the PC acts as a gateway between the PCs coming through the X.25 network and the AS/400; the AS/400 sees all the devices as if they were locally attached PCs. CA/400 can or cannot be used, depending upon specific products. The alternative to PCs is 5250 emulation.

FAX SERVICES

Users of OfficeVision/400 can use the product Office Facsimile Application (OFA) to receive and transmit documents to and from other remote stations through a fax server. A fax server is a PC or a PS/2 provided with special hardware (a card) and software for receiving and sending faxes. When transmitting, the user can prepare a document consisting of word-processor text, data belonging to AS/400 files, scanner-digitized documents, and/or previously received faxes; all these objects can be mixed in any combination. On the receiving end, the document can be highlighted on the screen, printed, or stored in special folders.

CHAPTER 9

Communications in APPN

Within an Advanced Peer-to-Peer Network (APPN), the AS/400 can communicate with any other IBM system provided with PU 2.1 functions (the PC, PS/2, RS/6000, S/36, S/38). As described in Chapter 6, "PU 2.1, LU 6.2., and APPN," the AS/400 also can function as an APPN network node (NN), end node (EN), or low-entry node (LEN). Furthermore, thanks to the 37XX communications controller, an APPN network can communicate with the resources of a traditional SNA network.

All the AS/400 application functions available under APPN are based on LU 6.2. The functions may use traditional lines (using the SDLC protocol), digital or analog lines (again, using SDLC), a packet-switching network (using the AS/400 X.25 interface and software), or a LAN (IEEE 802.5 protocols for Token-Ring and IEEE 802.3 for Ethernet).

In an APPN network, an AS/400 end user can use the functions discussed in Chapter 8 to access the AS/400 host (e.g., twinaxial 5250 terminals, ASCII terminals, CA/400 workstations, and so forth). Additional functions that allow the user to further navigate in an APPN network include the execution of remote commands, Display Station Pass-Through (DSPT), Distributed Data Management (DDM), Distributed Relational Data Architecture (DRDA), File Transfer Support (FTS), Interactive Communications Facility (ICF), System Network Application Distribution Services/Object Distribution Facility (SNADS/ODF) functions, and electronic mail distribution.

EXECUTION OF REMOTE COMMANDS

The OS/400 operating system allows commands to be executed on a remote AS/400; the command is entered on the same display station used for the input of requests addressed to a local AS/400. Before execution, a session must be established between the two remote systems; this connection is normally performed automatically when the AS/400 is powered on or when the communications link is activated. This function can be very useful for the control and management of remote systems and for the execution of applications using local or remote functions.

DISPLAY STATION PASS-THROUGH (DSPT)

This function allows the users of 5250 terminals connected to a system to access applications running on a remote system. The local and remote systems can be the AS/400, S/36, or S/38 in whatever combination. On request, users may be asked to identify themselves explicitly to the remote system, or they may be allowed to gain direct access to the application menus. If they have direct access, the password is passed automatically with the initial pass-through command.

The target system requires virtual controller and virtual device definitions to support the pass-through function. But in AS/400-to-AS/400 sessions, these definitions can be omitted because they can be generated automatically as needed. Figure 9.1 shows a typical pass-through environment. The DS1 box represents the display station using the pass-through to system B. DS1 is connected, locally or remotely, to system A. System A has the device description for the DS1 terminal. The virtual device description in system B, either entered manually or generated automatically, allows DS1 to access system B. Assuming that B is the name of system B, the user of DS1 can activate the pass-through function by giving a command as simple as

```
STRPASTHR RMTLOCNAME (B)
```

FIGURE 9.1
A Simple Pass-Through Environment

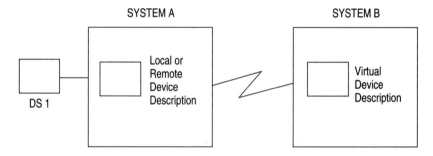

Once the function is activated, the person at the terminal proceeds as if operating on a remote system terminal. The terminal can activate up to two simultaneous working sessions on the remote system and, through special function keys, can return to the local system to manage one or two additional sessions. Depending on the user's needs, it is possible to switch from local to remote sessions, and vice versa, at any time. A reactivated session is resumed at exactly the same point where it was suspended. The application printer output on remote systems can be achieved easily on local systems through the SNADS/ODF function (explained later in this chapter).

Because DSPT enables access to resources of a remote system, based on the user's authority, DSPT can be a useful application instrument and means to control and manage remote systems. DSPT also can start remote diagnostic programs to identify and eventually correct possible problems.

DISTRIBUTED DATA MANAGEMENT (DDM)

DDM is based on LU 6.2; it is an OS/400 function that allows a source system application to gain transparent access to files, file members, or databases resident on a remote target system without requiring any program modification. The easy production of programs that can access distributed data via DDM allows data to remain where it is used most, without jeopardizing its access by the other network users. Thanks to DDM, every network user and application have at their disposal the same copies of files, with no redundancies, duplications, or differing data among the various copies. However, remember that access to a remote rather than a local file often means a longer waiting time. The operations available on a remote file or database (e.g., reading, updating, adding) are, as always, conditioned by the user's level of authority for the resource.

DDM also can be used to send CL commands to the remote system and to copy and/or transfer files, file members, or database members. But with very large files, the best transfer is established with SNADS/ODF or FTS rather than with DDM.

Figure 9.2 shows a simple DDM environment. The user at station DS1 is working with the APPL application in system A. The application needs to access a file or database in system B. To allow the access without modifying the application, a DDM file is created (a DDM file does not contain user data, but only pointers to the remote or target system) in system A that points to the real file (or database) in system B. To create a DDM file, use the CRTDDMF (Create DDM File) command, specifying the name of the file at the source system and the name of the file at the target system (where the file is located), and the name of the APPC application device that needs the function.

FIGURE 9.2
A Simple DDM Environment

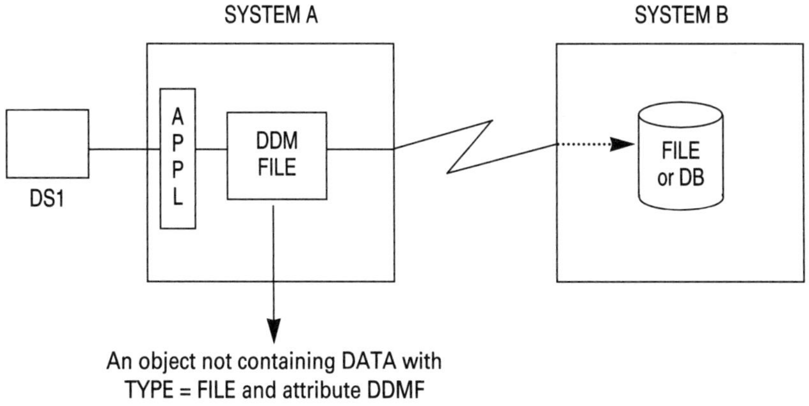

DISTRIBUTED RELATIONAL DATABASE ARCHITECTURE (DRDA)

This product, an integral part of System Application Architecture (SAA) (the overall IBM architecture at application level), allows access to distributed databases. There are two different ways to implement a DRDA connection: via the Remote Logical Unit of Work (Remote LUW), where access leads to one database; and via Distributed LUW, where access leads to databases on different remote systems. Presently, only the first function is available. With Remote LUW, an AS/400 application can gain access to a remote relational database on the AS/400, a PS/2, or the ES/9000. Similar applications on these systems can gain access to an AS/400 database.

FILE TRANSFER SUPPORT (FTS)

FTS allows the transfer of files or file members between any two AS/400s and/or S/36 systems. Although FTS can be directly activated by a terminal operator, it is more commonly called by CL programs or application programs written in RPG or COBOL. FTS can also be used outside of an APPN network via BSC and start/stop links.

INTERSYSTEM COMMUNICATIONS FUNCTION (ICF)

ICF software (Figure 9.3) allows conversation-based communications between applications running on remote systems. In this way, for example, an order-management application on the first system can transmit requests to the stock application on the second system to gain information about the stock on hand or other data related to the ordered goods. The main purpose of ICF is to cover up the complexity of the conversation interaction by reducing it, at least apparently, to the execution of an I/O operation on a local file. Hence, each of the two interacting applications must define an ICFFILE file. This file contains

- The detailed list of the data to be transmitted or received and their formats
- The specific list of "device" descriptions (or remote LUs) with which the conversation occurs
- The specific list (KEYWORDS) of commands for the control over the logical flow between the two applications (request for flow inversion, request for confirmation of reception, and so forth). By means of READ and WRITE statements the programmer interacts with the ICF file, which in its turn activates the ICF module. The ICF programming interface is available in RPG, COBOL, and C.

ICF can be used in an APPN network and in a non-SNA network (BSC or start/stop). When used in an APPN network, ICF uses the APPC (LU 6.2) interface for program-to-program communications. Through ICF, a program

FIGURE 9.3
ICF Functions in APPN (or PU 2.1) Network, Based on LU 6.2

Allows application-to-application functions. Requires the definition of an ICF file in both systems.

ICF
Intersystem Communications Function

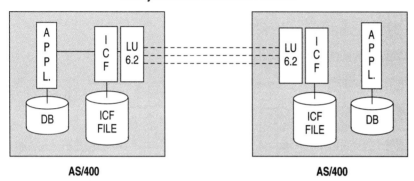

appl.-to-appl. sna: LU 6.2 (APPC) toward AS/400, S/36, S/38, S370/CICS
LU 0/ (SNUF) toward S/370/IMS, S/370 Banking System monitor, and toward S/36, S/38, or others.

can call and activate a remote program, exchange information, and then close the conversation.

The APPC variant of ICF has more functions than ICF based on BSC or start/stop connections; it can open any number of working sessions between two applications. These sessions can be previously activated (for example, at IPL time); thus the concerned program "acquires" one of the already activated sessions, calls the remote program, and initiates a conversation to exchange data. At the end, the program releases the conversation and closes the dialogue without closing the session. The session remains active and therefore can be used by any other program for a new conversation with any other application of the same remote system. A maximum of 256 remote "devices" or logical units can be defined on one ICFFILE, so programs on a given AS/400 can have up to 256 concurrent conversations with as many remote programs on one or more AS/400, S/36, or S/38 systems by means of the same ICFFILE.

Figure 9.4 shows the logical scheme and operating steps used by the source system to exchange data via ICF with a target system. Both systems are assumed to be AS/400s. Proceeding through the steps represented:

1. The line, controller, and device descriptions are activated.
2. The program on the source system is activated.

FIGURE 9.4
ICF Interactions: The Operations in the Source System

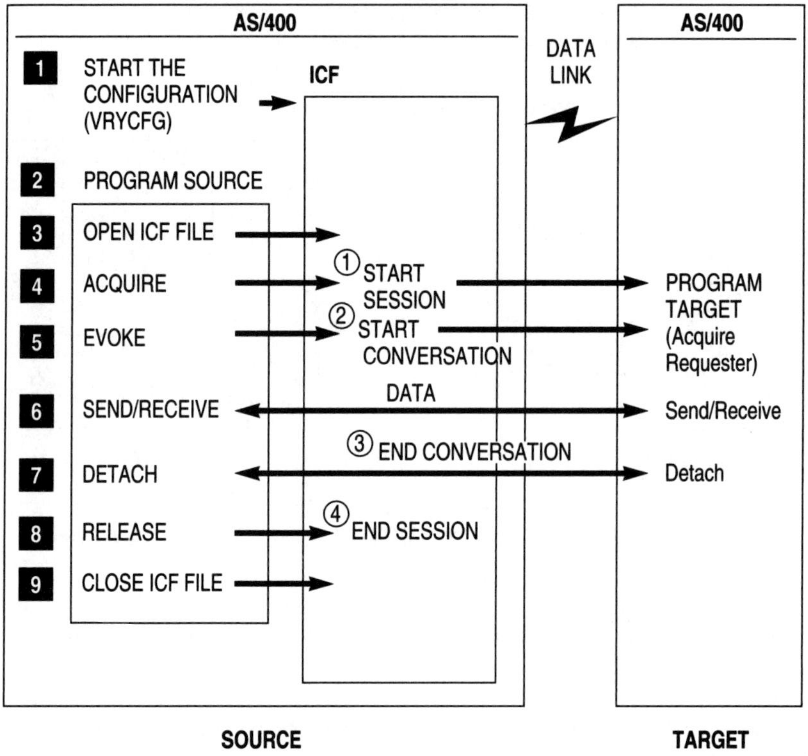

```
         AS/400                              AS/400
                              DATA
 1  START THE        ICF      LINK
    CONFIGURATION
    (VRYCFG)

 2  PROGRAM SOURCE

 3  OPEN ICF FILE
                      ① START                PROGRAM
 4  ACQUIRE             SESSION               TARGET
                      ② START                (Acquire
 5  EVOKE               CONVERSATION          Requester)
                        DATA
 6  SEND/RECEIVE                              Send/Receive
                      ③ END CONVERSATION
 7  DETACH                                    Detach
                      ④ END SESSION
 8  RELEASE

 9  CLOSE ICF FILE

         SOURCE                              TARGET
```

3. The program opens the ICF file.
4. An Acquire request activates a session with the target system (as identified in the ICF file).
5. A Write operation using the keyword Evoke activates the desired application on the target system. A conversation between the two programs is then started.
6. Data is exchanged via Read/Write operations.
7. One of the two programs, via a Write operation using the keyword Detach, ends the conversation. The session is still active, so it can be used by other conversations.
8. The Release operation ends the session with the remote system.
9. The program on the source system ends.

Figure 9.5 outlines the steps at the corresponding target system:

1. The line, device, and controller definitions are activated at the target system.
2. The received Evoke instruction activates the required program on the target system.
3. The program opens the ICF file.
4. The Acquire operation establishes the conversation with the remote source program.
5. Data is exchanged via Read/Write operations.
6. The Detach instruction ends the conversation.
7. The ICF file is closed and the program ends (or continues for local operations).

FIGURE 9.5
ICF Interactions: The Operations in the Target System

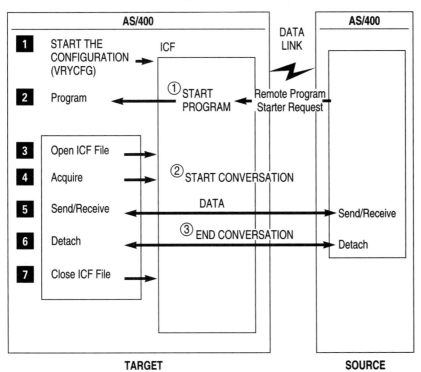

The program's interface through ICF allows it to identify the remote application (or program) required, specify the security parameters, maintain synchronization with the remote program, and change the data flow direction when needed.

SNA DISTRIBUTION SERVICES/OBJECT DISTRIBUTION FACILITY (SNADS/ODF)

SNADS is software that can be used on AS/400, S/36, and S/38 systems for the distribution of objects such as documents, files, programs, and job streams. SNADS is based on the concept of mailboxes, which are distribution queues (disk files where the objects to be distributed are stored) allocated for inbound and outbound information. SNADS uses a "store-and-forward" technique; therefore, the final destination system does not have to be online at the time of distribution. The object is transmitted gradually through intermediate systems until the addressee is reached. Once the destination is reached, the object is made available to the user via the user's mailbox.

When there are intermediate systems and the network is not APPN, the object is stored in the distribution queue of each intermediate system and then forwarded. If the network is APPN and the addressed system is ready, the object crosses the various intermediate systems and is directly stored in the addressed system, meaning that transmission is quicker and the intermediate systems must work less.

ODF is based on SNADS services; it allows the transmission of files, print and save files, programs, and job streams through the network. ODF is managed by a series of OS/400 commands that can be entered interactively or inserted in CL programs for later execution in batch mode. Transfer requests are received by the system, put in a queue, and then automatically executed. Operations can be requested to occur at a fixed time, and distribution lists can be used to distribute objects to several systems and users during the same operation. On the receiving systems, it is possible to define system parameters that cause actions to be taken on the received objects based on the source user profile. Jobs and programs, for example, can be rejected, stored, or automatically executed according to the sending user profile.

All this makes SNADS/ODF a useful instrument for the transfer of files with a fixed deadline (orders received during the course of the day, summaries, and the like). Thanks to its distribution services and automatic activation of programs, SNADS/ODF is also useful for managing unattended remote systems. Besides SNADS/ODF, DSPT and ALERT are useful for the same purpose; DSPT is useful for direct interaction with the remote system's resources and ALERT for distributing information about errors or abnormal events. ODF, when accompanied by DSNX (explained in Chapter 10), allows the AS/400 to distribute files or programs received from an S/370 to other systems connected within an APPN network.

ELECTRONIC MAIL DISTRIBUTION

Communications services include the functions of IBM's OfficeVision/400 product for the distribution of documents and personal notices and for services that support access to remote libraries. These services, too, are based on SNADS and allow the reciprocal exchange of documents, images, and PC objects contained in the OfficeVision/400 folders. These functions also can be invoked through system menus and through commands integrated into user-written application programs.

Finally, the AS/400 Communications Utilities product extends the distribution services to the S/370 environment, specifically for hosts running either the VM operating system and PROFS application or the MVS operating system and CICS/DISOSS.

CHAPTER 10

Traditional SNA Networks

This chapter discusses the role of the AS/400 when it operates in a traditional Systems Network Architecture (SNA) network in conjunction with a S/370/390 mainframe host. The connection between an AS/400 as a network distributed system and a S/370 mainframe is established according to the scheme represented in Figure 10.1. In this environment, the AS/400 functions as a distributed system that looks to the mainframe host for central services.

FIGURE 10.1
AS/400-to-Mainframe Connection

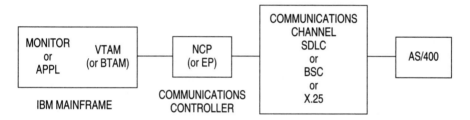

Most of the application functions for AS/400-host sessions listed in Figure 10.2 are available in an SNA environment. In this environment, Virtual Telecommunications Access Method (VTAM) is required on the host, Network Control Program (NCP) is required on the 37XX communications controller, and the AS/400 acts as PU 2.0 — that is, as a peripheral system capable of managing secondary logical units in session with primary logical units on the host. An AS/400 user can enter into session with applications running on any host in the SNA network (courtesy of VTAM, which acts as the System Services Control Point (SSCP)).

Some application functions can be used in non-SNA networks, too; for example, 3270 emulation also can be used when the 3270 BSC protocol is implemented. Support for 3270 BSC operations is available in both non-SNA and SNA networks; however, use of BSC 3270 in SNA networks is often discouraged because it adds overhead to NCP in the communications controller (which converts BSC 3270 data stream into SNA format).

Figure 10.2
AS/400 — Host Sessions: Application Functions

- CONVERSATIONAL ACCESS: From AS/400 to Host: 3270 Emulation
  From Host to AS/400: HCF
- FILE TRANSFER: RJE, N/DM-DSNX
- PRINT FILE TRANSFER: From HOST to AS/400: RJE, 3270 Emulation
- REMOTE FILE ACCESS: From AS/400 to Host: DDM
- APPL-TO-APPL: CICS: ICF (LU 6.2)
  IMS: ICF-SNUF (LU 0)
- DOCUMENT DISTRIBUTION: SNADS/ODF + BRIDGE MVS/VM
  From HOST to AS/400: N/DM-DSNX
- PROGRAM DISTRIBUTION: From HOST to AS/400: N/DM-DSNX
- NETWORK MANAGEMENT: HOST (NETVIEW), AS/400 ALERT Support

3270 EMULATION

3270 terminals connected to an AS/400 by means of their 3274 and 3174 controllers can access AS/400 applications (as described in Chapter 8) or they can pass through the AS/400 to gain access to conversational applications on the host. In the latter case, the protocols used to communicate with the cluster controller and the host are both SNA, so the AS/400 does not perform any protocol conversion. If, however, connections between the AS/400 and the host are achieved via BSC, the AS/400 converts from the SDLC line protocol (used to communicate with the cluster controller) into BSC (for the host), and vice versa.

Users of 5250 terminals also can gain access to conversational applications through the use of 3270 emulation software. In this instance, the AS/400 software converts the data stream into 3270 format. As in the case of 3270 access to AS/400 applications, 5250 access to host applications (using 3270 emulation) is constrained by operational differences in the two types of terminals. For example, 5250 keys must be mapped to 3270 equivalents; overlapping display enhancements are not supported, and bit-oriented graphics are not supported. (No such limitations exist when 3270 terminals attached to an AS/400 connect to host applications — this configuration enables the use of graphical applications, support for direct keyboard operations, and overlapping display enhancements.)

The AS/400 also supports the 3270 Application Program Interface (API). This interface allows a program to intercept all the data transmitted to or from the host to logically emulate a 3270 terminal. An additional program, System/370-PC File Transfer, supports file transfers in 3270 emulation between the host and PCs or PS/2s connected to an AS/400.

COMMUNICATIONS BETWEEN PROGRAMS

Interactions between AS/400 programs and programs on the host in conversational mode can be established via the Intersystem Communications Function (ICF) on the AS/400. ICF can be applied to the SNA network in two ways:

1. By using Advanced Program-to-Program Communications (APPC) (LU 6.2) for interactions with the Customer Information Control System (CICS) monitor on the host
2. Via ICF/SNA Upline Facility (SNUF) (LU 0) for interacting with the Information Management System (IMS) monitor

Functionally, the ICF/APPC combination is practically the same as that described for ICF between AS/400s in an APPN network. ICF/SNUF, on the other hand, has more limitations; in particular, only one session is possible between two applications. In both cases, the ICFFILE file definition — as discussed in Chapter 9 — is used to define the characteristics of the logical link between the AS/400 and the host.

CICS ON THE AS/400

The Customer Information Control System (CISC), the online transaction processing monitor so well known in the IBM mainframe environment, is now available on the AS/400. In terms of the AS/400, CICS can be used for two purposes: migration from an IBM mainframe to the AS/400, or mainframe-AS/400 coexistence in a transaction-processing environment.

For migration, or "rightsizing," applications based on CICS and developed in a mainframe environment can be transferred to an AS/400 with minimal conversion — COBOL presents some minor differences in the two environments, and the AS/400 does not support the mainframe DL/1 database. For coexistence, mainframe and AS/400 programs can communicate with one another using LU 6.2 services within CICS. This allows, for example, a transaction entered from an AS/400 terminal to be processed partially on the AS/400 and partially on the mainframe.

DISTRIBUTED DATA MANAGEMENT (DDM)

DDM enables applications on an AS/400 to access files residing on hosts supporting this function. Currently, DDM is available only under the CICS monitor and only for Virtual System Access Method (VSAM) files. DDM cannot be used to gain access to the central databases, even if interaction occurs with CICS. For database access, ICF must be used to communicate with a custom-written server program.

REMOTE JOB ENTRY (RJE)

The transmission of jobs and files to be processed by a central host has always been an important function available to distributed batch terminals and midrange systems, and signs point to continued and even increasing importance, especially in cases of heterogeneous networks and intercompany communications. IBM mainframes' various operating systems are provided with subsystems that support these batch-oriented functions:

- Multiple Virtual Storage (MVS) has Job Entry System 2 and 3 (JES2 and JES3).
- Virtual Memory (VM) has Remote Spooling Communication System (RSCS).
- Disk Operating System/Virtual Storage Extended (DOS/VSE) has Priority Output Writers, Execution processors, and input Readers (POWER).

The subsystems can work both in SNA networks (except VM) and in BSC networks (except DOS/VSE with POWER). By means of these subsystems, the host can accept peripheral jobs and files and, through the same subsystems, the host can send output files back to the remote device. These functions are collectively referred to as Remote Job Entry (RJE).

On the AS/400, the counterpart of these central subsystems is the AS/400 Communications Utilities program, which includes an RJE function. This program makes it possible to work with all the subsystems mentioned above using SNA or BSC links. In an SNA network, the RJE sessions use the LU 1 assignment while BSC networks follow the model established by the 3780 RJE workstation.

Jobs and data to be transmitted can be previously recorded on an AS/400 disk, or they can be inserted from the terminal in conversational mode with the RJE console function. Host print outputs can be inserted in the spool queues of OS/400 or can be printed immediately. The main tasks of the terminal equipped with the RJE console function are to control the flow between the two systems, to enable inquiries on the status of jobs previously sent (in process, waiting, ended, and so on), and to switch the sessions on and off.

RJE functions enabling the transmission of files in both directions can be used as an alternative to NetView/Distribution Manager-Distributed System Node Executive (N/DM-DSNX). The main purpose of RJE is transmission from the remote systems to the central host, while the main goal of N/DM-DSNX is to distribute information from a central host to remote systems.

BRIDGE MULTIPLE VIRTUAL STORAGE/VIRTUAL MACHINE (MVS/VM)

The AS/400 Communications Utilities product also contains the Bridge MVS/VM function. This function further extends the object distribution function available under SNADS/ODF in APPN networks to support the exchange of documents, mail, and files with mainframe hosts. Both SNA and BSC connections are supported.

BANKING MONITOR

As mentioned in Chapter 8, the Banking Monitor program provides an AS/400 with two operating modes:

- As the main system of a small- or medium-sized bank, with support for banking terminals and PCs or PS/2s with Financial Branch System Services (FBSS) software
- As a branch office communications server handling the same types of terminals and a connection to a S/370 host as well

In the second instance, the branch office AS/400 system can be provided with the following functions:

- Management of the branch office's distributed applications and related files
- Computer resources sharing service within the branch office
- Control and completion of transactions to be transmitted to the host
- As a log for local files of the transmitted transactions
- Concentration of traffic to and from the host

For communications to the host, the Banking Monitor uses the ordinary conversational functions provided by ICF/SNUF and enables access to central applications managed by CICS and IMS monitors.

HOST COMMAND FACILITY/DISTRIBUTED HOST COMMAND FACILITY (HCF/DHCF)

The host application Host Command Facility (HCF) is available under the MVS and DOS/VSE operating systems. HCF requires an application counterpart (DHCF) on distributed systems; this is available on the AS/400, S/36, S/38, S/1, 8100, and others. The SNA session between the HCF and the DHCF uses the software product ICF/SNUF and enables a 3270 system (or a PC or PS/2 using 3270 emulation) in the host environment to start a session with the remote system, such as an AS/400. Once connected to the AS/400 system, the 3270 terminal receives the log-on menu of the AS/400 remote system and is supported by the AS/400 in 5250 emulation. All the other systems provided with DHCF function in a similar manner.

It is therefore possible to use all the AS/400 applications, functions, and commands from the central 3270 workstation, depending on the authority granted to the user. The 3270 keyboard can be modified and personalized for better transmission of commands and requests to the remote AS/400 system.

Remarkably enough, there is no need for direct connections between the host and the AS/400 with HCF/DHCF. The HCF/DHCF can use any route of the SNA network and cross one or more 37XX nodes until the AS/400 is reached; from there, once the DHCF function is activated, DSPT can be used to gain access to another AS/400 distributed system by means of the PU 2.1 or APPN functions.

HCF/DHCF can be used for

Application access. The local or remote 3270 users of the host can gain access to the applications on an AS/400 system. From this point of view, HCF/DHCF is the functional counterpart of 3270 emulation, which allows AS/400 users to gain access to host resources. For this type of use, you must consider the following:

1. There can be a negative impact on terminal response time because data is transmitted via at least two sessions (one from the 3270 to HCF on the host, and a second from HCF to DHCF).
2. There are the usual operational constraints due to the hardware differences between 3270 and 5250 displays.

Printer output originated at the AS/400 site can be obtained at the host by using tools different from HCF/DHCF — for example, RJE or N/DM.

Analyses and solutions of problems on distributed systems. In networks with a high number of distributed systems, a pool of network and application experts is usually located in the central host location. With HCF-DHCF, these experts can gain access to remote systems experiencing anomalies; they can make inquiries about a system's configuration and, if necessary, modify it; or they can support a user facing problems on a particular procedure by using, for example, the Copy Screen Image function. HCF/DHCF is therefore a useful instrument for the centralized management of distributed systems.

NETVIEW/DISTRIBUTION MANAGER-DISTRIBUTED SYSTEM NODE EXECUTIVE (N/DM-DSNX)

The combination of N/DM on the host and DSNX on distributed systems (e.g., the AS/400, S/36, and others) enables the two-way transmission of files and other objects, and facilitates centralized management of peripheral application resources. When the number of peripheral distributed systems is high, a system identical to the distributed ones is often installed at a central location; this central system is used for the development, testing, and maintenance of the peripheral application resources. After the testing phase is successfully completed, the new applications or new versions of existing applications can be transmitted from the development system to the S/370 host by using RJE, DSNX, or other supports.

At the host level, N/DM enables distribution planning for the received objects; centrally records the transmissions made and their results; executes the transmissions to the remote DSNX system and also can receive, in turn, files and other objects sent from DSNX. Programs sent to the remote DSNX can be executed automatically. Furthermore, through SNADS/ODF, the receiving AS/400 can act as an intermediate node on behalf of other AS/400, S/36, or PC-to-PC systems that are not directly connected to the host.

At the central location, N/DM makes available the management instruments for the definition and execution of distribution plans for remote systems, a directory for network resources, log files for the recording of executed transmissions, the hour and date of the operation, the number of transmitted bytes, the name of the transmitted object, and the results of the individual transmissions.

DSNX and N/DM are valuable instruments for managing, planning, and controlling the centralized distribution of resources toward all of the distributed systems. No operator intervention is required once DSNX is activated on the AS/400. DSNX automatically transmits a "Return Code" to the host; this code shows the results of the received transmissions. N/DM-DSNX also can be used for unattended operation of a remote AS/400 centrally controlled from the host site.

NETWORK MANAGEMENT

Medium or large SNA networks require a central operator responsible for operations control and for solutions to network problems. The IBM NetView[1] product is the main support for these tasks. NetView enables the automatic execution of normal operating procedures such as switching on or off the whole network or single components; analysis of the conditions of the individual components; and, in addition to other functions, a centralized gathering of peripheral error messages (alerts). These alerts are stored on special central files and, depending on the importance of the error, can be automatically displayed on 3270 control terminals.

The AS/400 can originate and locally store alerts, allow an authorized operator to gain access to the alert files and, in the case of SNA networks, send them to a host system provided with NetView. The transmitted alerts are those generated on the AS/400 system and — when the AS/400 is defined as a focal point for the alerts — those coming from other systems connected via APPN networks. The central operator responsible for error analysis and resolution can make inquiries on the alerts received from the remote systems; the HCF/DHCF functions can then be used for further information and trouble-shooting.

---

[1] NetView is an IBM-supplied VTAM application specifically designed for network management tasks. For these tasks, NetView can interface, in turn, other complementary programs such as N/DM (NetView Distribution Manager) and HCF (Host Command Facility).

CHAPTER 11

OSI

So far, we have discussed the wide set of communications functions available to the AS/400 in IBM networks. From IBM's perspective, both the APPN and SNA architectures permit the connection of non-IBM equipment (for example, through start/stop attachments and 3270 emulation). When viewed from a non-IBM perspective, however, these network architectures are less than ideal. Therefore, although APPN and SNA remain the strategic architectures for all-IBM networks, the rest of the market has demanded the widest possible range of facilities to enable connections between all types of computers.

This need for connectivity between dissimilar systems is normally driven by real-life business situations (as opposed to technical requirements). For example

- A firm often chooses X supplier's systems for commercial applications, Y supplier's systems for CAD/CAM applications, and so on. Sooner or later, the computers (which are often incompatible) must be able to communicate with each other.

- Sometimes communications between incompatible computers are only needed "temporarily" (even though that period of time may extend to several years). For example, an organization chooses to add producer Y's new mainframe to its current X mainframe with the intent of gradually migrating all applications from the X mainframe to the new Y mainframe. Because of the large number of programs involved, a simultaneous conversion of all applications is often impossible, so the two systems must coexist for a fairly long time, thereby making communications between the two systems necessary for reciprocal file updating and application development.

- A group of businesses decides to create a consortium for one or more applications of common interest. It is unlikely that all the businesses will have the same type of system, so it is necessary to implement communications among them based on international communications standards, rather than on proprietary architectures.

- The communication of business data to the external world through Electronic Data Interchange (EDI) is becoming increasingly necessary; for example, to handle the "routine" business tasks of ordering, invoicing, and status inquiries. In these cases, too, the better solution is based on international standards.

To satisfy such needs, the AS/400 supports a series of additional functions beyond those seen so far with SNA and APPN. These functions are based on two sets of standards: those international standards resulting from the development of the OSI model, and the de facto standards that have resulted from the widespread use of the Transmission Control Protocol/Internet Protocol (TCP/IP) (for more information about TCP/IP, see Chapter 12).

OSI FUNCTIONS

We discussed the OSI conceptual model in Chapter 4. Those aspects of the OSI model that are particularly relevant to the discussion in this chapter are

- Levels 1 through 6 of OSI have been well defined and established in the current market. The more notable standards in these levels include the IEEE LAN specifications, the HDLC protocol definition, and the X.500 directory recommendation that handles object-naming conventions (e.g., user names, systems names) in a global network
- The application functions of the seventh level that have had the greatest visibility are those pertaining to the File Transfer, Access, and Management (FTAM) recommendation and the X.400 electronic message exchange recommendation. All these standards were completed some years ago. Formal completion of other application standards is progressing (e.g., for virtual terminals, for access to remote database)
- At the transmission level, the OSI model requires the use of geographical networks using X.25 packet switching and, in private areas, the IEEE 802 series of LANs (i.e., Token-Ring, Token-bus, and Ethernet)

To some extent, most major software suppliers have developed software that complies with the OSI standards. In particular, suppliers have been eager to provide products that support those standards defined in levels 1 through 6 and products that implement level 7 FTAM (file transfer) and X.400 (electronic message) functions. All these products are characterized by the use of X.25 software, Token-Ring, and Ethernet interfaces for transmission requirements.

IBM OSI PRODUCTS

Availability of OSI-compliant products on the AS/400 has been growing in recent years. At this time the AS/400 supports the following OSI products:

- OSI Communications Subsystem (OSICS), which corresponds to the standardized functions of levels 1-6 of the OSI model
- OSI File Services (OSIFS), for the transfer and management of files according to the FTAM standard; OSIFS also makes available an application interface for the personalization of services.

- OSI Message Services/400 (OSIMS), which corresponds to the X.400 electronic messages standard; the X.400 standard is becoming increasingly popular and important, and deserves a detailed description, which follows in the next section.

Thanks to OSICS, OSIFS, and OSIMS, the AS/400 can transmit files and electronic messages via X.25 networks to other IBM and non-IBM systems with software conforming to the same set of OSI standards.

ELECTRONIC MESSAGING SYSTEMS

Electronic mail (e-mail) is a network application for the exchange of objects such as notes and text-based documents between users. The electronic messaging system extends the application to objects such as files, faxes, telexes, and programs (see Figure 11.1 for the basic components of a standard X.400 e-mail system).

FIGURE 11.1
X.400 Message Handling System

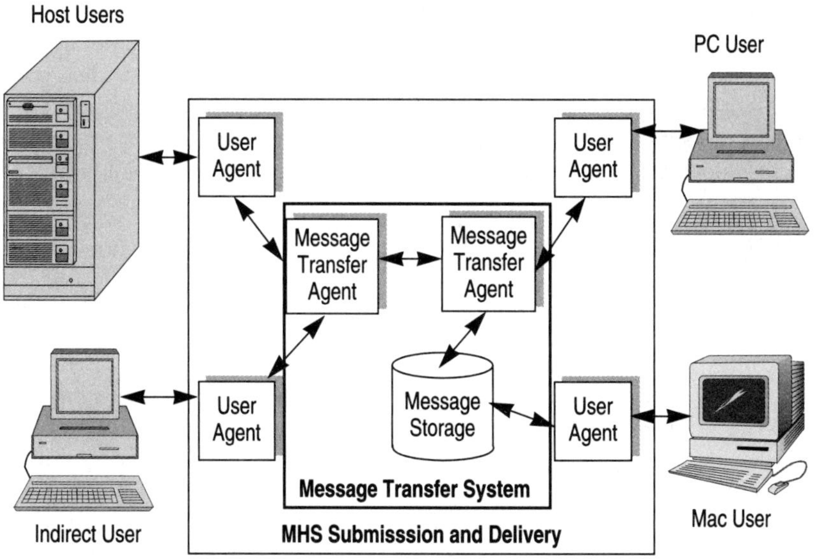

X.400, the standard for e-mail systems, divides the functions into those of the user agent (the client, responsible to the end user) and the message transfer agent (the server, responsible for the message transmission). A component, the message store, supports user agents for PCs with or without a fixed disk permanently connected to the network. An access unit allows interchange of the message with other communications services such as telex, telefax, and fax or with normal mail services and their users.

Electronic messaging is a popular application among a range of different wide- and local-area networks. Although it is hard to economically justify the network implementation of this application alone, e-mail often is an easy-to-use and functional added value. E-mail applications based on proprietary protocols and systems exist on all the major products on the market. IBM offers DISOSS and PROFS on mainframes, and SNADS/ODF and OfficeVision/400 on the AS/400; DEC offers All-in-One and VMS-Mail on VAX systems; HP uses HPOffice on its HP3000 systems; and Unix and other systems using TCP/IP have the SMTP function. Among the most popular solutions for LANs are Microsoft Mail, Lotus cc:Mail, and DaVinci Email.

Many of these products have specific APIs that allow data to be imported from other applications and inserted in the text to be sent. The opposite sometimes is also possible: Traditional end-user applications can call the e-mail package. In both cases, data and text integration is possible, so communications to the internal users of the originated documents is completely automated.

When a large organization decides to unify its different local- or wide-area networks into a single global network, it often faces — in addition to many other problems — the problem of interconnecting two or more e-mail applications that potentially run on different systems and use incompatible application and communications protocols. In such cases, X.400 is often an ideal solution because it is based on OSI standards and is therefore independent from the system and the supplier. X.400 e-mail software is now available on a wide range of systems, including virtually all those that also have a proprietary solution.

THE X.400 STANDARD

X.400 is a set of protocols defined by CCITT for a standard electronic messaging system that has been incorporated into the OSI reference model for open systems. Thus, an e-mail implementation based on X.400 is completely consistent with OSI. X.400 defines the rules for the setup of the message, its delivery to the transmission system, its transmission, the delivery to the addressee, and notification to the source.

Like SNADS, X.400 uses a store-and-forward technique that queues mail objects in disk files until they are ultimately delivered to a user mailbox. X.400 can be used on all networks that support OSI and therefore on X.25 networks and all LANs using IEEE 802 standards. Many software suppliers have implemented specific gateways between their proprietary e-mail and X.400, either in addition to or instead of direct support for the full range of X.400 functions.

Two versions of the X.400 standard exist: the 1984 and the 1988 specifications. Presently, many of the products on the market correspond to the 1984 specifications. The 1988 specifications, however, define new functions for enhanced security, more flexibility, and easier implementation. Among other things, access to the service via switched line and start/stop protocol has been defined, which is a significant extension from the original version.

X.400 defines two main entities: the User Agent (UA), for service between the end user and the other main entity; and the Message Transfer Agent (MTA), whose role is that of server for the transmission. This client/server relationship between the UA and the MTA and the fact that OSI is based on a peer-to-peer relationship point to the interesting and much-discussed design of X.400 — that of a client/server relationship in a peer-to-peer network.

UA AND MTA FUNCTIONS

The UA offers a set of functions to guide the end user to set up the message and enter it in the mailbox for transmission. The UA is responsible for message input, for presentation services, message editing, definition of the security parameters, and the definition of transmission priorities. In terms of output, the UA is responsible for delivery of the message and notification of acceptance to the sending user.

The MTA routes and forwards the messages received by UA. Among the MTA's tasks are selection of the network route, transmission to the next MTA on the selected route, and protection of the message during transmission. When a message is extracted from the UA's sending queue, the first task of the MTA is to see whether the destination is served by a directly connected UA; if so, the message is sent directly to the addressed UA. Otherwise, the MTA selects the network route to be used and the message is sent to the next MTA on the selected route. All subsequent MTAs will act in the same way until the message arrives at the final UA and is delivered to the destination user.

A set of MTAs make up a Message Transfer System (MTS). In 1988, a new entity was added internally to the MTS: the Message Store (MS). MS is a component capable of storing incoming messages that allows eventual message searches and extractions from an authorized UA. In practice, MS is a message database system. It is particularly useful for supporting terminals and PCs that may not always be connected to the network.

Another entity, the Access Unit (AU), establishes MTS connections to other services such as telex, facsimile, and mail services. In 1988, specific AUs were defined for these three services.

SENDING THE MESSAGE

Conceptually, X.400 is similar to mail services: The message is the letter to be sent, and the UAs and MTAs provide the mail service. The messages are inserted in special folders called envelopes. The information needed for the transmission is written on the envelope: the destination (or a list of destinations), the format of the text, and the code used. X.400 users can send their objects to other X.400 users, as well as to the users of other communications services.

As with mail service, there must be a way to identify exactly who the addressee is, regardless of location. In X.400, the basis for the identification is the user's name. On the basis of the name, a directory provides the corresponding address identification. Addresses are based on the X.121 international standard (another CCITT standard). The X.121 address identifies the country in its first part, and then the user within the country. In addition to the user address, the dictionary also supplies the serving UA's identification, the owning domain identification, and other textual information, such as the formal name of the user, the user's address (e.g., street, city), and, possibly, the firm or organization.

X.400 mail service also transfers "probes." A probe consists of an empty envelope that can be used for tests before preparing and sending long and important messages to a specific user. The user may never have been contacted before and the test determines whether the user can be reached.

X.400 Protocols

Several protocols define the relationships between the different X.400 entities. Specifically, P1 defines the interaction between two MTAs, and P2 defines the exchange between an X.400 user and external communications services, such as telex. In 1988, specifications relating to telex and fax Group III services were added to the existing P2 specifications; these new specifications also define the relationships with a number of text processors, enabling the electronic communications of computer-originated documents.

The P3 protocol defines the rules to be followed in delivering a message from the UA to the serving MTA and the reverse exchange at the destination. P3, as originally defined in 1984, requires that the addressed UA always be active and connected to the network; no provisions were made for UAs intermittently connected to the network, a typical situation when the UA is implemented on a portable PC.

To overcome these shortcomings, the Message Store (MS) entity was introduced in 1988, and the P7 protocol was defined to address the relationships between UAs and MSs. The P7 protocol allows an MS to store messages for UAs that are not connected. In addition, the same protocol defines how to search, list, retrieve, or cancel previously received messages.

Directory and Security

For directory purposes, the 1988 specifications suggest using the X.500 standard, also defined by CCITT. Specifically, the X.500 standard exists to provide a central directory of the names, distribution lists, and addresses of UA profiles and to provide a procedural definition for reciprocal authentication of users. Using this standard, the user can avoid implementing the actual complicated structure of names, which is replaced by a simpler and more familiar one.

In 1988, security specifications were significantly improved, with the definition of functions for source authentication, functions to control exit from the transmission, and functions to check that the message has not been partially or totally changed. Yet requests exist for even more improvements in this area. For example, controls and facilities must be developed to prevent simulation of an entire domain or of one of its subsets, the risk of a user "masquerading" for another, and so on.

X.400 SUMMARY

X.400 is now one of the options for implementing networks for e-mail and, for this purpose, is an alternative to many existing proprietary solutions. Its advantages lie in its independence from a particular supplier and its positive international reception. In terms of supplier independence, X.400 can offer the best solution for a proprietary network that needs to support different suppliers' systems. In terms of its international appeal, X.400 will be a fundamental tool in the implementation of solutions to interconnect incompatible proprietary solutions. Its capacity to transfer objects among incompatible systems may help X.400 systems become the transmission vehicles for important network applications involving more than one company, as is the case with Electronic Data Interchange (EDI).

EDI standards such as EDIFACT, Odette, ANSI X.12, and others have been defined to allow the transmission, via communications networks, of standardized records corresponding to company documents, such as invoices, orders, and transport documents. EDI implementations are becoming very popular because of advantages such as speed, accuracy, and cost-effectiveness that they offer to companies. X.400 can be the foundation on which to implement or extend these applications.

The OSI Message Service/400 currently implements the MTA X.400 function. This function can be used in conjunction with AS/400 Office to facilitate communications with other X.400 users.

COMMUNICATIONS AMONG INCOMPATIBLE SYSTEMS: STANDARD AND NON-STANDARD SOLUTIONS

The set of international standards known as OSI has some remarkable advantages: It is well defined and functionally rich; it has received international recognition; and virtually all the communications software suppliers provide OSI software covering all layers from 1 to 6 as well as applications complying with the FTAM and X.400 standards. Ultimately, when work on other OSI application standards is complete — such as those for remote database access and virtual terminals — and these standards are translated into products, OSI has the potential to become the universal solution for every computer communication.

However, a slightly different view is that there will be multiple communications architectures in the future; for example, OSI and SNA.

The market will always offer many products, each meeting the requirements of specific customers, even when the products are non-standard. And OSI does have some specific weak points, such as its rough definition, at present, of the virtual terminal function. But the main problem with OSI as the universal solution is that single products are rarely ever the best answer to customers' requirements. This is, to us, the main reason why OSI will be neither the only architecture nor the only solution for communications between incompatible systems. Indeed, the not-so-long history of data communications is full of examples of standards that received only partial market acceptance: HDLC and X.25 are two.

Let us consider a few fictitious examples to demonstrate that different products can receive different acceptance from the customer, depending on that customer's requirements.

Let's imagine an IBM system provided with an SNA network and a Bull system with its proprietary network (termed DSA). The OSI solution for their interaction would be as shown in Figure 11.2. This is a symmetrical solution, requiring equal software on both systems to implement the common OSI functions.

FIGURE 11.2
OSI Solution for SNA-DSA Network Interaction

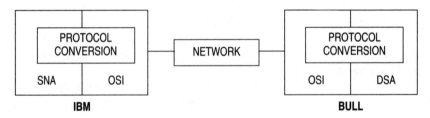

Alternatively, a gateway could be used as shown in Figure 11.3. In this example, the gateway appears as a native connection to each system and bears the processing burden for protocol conversion and data manipulation; no additional load is introduced to the two systems.

A third solution is also possible, as shown in Figure 11.4. This solution, in contrast to the other two, is an asymmetrical solution that places an additional load in only one of the systems; the other remains unaffected.

Now let's suppose that all three solutions are available and that all are equal in function, cost, performance, and system prerequisites (in reality, a very unlikely scenario). Which solution should be used?

The supporters of standards say the first because it introduces common, well-defined standards to both proprietary systems. Unfortunately, adding the

FIGURE 11.3
Gateway Solution for SNA-DSA Network Interaction

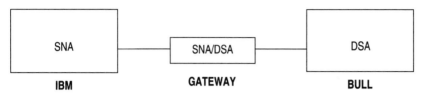

FIGURE 11.4
Asymmetrical Solution for SNA-DSA Network Interaction

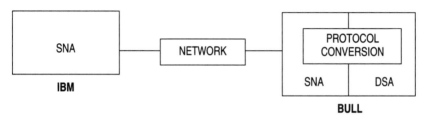

standards-based software to both systems has an impact on those systems. If the processing load for either of the two systems is close to its maximum capability, then this approach is unrealistic. If, however, both systems have resources to burn, this approach is both realistic and highly feasible.

If the utilization of existing system resources is an issue, then the best solution is the use of a gateway because it does not (in most cases) add any additional load to either of the systems. Also, a gateway can often provide superior performance because gateway hardware and software are typically optimized for their tasks.

Finally, if one of the two systems has unused power, then the third solution is probably best. The advantage of this approach is that it is simple to implement and is potentially the least costly approach of the three.

But there are some cases where OSI is functionally not the best solution, or where it cannot be implemented at all. A particular example is as follows: Suppose that remote Bull terminals need to access a Bull system and an IBM host, and that remote IBM terminals also need to access both the Bull and IBM systems. A solution to this problem is shown in Figure 11.5, where two remote devices (cluster controllers, for example) let the traffic pass unchanged from a terminal to its compatible host while converting the protocols for the data to be sent to the incompatible host.

Compared to the OSI virtual terminal concept, this solution has some advantages: It avoids an extra load on the hosts, and the communication is directly

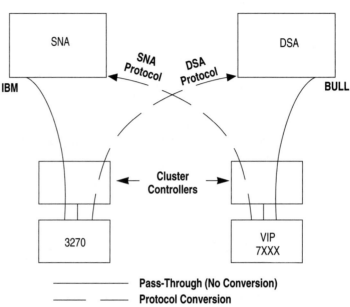

FIGURE 11.5
Protocol Conversion at Cluster Controller Level

established without the need to pass through an intermediate (and maybe overloaded) node. This approach also reveals another interesting point: Often what is needed for multivendor connectivity is not application-to-application capability between incompatible hosts but, instead, access to both environments from a single terminal.

Finally, enterprises sometimes have no need to implement communications among incompatible systems, but they do have a need to implement a common multiprotocol network that can be used concurrently by all of the attached systems. As shown by Figure 11.6, this network provides common connectivity, but the actual traffic patterns are IBM-to-IBM, DEC-to-DEC, and so forth. In a leased-line environment, this strategy can be accomplished through the use of Time Division Multiplexers (TDM). In a LAN/WAN environment, multiprotocol routers can be used to direct traffic to the appropriate LAN segment.

The conclusions we can draw from these examples are that standards, no matter how important, are and will be judged by the market as all other products are: by the functions they offer, their prerequisites, and their performance, cost, and potential value. This means that other solutions, such as gateways, protocol converters, emulation software, Time Division Multiplexers, multiprotocol routers, and TCP/IP, will continue to be offered as alternatives to the OSI methodology of connectivity.

FIGURE 11.6
Multiprotocol Network

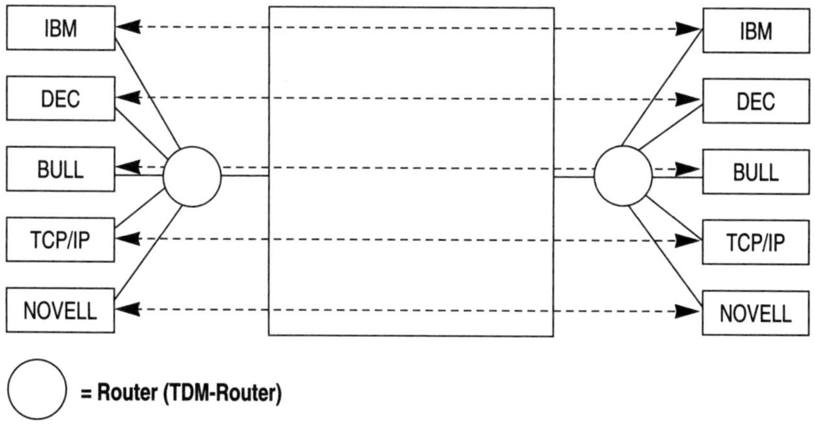

```
IBM  <------\         /------>  IBM
DEC  <-----\ \       / /----->  DEC
BULL <----\ \ \     / / /---->  BULL
TCP/IP <--/ / /     \ \ \---->  TCP/IP
NOVELL <-/ / /       \ \ \--->  NOVELL
```

○ = Router (TDM-Router)

OSI vs. SNA

To give you a broader understanding of OSI in the context of other midrange architectures, this section focuses on a comparison of OSI with the SNA architecture, which lies at the base of AS/400 communications. Figure 11.7 lists the functions defined in the layers of the two respective architectures. For comparison, let's start with some general considerations. The most important similarities are that both architectures have seven layers, ranging from the physical interface up to the application layer, and most of the functions in each layer correspond. In both cases, the three upper layers are devoted to the functions needed to establish communications between two network users, the middle layer is devoted to the establishment of reliable end-to-end network communications, and the last three layers are dedicated to the tasks of transmission through a network connecting the two end users.

There are also some significant differences. Traditional SNA is based on a master-slave relationship (APPN is a new approach in this sense), while OSI is based on a peer-to-peer relationship. OSI has more precise definitions for every function and for the relationships between the different entities (this is not surprising, because the OSI reference model was defined years after the implementation of SNA). As an example, OSI defines a specific header for every layer, while SNA has only a request header for layers 5 and 6, and a transmission header for the functions of layers 3 and 4, in addition to the data link layer.

Other differences are that OSI does not consider the role and specific functions of intermediate nodes, defining only the logical relationships between the two end users and leaving all the rest to other standards. On the other hand, SNA gives great emphasis to the functions of the intermediate nodes and

Figure 11.7
SNA vs. OSI Functions

SNA TRANSACTION	OSI APPLICATION SERVICES
Configuration Services • Activation and deactivation of lines and components • Application program load and unload • Network reconfiguration and restart • Network name and address management • Control and management of lines and NAU **Management and Maintenance Services** • Error identification and analysis • Test data and error statistics collection **Operator Control Services** • Tools for communications with network operator **Session Services** • Session setup and reset • Verification of application authority of the concerned LU • Choice of the protocols to be used • Selection of the virtual route • Startup of the requests queue **Application-To-Application Services** • Session activation • Synchronization between programs	**Application Management** • Program activation and deactivation • Recognition and prevention of lock situations • Security • Checkpoint/restart **System Management** • Activation/deactivation of network resources • Network reconfiguration and restart • Network status control and reporting • Error identification, analysis and resolution • Network statistics **Application Services** • Definition of internal resource availability • Partner identification • Agreements re. dialogue protocols, re. error resolution procedures, and re. data integrity controls • Service quality determination • Network resource availability determination • Information transfer • Application synchronization • Agreement re. data privacy controls • Remote user authentication • Choice of data syntax formats
SNA PRESENTATION SERVICES	**OSI PRESENTATION LAYER**
• Data formats selection • Data compression • Display map handling	• Data format and syntax • Conversion of syntaxes • Data formatting protocols
SNA DATA FLOW CONTROL	**OSI SESSION LAYER**
• Choice of send/receive modes • Message chain grouping • Bracket protection • Control of the request/response sequences • Applications' synchronization • Normal flow interrupt • Urgent messages	• Applications' interaction handling • Quarantine service • Brackets handling • Synchronization • Flow parameters selection • Transmission stop and restart • Urgent message • Exceptional conditions reporting • Security Management

Figure 11.7 Continued

FIGURE 11.7 *CONTINUED*

SNA TRANSACTION CONTROL	OSI TRANSPORT LAYER
• Flow pacing • Sequence handling and control • Virtual route sharing among multiple sessions • Transmission header handling • Data encryption	• Flow control • Sequence handling • Identification and resolution of error (at end-user level) • Session multiplexing in network • Service quality control • Windows • Address conversion from transport to network level • Data segmentation, blocking and chaining
SNA PATH CONTROL	**OSI NETWORK LAYER**
• Route selection • Explicit route sharing among multiple virtual routes • Message segmentation and repackaging • Segment and message sequencing • Sequencing in transmitting on a transmission group • Resequencing of blocks received on a transmission group (having lines of different speeds) • Priority transmission • Pacing on a virtual route	• Sequencing in transmission • Interrupt at request of the message flow • Multiplexing • Message segmentation and repackaging • Priority transmission • Network reset services • Clear at request of network connections
SNA DATA LINK CONTROL	**OSI DATA LINK LAYER**
• Data formatting in SDLC frame • Master-slave relationships • Synchronization (line level) • Transmission • Line errors identification and recovery	• Use of multiple links for a line connection • HDLC framing • Asynchronous balanced mode relations • Synchronization (line level) • Pace control (line level) • Transmission • Line error identification and resolution
SNA PHYSICAL INTERFACE	**OSI PHYSICAL INTERFACE**
• Bit transmission according to the physical, electrical, logical, and mechanical characteristics of the line interface use	• Bit transmission according to the physical, electrical, logical, and mechanical characteristics of the line interface use

defines their exact tasks and their relationships with the systems hosting the two end users, as demonstrated by the definitions of the SNA PU set. Other differences show up in a detailed analysis of the functions of the seven layers, as shown in Figure 11.7:

- *Application layer.* Both architectures support conversational and batch exchanges between the two end users and provide functions for store-and-forward mechanisms. Unfortunately, the user interfaces for each service are rather different, meaning that the implementation of applications compatible with both architectures is not an easy task.
- *Presentation layer.* There is only one significant difference here between OSI and SNA. SNA assigns the tasks of data encryption and data compression to this layer, while OSI assigns them to other layers below. Otherwise, the two layers have the same functions.
- *Session layer.* This layer is functionally richer under OSI. There are provisions to handle the session in half or full duplex, to control the authentication of the remote user, to charge the cost of the session, and to control the status of the involved resources. All this can be very important in implementing a heterogeneous network, especially when there are specific requirements for network security.
- *Transport layer.* The only significant difference in this layer is that OSI formally defines a set of different classes of transport to ensure reliable transport through networks having different levels of reliability. SNA has no such formal definition and flexibility.
- *Network layer.* There are other significant differences here. OSI is functionally rich in defining the external requests to this layer, which are responsible for the routing in the network. But OSI does not define at all how to pass through the network. The fact that OSI suggests using X.25 in wide-area networks does not mean too much in this instance — X.25 defines the external relationships between a user node and a packet-switching node, not how the network must work internally. SNA, on the other hand, defines the tasks of every network component and how the network routes are selected and used. Briefly, this comes from the fact that SNA takes into account all the components of a proprietary network, while OSI considers only the relationships between the two systems hosting the two end users.
- *Data link layer.* SNA SDLC protocol only includes master-slave relationships, which are very useful in the case of multidrop lines (and also is applied by exception in cases of point-to-point lines). Other SNA-compliant protocols — such as those applied to LAN and X.25 networks — are peer oriented. OSI is equal to SNA in this aspect.

As you can see, OSI's specific advantages lie mainly in a richer functionality and more precise definitions of the entities. Likewise, SNA, an important market reality for a long time, has some specific advantages — mainly that it carefully considers all the functions of the network components and their relationships.

THE FUTURE OF OSI

Saying that OSI is not likely to become the only communications architecture in the future does not mean that it does not have a future. Actually, we can expect a strongly positive market acceptance when the complete set of applicative standards is defined. The problem, of course, is the long wait required for new OSI standards to emerge.

In the meantime, the widespread adoption and use of OSI as a multivendor solution is being challenged by TCP/IP — in fact, TCP/IP has become the de facto standard for multivendor networking. This does not, however, mean that OSI is dead. Many OSI standards — X.400 and X.500 in particular — have been accepted by the data processing community and are now looked on as preferred solutions. The most likely scenario is that the future of multivendor computing will embrace both TCP/IP and OSI.

CHAPTER 12

TCP/IP

The Transmission Control Protocol/Internet Protocol (TCP/IP) was originally developed by the United States Department of Defense to facilitate communications and information exchange between government agencies and private contractors. The popularity and flexibility of TCP/IP allowed it to make a transition to the commercial market and, since that time, TCP/IP has become a de facto standard for communications between computers of different manufacturers. There are several reasons why TCP/IP is so important:

- It is a mature, time-tested environment.
- It can operate with equal efficiency in both LAN and non-LAN environments.
- It is based on a client/server relationship.
- It is the network of choice for UNIX systems; therefore, as UNIX and UNIX-derivative operating environments grow and prosper, so does TCP/IP.
- It is available on a large number of non-UNIX systems from different suppliers.
- It is the underlying network for many multivendor distributed environments, such as Open Software Foundation's (OSF) Distributed Computing Environment (DCE), Sun MicroSystems' Network File System (NFS) and Solaris operating system, and X-Windows.

Potential TCP/IP hosts include every system from a high-end IBM mainframe to a low-end PC (Figure 12.1). Thanks to TCP/IP gateway functions, a TCP/IP host on network A can communicate with another TCP/IP host on network B. These two networks can be of different types, such as Token-Ring or Ethernet LAN, X.25 WANs, and others. Conceptually, the two networks, A and B, set up a new network, C, which includes the other two. Using the same (or a different) gateway, network C can also form an additional network with network D, and so on. A TCP/IP gateway can be any host connected to two or more different networks; hence, it is identified by different TCP/IP addresses, one address for every different network.

Because TCP/IP is a symmetrical communications solution, TCP/IP functions must be on both systems for communication to occur. Specifically, the two systems must have the TCP/IP functions defined at levels 3, 4, and 5 of the corresponding OSI model (Figure 12.2), plus the application functions that the two

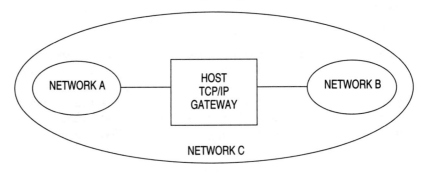

FIGURE 12.1
Networking Using TCP/IP

FIGURE 12.2
TCP/IP Structure

L 6-7	FTP	TELNET	SMTP	SNMP	NFS	...
L 4-5	TRANSMISSION CONTROL PROTOCOL			USER DATAGRAM PROTOCOL		
L 3	INTERNET PROTOCOL					
L 1-2	NETWORK DRIVERS AND ADAPTERS					
	TOKEN RING	ETHERNET	---	X.25	X.21	---

users intend to use (e.g., File Transfer Protocol (FTP), TELNET, and so on). These systems are then called TCP/IP hosts.

A client/server relationship can be started between two hosts by a specific user requesting a specific service. This relationship is dynamic. The system asking for the service is the client and the system providing the service is the server. In a given situation, two systems can be servers of each other for two different service requests concurrently. For example, system A can be a TELNET server and an FTP client to system B at the same time.

TCP/IP's basic structure includes the Internet Protocol (IP), the Transmission Control Protocol (TCP), and the User Datagram Protocol (UDP) modules. IP has functions roughly comparable to those of the OSI model's third layer, while TCP and UDP relate to OSI layers 4 and 5. The main function of the IP module is to handle the data transmission between two hosts of the same or different networks.

The format of TCP/IP addresses is fundamental for this; that address structure consists of a 4-byte code that has at the beginning the network identification and at the end the host identification within that network. When IP processes a message, it looks at the destination address. If this points to a host of the same network, the message is sent directly to it. When the network is different, IP looks at a routing table that associates each external network with a specific gateway.

A gateway, because it is connected to two or more networks, has as many different TCP/IP addresses as the number of different networks to which it is connected. In addition, gateways have "knowledge" of the overall topology of the interconnected networks via a topology table that is dynamically updated. Because it has this topology information and specific routing algorithms, a gateway can forward the message directly to the final destination or to another gateway. The receiving gateway, and any subsequent gateways involved along the selected route, act in the same way until the message is delivered to its final destination.

IP uses an interesting technique to handle messages. This technique is called, in OSI parlance, the "connectionless" mode. In this mode, the sending node has only the task of transmitting the message to another node, without asking or waiting for a positive or negative acknowledgement of the transmission. As a consequence, IP does not provide for error recovery. The receiving node rejects the message if it contains errors; otherwise, the message is accepted.

Paradoxically, many find this "connectionless" transfer mode to be quite efficient, because the intermediate nodes do not have excessive processing loads resulting from acknowledgement exchanges. Furthermore, they do not have to reserve a large memory or disk space to keep copies of messages for possible retransmission in case of errors, nor do they impose similar charges to the near nodes. As a result, overall performance is generally good.

The responsibility for handling errors in the client/server session is left to the TCP modules of the two involved systems. TCP modules provide for error recovery, for data integrity, for the sequencing and related control of the transmitted messages, for the pacing of their exchange, and for synchronization of the two applications involved in the connection.

The "connectionless" mode, made popular by TCP/IP, has a significant future because networks based on optical fibers have a very low error rate during transmission. According to some experts, a reasonable average error rate in an all-optical network might be one bit in error out of every million of a billion (1015) transmitted bits.[1]

---

[1] P. E. Green, Jr., T. J. Watson Research Center, Hawthorne, IBM ("The Future of Fiber-Optics Computer Networks," IEEE, 1991).

In such a scenario, it is perfectly justifiable to leave the task of error recovery to the end-user systems rather than to the intermediate nodes because error recovery should be a seldom occurrence. This approach, used in developing technologies such as B-ISDN and ATM, constitutes the most important difference between X.25 networks (where recovery tasks are assigned to the intermediate nodes) and frame-relay networks.

A third TCP/IP module — UDP — can be used instead of TCP on an application-by-application basis. UDP allows the two end-user systems to avoid responsibility for the tasks related to the connection controls and features. So in contrast with TCP, UDP does not provide any error-recovery procedures. Because of this, a good suggestion is to use UDP in very reliable networks, or when the loss of a message does not lead to serious consequences, or when error-control and error-recovery functions are handled by the user-written applications. As with IP, UDP places a minimum load on the nodes and improves message-propagation delays, having eliminated all the error-recovery functions in all the nodes.

TCP/IP-transmitted frames have a header made of IP and TCP (or UDP) headers, followed by the user data and a Frame Check Sequence (FCS) field for transmission-error discovery. Once the message arrives at the destination node, TCP or UDP passes the user data to the interested TCP/IP application through a specific software channel called a "socket."

In the simplest terms, a socket is a numeric port assignment within a given TCP/IP host. For example, the TELNET service is normally assigned to socket "23" in every TCP/IP host. When one TCP/IP program wants to communicate with another program on a different host system, the program requests a connection, via TCP or UDP, to the target host and specifies a socket assignment. If the assignment program for that socket is available, the two programs are logically linked together and can exchange data. This methodology is the underlying structure for TCP/IP client/server communications.

As you may have noticed, the TCP/IP general design does not include data-link control and physical interface functions. Quite simply, IP has been given a significant number of "network drivers" to be selected and used for transmission on a wide range of possible networks. Every network used (X.25, Token-Ring, Ethernet, serial lines, etc.) is considered simply as a transport network.

Now let's consider a given number of TCP/IP hosts on LAN 1, and another number of hosts on LAN 2, with the two networks interconnected via a TCP/IP gateway. As already said, any LAN host can ask for service from any other host, including those of the other LAN. So how is the problem of addressability solved? In most cases, the user requests access to the host based on a unique name. This name can be translated into an actual TCP/IP address through one of two mechanisms:

1. The source host can use an internal table (disk file) to which it has access and obtain the TCP/IP address based on the target host name.
2. Domain name servers can be employed to supply TCP/IP addresses for all hosts. In this case, one or more systems within each logical network maintain the list of host names and addresses. Systems requiring the translation of a name into an address simply request this service from a name server.

Finally, because the LAN-connected systems are ultimately addressed via the LAN adapter address rather than by the TCP/IP address, special protocols — the Address Resolution Protocol (ARP) and Reverse ARP (RARP) — allow the TCP/IP address to be further translated into the actual hardware address of the LAN adapter in the target host (and vice versa).

Above the TCP/UDP layer are the application functions. Those application functions will be discussed in the subsequent sections of this chapter.

TCP/IP VS. SNA

A comparison of TCP/IP to IBM SNA reveals the following points of interest about TCP/IP:

- TCP/IP is available on a large variety of computer systems.
- TCP/IP has been designed as a peer-to-peer solution.
- TCP/IP is easy to implement and easy to use.
- TCP/IP easily passes through any number of interconnected networks.
- TCP/IP performance is generally good, but it is influenced by instantaneous load on networks.
- TCP/IP is oriented toward human intervention rather than toward automated processing.

By contrast:

- SNA is specifically designed for automated processing.
- Because SNA is designed for automated processing, it has a functionally rich capability for application-to-application communications.
- SNA offers stable performance under reasonably variable network conditions.
- SNA offers either master-slave or peer-to-peer solutions.

TCP/IP IMPLEMENTATION ON THE AS/400

Before OS/400 V3R1, support for the core TCP/IP protocols (e.g., IP, TCP, and UDP) — as well as support for all the application functions — was provided in a separate licensed product. Starting with V3R1, however, the core TCP/IP protocols are integrated with OS/400 — just like APPN/APPC — and most of the application functions are provided as no-charge options. The provided application functions include

- *File Transfer Protocol (FTP)* — As the name implies, FTP is for file transfer. FTP is easily activated either interactively by an operator at a terminal or via batch files. The AS/400 can function as an FTP client or server.

- *TELNET* — Using TELNET, a terminal can be connected to a remote system over the network and function as if it were a terminal physically attached to the remote system itself. TELNET supports a variety of ASCII terminals, including character-oriented, line-mode, and full-screen terminal types. The AS/400 supports general ASCII terminal emulation, Digital VT100 emulation, and full-screen 3270 or 5250 emulation. The AS/400 can receive TELNET connections from other systems or can initiate TELNET connections to other systems.

- *Simple Mail Transfer Protocol (SMTP)* — SMTP provides a simple mechanism to carry interpersonal messages. Unlike most e-mail applications, SMTP uses no mailboxes and requires that both systems (source and destination) be online. The AS/400 supports an optional bridge between SNA Distribution Service (SNADS) and SMTP that enables the exchange of notes and texts between the users of SNADS and those of SMTP. The system controls the conversion of formats, addresses, and rules.

- *Line Print Remote/Line Print Daemon (LPR/LPD)* — These two functions work together to allow one system to send output files to another system for printing. The LPR function initiates the transfer of an output file and the LPD function is responsible for receiving and printing the file. The AS/400 supports both the LPR and LPD functions.

- *Sockets* — TCP/IP sockets refer to the interfaces used by programs to communicate with one another in a TCP/IP program. The AS/400 supports access to TCP/IP sockets from the Pascal and C programming languages.

- *Simple Network Management Protocol (SNMP)* — SNMP provides basic network troubleshooting and configuration functions in support of automated network management. While waiting for the final standardization of OSI protocols for network management (i.e., CMIS and CMIT), many suppliers now offer network management solutions for heterogeneous networks based on SNMP. The AS/400 implementation of SNMP allows the AS/400 to act as an SNMP agent. As an agent, the AS/400 will report information to an SNMP management program (e.g., an HP9000 running OpenView) and will also permit limited configuration changes initiated from the management program.

In addition to these included functions, the following application functions are available as licensed products for the AS/400:

- *Network File System (NFS)* — This application function provides a network-based file architecture that permits groups of files on a server system to be "mounted" as file sets on a client system. NFS is similar in concept to the Novell implementation of a PC file server; however, many TCP/IP hosts can be both an NFS server and client concurrently. The AS/400 implementation of AS/400 can function only as a server.
- *Distributed Computing Environment (DCE)* — DCE enables a number of client/server functions, but the most notable function is support for Remote Procedure Calls (RPC). RPC is a set of protocols and functions that allow a program to activate and communicate with remote programs or subprograms. RPC is similar to TCP/UDP sockets in that it facilitates program-to-program communications between systems; the significant difference is that RPC provides a sophisticated and structured interface, whereas sockets are, for the most part, a "grow your own" approach.
- *Internet applications* — A variety of TCP/IP applications have been introduced to the AS/400 so it can function on the Internet. These applications include World Wide Web (WWW) server software and Gopher server software.

ANYNET

As you should be able to see by now, SNA and TCP/IP share many similarities but they also have many differences. In real life it is often necessary to choose between these two protocols based on external factors instead of on their own merits. For example, if you need to integrate an AS/400 into an existing UNIX TCP/IP network, using AS/400 TCP/IP is far more desirable than introducing SNA into the network. Similarly, if you operate a multivendor network, you might want to consolidate as many operations as possible into TCP/IP to reduce the number of protocols you need to support.

Unfortunately, many AS/400 capabilities — especially AS/400 client/server capabilities — were designed to run on an SNA network and cannot make the transition to a native TCP/IP environment. For example, Display Station Pass-Through (DSPT), Distributed Data Management (DDM), and CA/400 were all designed around the SNA LU 6.2 communications format. You cannot simply remove the SNA network services below these programs and replace them with TCP/IP network services.

IBM did, however, recognize this limitation and addressed it by introducing "AnyNet" technology to the AS/400. Using AnyNet, traffic from an SNA application function (e.g., CA/400, DSPT, or DDM) can be encapsulated into TCP/IP format for transmission over a TCP/IP network. When the TCP/IP traffic arrives at its destination, the SNA information is extracted from the TCP/IP data and passed on to the SNA application function. The beauty of AnyNet is that the sending and receiving SNA application functions are totally unaware that the data they are sending and receiving is being translated into and out of TCP/IP format — as far as the application functions can tell, they are operating over a standard SNA network.

Hopefully, AnyNet is the first of many steps that IBM is taking to allow AS/400 functions and services to operate in a variety of network environments. Future implementations of AnyNet will support SNA traffic carried in NeBEUI networks (i.e., IBM LAN Server and Microsoft LAN Manager networks) and IPX networks (i.e., Novell NetWare networks).

AS/400-RS/6000 COMMUNICATIONS

With the increasing popularity and acceptance of the UNIX operating system and the growing acceptance of IBM's RS/6000 as a working partner in midrange shops, AS/400 managers face the issue of interconnecting the two systems. The RS/6000, which was specifically designed for graphical and scientific applications, uses the AIX operating system, IBM's version of UNIX. Hence, the RS/6000 often uses TCP/IP software, which is very popular in the UNIX environment.

IBM offers two software products for the RS/6000 to establish communications with other IBM systems, and in particular with the AS/400:

1. *AIX AS/400 Connection Program/6000*. This product has been specifically designed for the connection of the two systems. It is based on a client/server relationship with the RS/6000 always in the role of the client and the AS/400 always in the role of the server. The connection can be established via a switched or leased line or via a Token-Ring or Ethernet LAN.

   The goal of this product is to offer RS/6000 workstations functional support and access to AS/400 resources roughly comparable to that of PC Support. The communications protocols can be SNA, TCP/IP, or both. The functions offered are not, however, the same. The following functions are available via SNA:

   - 5250 emulation
   - Bidirectional file transfer
   - Remote AS/400 command execution

   The product also includes an API that lets you call the file-transfer function from user programs written in C. Via the TCP/IP protocol, the product makes available only the 5250 emulation function to the

RS/6000 client. Of course, this product does not necessarily have to be used for communications between the two systems.

2. *AIX SNA Services/6000.* This product implements, under AIX V.3, the following SNA functions:
   - PU 2.1 support
   - Support of LU types 0, 1, 2, 3, and 6.2

   In this way, the RS/6000 can communicate with traditional SNA mainframes as a secondary or remote system and also have peer-to-peer communications with other midrange systems that support PU 2.1. Note, however, that this solution does not include 5250 emulation or ready-to-run file transfer functions.

In addition, non-IBM products exist that allow UNIX to communicate with the AS/400. Following is a summary of three typical approaches.

AS/400-TO-RS/6000 COMMUNICATIONS VIA THIRD-PARTY SOLUTIONS

Among the many non-IBM solutions to connect UNIX-based systems to the AS/400, two deserve some comment because they do not need TCP/IP software on the AS/400. A third solution also will be discussed because it is simple and easy to use.

Forest Computer. This company offers a line of gateways to interconnect IBM midrange systems (the AS/400 in particular), IBM mainframe systems, Digital systems, and TCP/IP systems.

OpenConnect Systems (formerly Mitek). This company also supplies a comprehensive line of gateways to accommodate the interconnection of IBM midrange, IBM mainframe, and TCP/IP systems.

The gateway products offered by both Forest Computer and OpenConnect Systems provide the following functions:

- Bidirectional file transfer — files can be transferred from one type of system to another, with the contents translated between ASCII and EBCDIC or left unchanged (binary transfer).
- Bidirectional virtual terminal support — a TELNET client can appear to the AS/400 as a native 5250 workstation and a 5250 workstation can appear to a TCP/IP host as a VT100 or VT200 TELNET client. Mainframe support featuring 3270 emulation is also available.
- Application-to-application communications — a TCP/IP program can use sockets to communicate with an IBM program using APPC.

As noted, the offering of both products is extremely similar, including the fact that TCP/IP software is not required on the AS/400. But some feature differences do exist; for example, OpenConnect Systems provides SNMP support, and Forest Computer provides queue-to-queue printer sharing. In general, though, the two companies differ more in philosophy than technology.

Another alternative is offered by Andrew Corporation. The Andrew Corporation product, Handshake-Alliance/6000, which consists of a micro-channel board for the RS/6000, allows the connection of an RS/6000 to AS/400 twinaxial cable. Each Handshake-Alliance board can support up to seven concurrent sessions for interactive 5250 and printer emulation and for file transfer. File transfer converts from EBCDIC to ASCII and vice versa, and can be scheduled for later transmission.

The market also offers many other products that are more or less similar to the ones described above, such as products from Apertus, Wingra Technology (formerly Joiner Software), and Soft-Switch; but the ones discussed are representative examples.

CHAPTER 13

The AS/400-DEC Connection

As mentioned in previous chapters, the proliferation of computing equipment leads to a growing need to connect systems of different manufacturers. The possible combinations could fill a book, so we will focus on a specific case — the interconnection of AS/400 and Digital Equipment Corporation (DEC) systems and networks. Why DEC? Because DEC systems have a large market, and a company often has both IBM and DEC equipment — IBM for corporate applications and DEC for departmental or technical applications, for example — with a need to interconnect the two environments.

DEC has always put a strong emphasis on networking functions, with a particular interest in interconnecting its systems to IBM mainframe systems. Although DEC's ultimate intent may have been to replace centralized IBM mainframe solutions with DEC distributed processing systems, DEC realized that to successfully market and sell departmental solutions, had to integrate those solutions with the corporate mainframe systems. Unfortunately, not many DEC products exist for interconnection to the AS/400, which DEC views as a direct competitor of its VAX computer line.

Let's first discuss the DEC attitude toward networking in general. Traditionally, the DEC marketing approach has been very different from that of IBM and often consists of going directly to a departmental, office, or technical service manager and offering that manager a specialized set of hardware and software as the solution to a specific problem — "This system for this problem of yours," in essence. To answer some possible objections to this basic approach (for example, "What if my system needs additional resources?" or "What if I need to interact with other departmental systems or with the central mainframe?"), it has always been necessary for DEC to offer advanced networking functions as well as interconnection tools for mainframe suppliers (IBM first, but also CDC, Sperry, etc.).

DIGITAL NETWORK ARCHITECTURE (DNA) AND DECNET SUMMARY

DEC's networking architecture, Digital Network Architecture (DNA), was announced just one year after IBM introduced SNA. DNA is best represented by "DECnet," DEC's suite of protocols and services that operate in an Ethernet and wide-area environment. In general terms, DNA's goals are

- To provide a networking solution that allows communications among all DEC systems
- To enable the use of any transmission facility or public network

- To provide connections with products and systems of other suppliers

In pursuit of these DNA goals, DECnet exhibits the following architectural characteristics:

- DECnet solutions are based on distributed functions to avoid single-point-of-failure risks.
- DECnet is based on a hierarchy of functional layers, roughly comparable to that of IBM's SNA.
- DECnet allows remote access to any DEC resource.
- DECnet solutions are flexible and adaptable, and capable of self-modification under whatever circumstances.
- DECnet uses network algorithms and strong, stable techniques to assure high availability and good performance.

DECnet interconnects DEC systems in meshed networks based on a peer-to-peer approach. In fact, the DECnet and APPN approaches are similar: Both include networks with every kind of configuration, transit (routing) nodes and end (non-routing) nodes, self-reconfiguration capability, adaptive techniques for routing, network applications based on peer-to-peer relationships, and so on.

DEC has pioneered the research in commercial LANs and has traditionally placed a strong emphasis on connections using Ethernet. Today, DEC also supports Token-Ring and FDDI connections and, in more general terms, is putting more of an emphasis on openness. This commitment to openness can be seen in the incorporation of OSI standards into DECnet, and in the DEC involvement with the Distributed Computing Environment (DCE) sponsored by OSF.

The major functions offered in DECnet are

- Remote terminal log-ins, allowing a single terminal to concurrently log in to any number of computers in the local- or wide-area network
- Task-to-task communications between application programs
- Remote file access, allowing file transfer between any two systems, and also allowing a user or program to open a remote file for read/write access
- Message-handling applications, including both simple mail handing and sophisticated office applications through DEC's All-In-One software offering
- Distributed print services, allowing output to be directed to any printer in the network

In addition to its proprietary VMS operating system, DEC offers its own version of Unix, called Ultrix, and the OSF version of UNIX, OSF/1. DEC traditionally has received solid acceptance for applications such as process control, plant automation, scientific and technical applications, CAD/CAM, and office automation.

THE AS/400-DEC CONNECTION: IBM TOOLS

IBM has several approaches that can be used to integrate DEC and AS/400 environments:

- Because the AS/400 supports APPN functions over Ethernet, a PC can, with suitable software, gain access equally to both IBM and DEC resources over a common Ethernet LAN. For example, a PC can access an AS/400 via CA/400 and DEC systems via TCP/IP or Pathworks (DEC's equivalent of CA/400).

- DEC's VTXXX terminal family or compatible can be connected to an AS/400 through the ASCII controller or via the 5208 protocol converter. In both cases, the connection can be local or remote via modem and AS/400 support is via 5250 emulation.

- The IBM LAN Asynchronous Communications Support (LANACS) product can be placed in a dedicated PC to allow it to act as a gateway for Token-Ring-attached PCs. Using this method, a LAN-attached PC can connect to the LANACS gateway and access an asynchronous port on the gateway connected to a DEC system or DEC terminal server.

- The AS/400 Intersystem Communications Function (ICF) can also be used to communicate with a DEC system over an asynchronous connection. This option requires user programming.

- TCP/IP is available for all DEC systems; therefore, AS/400 TCP/IP services can be used for connectivity.

- The AS/400 OSI application functions (FTAM and X.400) can interoperate with the DEC product counterparts over an X.25 network.

- The IBM Message Queue Interface (MQI) is a generalized, queue-based messaging system that can be implemented on a number of non-IBM systems, including DEC systems. Custom programs must be developed on the AS/400 and DEC systems to utilize this interface. The AS/400 side of MQI is provided by the Message Queue Manager/400 (MQM/400) licensed product.

THE AS/400-DEC CONNECTION: DEC TOOLS

Except for the above-mentioned OSI and TCP/IP solutions, DEC presently does not offer any AS/400 connectivity tools of its own. Instead, DEC recommends third-party solutions, such as those discussed in the next section.

THE AS/400-DEC CONNECTION: THIRD-PARTY SOLUTIONS

Third-party offerings provide the widest set of connectivity tools in the IBM-DEC arena. The major players in this field are

- Forest Computer's line of gateways that interconnect IBM midrange systems, IBM mainframe hosts, TCP/IP systems, and DEC systems (via DECnet)
- OpenConnect Systems' line of gateways that interconnect IBM midrange systems, IBM mainframe hosts, and TCP/IP systems
- Apertus line of software products that interconnect IBM midrange systems, IBM mainframe hosts, TCP/IP systems, and DEC systems (via DECnet)

Forest Computer's and OpenConnect Systems' products are based on network-attached hardware gateways. In contrast, System Strategies' products are software products that operate in some (or all) of the interconnected systems. The product offerings of all three companies provide, for the most part, the same set of services in the AS/400 and DEC market:

- DEC-to-AS/400 terminal access (5250)
- AS/400-to-DEC terminal access (VT100 or VT200)
- Bidirectional file transfer
- Bidirectional job submission
- Program-to-program communications

A detailed look at these products will, in fact, show differences between the offerings. For the scope of this discussion, however, they are all more or less equal in that they facilitate a number of interoperability functions between AS/400 and DEC systems.

Other companies offer solutions that are less encompassing in scope, but quite effective nonetheless. These include the following:

- IDEAssociates offers a combined terminal controller/protocol converter that allows 5250 and ASCII terminals to access IBM mainframes, the AS/400, and DEC VAX systems. IBM 5250 (or 3270) terminals can be connected to the unit via twinaxial (or coaxial) cable and ASCII terminals are attached via an asynchronous interface. With IDEAssociates-supplied software, either type of terminal can access any attached host.
- Wingra Technologies, Boston Software, and Soft-Switch offer software products that permit the exchange of e-mail between OfficeVision/400 and DEC's VMS Mail and All-In-One products.

An additional category of third-party AS/400 and DEC connectivity solutions includes products that are focused solely on file transfer between the two environments. These products will be discussed in the next section.

HETEROGENEOUS NETWORKS AND FILE TRANSFER

File transfer is a common way to make data that originated elsewhere available to a computer. Developed as a more efficient alternative to transporting files via punched cards and magnetic tape, file transfer has become an economical remedy to the burden of having several distributed systems. But at the heart of file transfer technology is its origin in the batch-oriented processing environment, where the entry of data and the subsequent processing of that data were separate activities.

Given the variety and sophistication of modern distributed processing environments, one would think that file transfer should be a dead (or dying) technique. But in fact, file transfer has a strong future for a number of reasons, including the following:

- Implementing interactive communications between application programs requires sophisticated programming techniques and is therefore recommended for use only when needed. By contrast, file transfer is easier to use and implement; and it imposes fewer operating and technical constraints.
- With the success of distributed processing, it is unavoidable that files, programs, and texts need to be shared among those systems. The benefits of file transfer in a distributed-processing environment include simplicity of operations, minimization of transmission costs, and ease of software distribution, to name a few. Furthermore, file transfers in a heterogeneous network compensate for the differences between systems (e.g., ASCII/ EBCDIC encoding, record structures, blocking factors).

Consequently, virtually every network architecture includes a file-transfer function: OSI has FTAM; TCP/IP has FTP; APPN has SNADS; and SNA has SNADS, RJE, and other file-transfer utilities. Beyond the realm of proprietary architectures, the market offers some independent products that are focused on the issue of file transfer. With these products, the file-transfer functions cover the IBM-DEC relationship, and beyond.

The following products, known by us to have significant market acceptance, are summarized here according to their functions as examples of heterogeneous network solutions many companies may be seeking.

Two products from the United States are Network Data Mover (NDM) from System Center and XCOM 6.2 from Legent (XCOM 6.2 was originally developed by Spectrum Concepts, but Spectrum was acquired by Legent). Both provide not only file transfer among AS/400s and between the AS/400 and other systems, but also the software tools for organizing, planning, and controlling distribution flow. Additional tools are provided to end users and programmers to allow them to submit requests interactively, via menus, via batch files, or through an API for batch and interactive applications.

In both offerings, the actual transfer can be activated immediately or postponed for later execution. Transfers are flexible in terms of handling different record lengths and block sizes, and are further supported by functions such as checkpoint-restart and data compressions, and user security.

NDM supports IBM mainframes under MVS, VM, and DOS/VSE operating systems; the AS/400, PCDOS and OS/2; and DEC VAX VMS and TANDEM.

XCOM 6.2 is available on IBM's MVS and VM, the AS/400, S/38, S/36, S/88, PC DOS and OS/2; Stratus; DEC VAX VMS; and Data General.

Two European products also focus on the issue of file transfer:

Interpel, developed by Netsys (France), probably has the widest range of supported systems: IBM's MVS, VM, DOS VSE, the AS/400, S/36, S/38, PC DOS and OS/2, and the RS/6000; Bull's DPS 6, DPS 7, and DPS 8; Unisys; ICL; Prime; Tandem; Sun; DEC's VAX; the HP 9000; and UNIX. Every system uses a system mailbox for input/output files, providing the basic mechanism for store-and-forward transmission. Communications functions are based on SNA links when possible; otherwise, the transmission is based on X.25. Other functions provided are practically the same as in the previous products.

The last product is Spazio, by Primeur (Genova, Italy). Spazio supports IBM's MVS and DOS/VSE, the AS/400, PC DOS and OS/2; UNIX; and DEC's VAX. SNA, TCP/IP, OSI, and DECnet can be the transmission platforms. Also based on mailboxes (but one per user and not per system), Spazio offers the same file-transfer functions as those above. Unlike the other file-transfer products, however, Spazio is a sophisticated "mid-ware' package that provides additional functions such as a query language, an event scheduler, a virtual terminal API, and an electronic mail facility.

Certainly, other products exist on the market that offer similar functions for heterogeneous environments. Their exclusion from this summary is due only to lack of information by the authors and does not indicate a judgment of their value.

Appendix A

AS/400 Network Entities

A prerequisite to the use of communications functions and their application on the AS/400 is the establishment of various entities that define and control the communications process. The first entity is a set of system-level variables known as the "network attributes." These variables define default assignments and global characteristics, such as whether the system functions as network node on an APPN network, whether the system gathers error messages (ALERTs) from other systems, and what mode will be used as a default. Network attributes can be viewed through the DSPNETA command.

In addition to the network attributes, each system requires a definition of the following elements:

- *Line* — The line definition defines the physical adapter to which the line is connected, the type of line (e.g., dedicated, switched, point-to-point), the protocol used (e.g., SDLC, start/stop, BSC), and other parameters.
- *Controller* — Generally speaking, a controller can be considered the same as the SNA PU concept; therefore, a workstation controller, another AS/400, or a PC acting as a PU 2.1 node are all controllers. Each controller involved in communications on the line must be defined separately.
- *Device* — The device describes the characteristics of the physical device or logical application associated with the controller. In SNA networks, the concept of device corresponds to the concept of LU. The device entry defines its related controller, the name of the remote system, whether single or multiple sessions are supported, the mode to be used (only within SNA environments), and other parameters.
- *Modes* — Modes are only used in an SNA environment and define the environment to be used for APPC (LU 6.2) communications — the maximum number of sessions, the maximum length of messages, flow-control parameters, and the class of service (if the network is APPN).
- *Class of Service (COS)* — The COS is only used in APPN networks, and determines the parameter values used for the selection of the route to be used by the session in APPN networks. See Chapter 6 for a discussion about route selection in an APPN network.

Depending on the function to be used, these definitions may be accompanied by other definitions; for example, the use of ICF requires a definition of ICFFILE, and the use of RJE toward a host requires a definition of entities such as readers and writers. Special CL commands are available for defining all these entities.

APPN networks may lack device definitions. In this case, the central processing system, when necessary, automatically generates the device definitions and then refers them to the default modes and COS predefined by IBM. This implicitly means that users do not have to define their own modes and COS; at least initially, they can use the default IBM definitions until they have enough experience to define their own.

When an AS/400 is connected to a Token-Ring or Ethernet LAN, the definitions relative to devices and controllers can be spared for all PCs or PS/2s connected on the same local-area network that may need access to the system. The AS/400 can generate these definitions automatically when sessions are requested. In this case, the only definitions required are those of "LAN line" and of a controller model, which is the basis for the automatic definition of all the necessary controllers.

All of these definitions can be entered through special commands of the "work" type (e.g., WRKLIND, WRKCTLD, WRKDEVD) or through commands of the "create" type (e.g., CRTLINSDLC). The latter are specially designed for the creation of entities, while commands of the "work" type enable both modification and creation. When defining the entities and their parameters, help is available through the Help function key.

CREATING NETWORK ENTITIES

Network entities are established through "create" commands; however, lines, controllers, and devices support several different create commands. The differences between the commands allow the AS/400 to display parameters that are appropriate for the type of entity being defined. For example, both CRTLINASC and CRTLINSDLC are line creation commands — CRTLINASC is used for start/stop (asynchronous) lines and CTRLINSDLC for SDLC lines — but the menus displayed by these commands are different because they contain parameters specific to that type of link.

Following are more specific details about the commands used to create the various entity definitions.

Line definition. The line defines the characteristics of the physical attachment. The creation command is CRTLIN<type>, where <type> means

- ASC for the definition of a line using a start/stop protocol
- BSC for a non-SNA line using binary synchronous communications
- SDLC for an SNA line using the SDLC protocol
- TDLC for a twinaxial line
- TRN for a Token-Ring LAN connection

- ETH for an Ethernet LAN connection
- X25 for connections to an X.25 packet-switching network

Controller definition. The controller defines the functional characteristics of the remote system. The creation command is CRTCTL<type>, where <type> stands for

- APPC if a remote PU 2.1 system is being defined
- ASC for the description of a system supporting start/stop protocols
- BSC for a BSC protocol system
- FNC (finance) for the description of a 4700 banking system connected to an AS/400
- HOST for the description of an S/370, which can be connected for 3270 emulation, RJE or N/DM-DSNX applications
- LWS for local terminal controllers
- RWS for remote terminal controllers (i.e., the 5294, 5394, 3174, and 3274). When using switched lines, the controller may refer to a group of lines, which must all be of the same kind

Device definition. The device defines the characteristics of the physical device or logical application associated with the controller. The creation command is CRTDEV<type>, where <type> stands for

- APPC for the definition of LU 6.2 sessions (this is the type of device normally defined for AS/400-to-AS/400 links)
- ASC for the description of a terminal connected to a start/stop controller
- BSC for connections to hosts in 3270 BSC emulation or in ICF applications with BSC connections between an AS/400 and a S/36 or S/38
- FNC for the connection of a 4702 and its related applications
- HOST for sessions with a host S/370 and, in particular, for RJE and HCF-DHCF sessions
- SNUF for interactive applications with a host S/370 using LU 0 and for sessions with IMS (possible with CICS, too) via ICF/SNUF and N/DM-DSNX sessions

Remember that in APPN networks, controller and device definitions of the APPC type can be omitted because they can be generated automatically by the AS/400 when necessary.

Mode definition. At least one mode description is required for APPC links. This description is created through the CRTMODD command. No variations of this command are supported. Consult the next section of this appendix for more information about modes.

Class of Service (COS) definition. At least one COS description is required for APPN networks. A COS description is created through the CRTCOSD command. No variations of this command are supported. Consult the next section of this appendix for more information about COS.

MODES AND CLASSES OF SERVICE

When the applications used are based on APPC (such as ICF, DSPT, DDM, and SNADS/ODF), the APPC device description references a specific mode. If the user does not define the specific name of the mode, the definition refers to a default mode defined by IBM.

The mode serves to further define the operating characteristics of the APPC device — the highest number of sessions that the device can use, whether the central processor must pre-establish some or all the sessions at IPL time or whether they must be activated upon a user's request, the maximum length of the message, and the pacing values in input and output.

In an APPN network, what matters most is that the mode references a specific COS. The COS description contains the necessary information to choose the route in the network, depending on the characteristics of the lines, the nodes included in the various possible routes, and the other criteria discussed in Chapter 6. A COS also specifies the transmission priority (low, medium, high) the session blocks will have when crossing the network on the established route. IBM supplies a few sets of default COS definitions.

SOME EXAMPLES OF NETWORK ENTITY DEFINITIONS

Following are definitions related to two very simple networks. The first is for two systems, named AAA and BBB, connected via a leased SDLC line in an APPC environment (i.e., an environment where SNA functions such as DDM, DSPT, and ICF can be used). The second example shows an APPN network consisting of a network node, BBB, connected via leased lines to two end nodes, AAA and CCC. The purpose of these two examples is to give a more precise idea of entity definitions.

You will note that there are not many defined parameters, which is often the case. Of the values given to the parameters, those starting with "*" have been chosen from among the possible default values suggested by the system.

In the first example, in addition to the line and the controller, the device must be specified because we are assuming it is a network that is not using APPN. The line definition refers to the line connected to the system, while the controller and the device description refer to the remote entities connected to the same line.

APPENDIX A AS/400 Network Entities **131**

FIGURE A.1
Definitions of Network Entities for Two Systems Not Using APPN

```
1)                    SYSTEM AAA              SYSTEM BBB
2)    CRTLINSDLC   LIND ( LINE AAA)      CRTLINSDLC  LIND (LINE BBB)
3)                 RSRCNAME (LIN011)                 RSRCNAME (LIN 08)
4)                 ROLE (*NEG)                       ROLE (*NEG)
5)                 STNADR (01)                       STNADR (02)
6)    CRTCTLAPPC   CTLD (UNBBB)          CRTCTLAPPC  CTLD (UNAAA)
7)                 LINKTYPE (*SDLC)                  LINKTYPE (*SDLC)
8)                 APPN (*NO)                        APPN (*NO)
9)                 LINE (LINEAAA)                    LINE (LINEBBB)
10)                STNADR (02)                       STNADR (01)
11)   CRTDEVAPPC   DEVD (DEVBBB01)       CRTDEVAPPC  DEVD (DEVAAA01)
12)                LOCADR (00)                       LOCADR (00)
13)                RMTLOCNAME (BBB)                  RMTLOCNAME (AAA)
14)                LCLOCNAME (AAA)                   LOCLOCNAME (BBB)
15)                APPN (*NO)                        APPN (*NO)
16)                CTL (UNBBB)                       CTL (UNAAA)
```

Figure A.1 shows the command syntax for establishing these definitions on each of the two systems. Following is an explanation of each row of the figure:

Row 1 — gives the names of the two systems.

Row 2 — contains the CRTLINSDLC command and the name assigned to each line on each system. The line name is used to logically link the line definition with the controller definition (see Row 9).

Row 3 — shows the name given at the hardware component used by the line.

Row 4 — identifies the role (primary, secondary, or negotiable for SDLC purposes) that the system has on that line. The value of "*NEG", meaning negotiable role, is the recommended choice for mid-range systems.

Row 5 — specifies the line address. Note that the same address must be given in the controller definition of the remote system.

Row 6 — contains the CRTCTLAPPC command and the name assigned to each controller in the two systems.

Row 7 — indicates that the line servicing the controller uses SDLC.

Row 8 — shows that the relationship is not APPN.

Row 9 — gives the name of the line servicing the controller.

Row 10 — gives the line address used by the controller. This is the same as the line address in the line definition of the remote system.

Row11 — contains the CRTDEVAPPC command to create an APPC device (LU 6.2, in SNA parlance) and the name assigned to the device on each system.

Row12 — sets LOCADR equal to 00, which means that the LUs are independent and the system can start the session. Other values mean a dependent LU that must wait for the start from the remote site. Between midrange systems, the suggested value is 00.

Row13 — gives the name of the remote system. This name must correspond with the local system name defined on the opposing system.

Row14 — gives the name of the local system. This name must correspond with the remote system name defined on the opposing systems.

Row15 — indicates that APPN is not used.

Row16 — links the APPC device generated with its controller.

In this example, the device definition does not specify a mode. This means that an IBM-supplied default mode for the APPC session will be used. Once the definitions are established and the physical link is connected, the definitions must be activated for use. This can be done either via the VRYCFG (Vary Configuration) command or via the "On" option of the "Work with the Configuration Status" (WRKCFGSTS) display. After that, a user can activate DSPT, DDM, ICF, or other SNA functions available in peer-to-peer networks.

Figure A.2 shows the network and the names of the systems for the second example. Because this is an APPN network, the device descriptions are omitted because they can be self-generated. Also note that some network attributes of the systems must be given with the CHGNETA (Change Network Attributes) command.

FIGURE A.2
An APPN Network with Two End Nodes and One Network Node

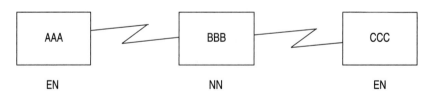

AAA	BBB	CCC
EN	NN	EN

COMMANDS: CHGNETA   to define the system network attributes at system level
           CRTLINSDLC to define the line
           CTRCTLAPPC to define the controller

APPENDIX A AS/400 Network Entities   133

FIGURE A.3
Network Definitions for an APPN Network

	COMMAND	PARAMETERS	AAA VALUE	BBB VALUE		CCC VALUE
1)	CHGNETA	LCLNETID	XYZ	XYZ		XYZ
2)		LCLCPNAME	AAA	BBB		CCC
3)		NODTYPE	*ENDNODE	*NETNODE		*ENDNODE
4)		NETSERVER	BBB	—		BBB
5)	CRTLINSDLC	LIND	LINEAAA	LINEBB1	LINEBB2	LINECCC
6)		RSCNAME	LIN23	LIN07	LIN08	LIN01
7)		ROLE	*NEG	*NEG	*NEG	*NEG
8)		STNADR	01	02	02	01
9)	CRTCTLAPPC	CTLD	CTLBBB	CTLBB1	CTLBB2	CTLBBB
10)		LINKTYPE	*SDLC	*SDLC	*SDLC	*SDLC
11)		LINE	LINEAAA	LINEBB1	LINEBB2	LINECCC
12)		RMTCPNAME	BBB	AAA	CCC	BBB
13)		STNADR	02	01	01	02
14)		NODTYPE	*NETNODE	*ENDNODE	*ENDNODE	*NETNODE

Figure A.3 shows the command syntax for establishing definitions on each of the three systems. Following is an explanation of each row of the figure:

Row 1 — shows the CHGNETA command, indicating the name given to the network, which is XYZ in all systems.

Row 2 — identifies the name of the local systems.

Row 3 — indicates that AAA and CCC are end nodes while BBB is a network node.

Row 4 — specifies which network node serves the end node.

Row 5 — shows the command CRTLINSDLC with the name given to it in the systems. Please note that in BBB there are two lines and two controllers defined — the first pair toward AAA, the second pair toward CCC.

Row 6 — gives the name of the line connection used by the line.

Row 7 — shows that the role at the SDLC level is negotiable.

Row 8 — indicates the line address. Again, this address must refer to the definition of the controller at the other end of the line.

Row 9 — shows the CRTCTLAPPC command with the name given to the controller.

Row 10 — states that the used line is SDLC.

Row 11 — gives the name of the line used.

Row12 — gives the name of the system at the other end of the line.

Row13 — indicates the line address used.

Row14 — shows that AAA and CCC are end nodes and BBB is a network node.

After activation of the defined entities, the APPN applications can start using the network. Each system can define APPC devices for sessions with both of the other two.

Appendix B

Application Synchronization

The terms "synchronous" and "asynchronous" can refer to line protocols and to the relationships between applications running on different hosts. The application of synchronous and asynchronous behavior to line protocols is discussed in Chapter 2; this Appendix will focus on the issue of synchronous and asynchronous behavior at the application level.

Two applications are synchronous when they are jointly involved in the handling of a single transaction and this interaction does not exceed a given time limit. People talk about real-time, simultaneous, synchronous, or session-oriented (connection-oriented) applications. Maybe the most useful definition is that of an exchange of individual transactions based on a session or connection.

Under the transaction exchange scenario, data exchanges occur within one session, or connection, that has been previously established between the two applications. This also implies that both applications are available when the sessions are active and that the failure of one implies the interruption of the connection, and thereby of the exchange. Traditional services based on conversational or transactional sessions are those acting, for example, between an intelligent workstation application and the central system responsible for the correct and immediate processing of the peripheral transactions.

Consider this example of session-based synchronous communications between two AS/400s: A bank has two AS/400s, one in Milan and the other in Rome. The first serves all the branch offices' terminals in northern Italy and manages the related customer database; the second fulfills the same services in southern/central Italy and manages the database of central/southern Italian customers. In addition to other functions, the session between the two systems is useful for accurate and immediate transaction management for southern clients wanting to be served in a northern branch office, and vice versa. These transactions are moved from the receiving AS/400 to the other one.

Obviously, this service requires the active presence of both computers and that the transactions be conducted in real time so that response to the peripheral terminal can be sent within a reasonable time. Thus, the interactions between the session-based (or connection-based) conversational applications in this example can be said to be synchronous.

But the relationships between applications allow another approach, which is based on the concept of message queues, as shown in Figure B.1. The queues are disk space reserved for inbound and outbound messages and transactions. Almost all mail or electronic messaging applications are based on this principle. Messages that have entered APPL 1 and are addressed to APPL 2 users

FIGURE B.1
Asynchronous Communications Between Two Applications via Queues

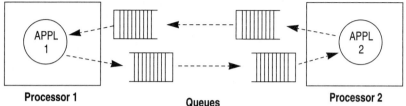

are placed in the output queue of the computer instead of being transmitted directly. The actual transmission occurs later, with the condition that APPL 2 is ready to receive the messages. This is the principle underlying store-and-forward communications, typical of electronic-mail and message-switching applications.

Compared to the scheme based on connections or sessions, this scheme allows more freedom. The two systems do not have to be active at the same time to accept, control, and store the messages. This relationship between two applications is called asynchronous or non-connection oriented.

In an asynchronous application environment, each system informs the other systems of its availability to send and receive application messages when it starts up. This process also includes handling any messages that remained in any queues when the system became unavailable. In other words, the receipt and delivery of messages into and out of queues is handled at the system level, regardless of the status or availability of the individual programs that handle the messages.

You may rightfully ask whether this type of relationship can be useful for applications different from electronic mail. Indeed, all too often the idea of distributed applications is coupled with the idea of a single transaction being processed by multiple systems in real time. In other words, too often the idea of distributed applications is coupled with that of synchronous relationships among the applications.

There are obviously cases, as in the example of the two bank systems, where synchronization is absolutely necessary. But its implementation leads to various problems and constraints. Imagine a transaction that must reach different systems, all of which are dedicated to specific applications, and the transaction must update the database of each system. To maintain databases consistent with each other, the transaction must always be either accepted or rejected by all systems. This situation poses "commit" problems that are related to the updating of a distributed database; these problems have solutions that leave high-risk margins. For example, a computer could send others its updating commit and then fail without having updated its database. Furthermore, the "commit" approach results in increased traffic and a longer transaction processing time when the number of involved systems is significant.

In addition, generally high availability of systems and communications lines in a synchronized application environment must be guaranteed; components ensuring good service and performance must be used; and alternative backup solutions for lines, components, and systems must be determined and implemented. The synchronous solution is therefore less flexible and more expensive than the asynchronous solution.

When planning networks for distributed applications, it would be wise to consider assigning application tasks to the various systems so that each system has a degree of autonomy. Imagine, for example, a company that has one system for marketing applications and a second system for accounting applications. Is it really necessary that the events stored in the first system be transmitted in real time to the second system? A daily series of file transfers would probably suffice. If daily file transfer is not frequent enough, communications could be performed on a store-and-forward basis at various times throughout the day.

By using an asynchronous solution, the two systems in this example would be more independent and flexible, roll-back procedures for erroneous transactions would not have to be done "on the fly," transmission would have only minor constraints and minor cost, and exposures and risks regarding the data integrity would be minimal.

Selecting a synchronous or asynchronous relationship between applications is rarely affected by the choice of line protocols, which can also be synchronous and asynchronous. Rather, that selection is largely influenced by the interaction required between the two applications.

A synchronous relationship between two applications essentially means that both applications must be simultaneously active and that a transaction session or connection has been established between them. Exchanges occur within the session and are also subject to time constraints.

When time limits between the transaction processing at the two systems are loose and the systems' applications are consistently independent, an asynchronous application relationship can be established between them using store-and-forward techniques. These techniques provide more independent and flexible systems and are easier to manage than those involving synchronous relationships.

Glossary

A

Abbreviated dialing A feature of some telephone switches that permits users to establish calls by entering fewer digits than would otherwise be required; speed-dialing directories are predefined, though usually changeable by the user; also, speed dialing.

ABM *See* Asynchronous Balanced Mode

Access charges FCC-specified tariffs levied for access to a local exchange carrier (LEC), either for private-line access by users or for access to the LEC by interexchange carriers (IECs).

Access line That portion of a leased telephone line that permanently connects the user with the serving central office or wire center.

Accunet Data-oriented digital services from AT&T Communications, including Accunet T1.5, terrestrial wideband at 1.544 Mbit/s; Accunet Reserved T1.5, satellite-based channels at 1.544 Mbit/s primarily for video teleconferencing applications; Accunet Packet Services, packet-switching services; Accunet Dataphone digital service (DDS), private-line digital circuits at 2,4, 4.8, 9.6, and 56-kbit/s; Accunet Switched 56.

ACF Advanced Communications Function; family of IBM communications software products that add to other systems software the functions of SNA network operation, control, and management; performs critical control functions for IBM SNA networks; ACF/NCP/VS (ACF/Network Control Program/Virtual Storage); also, ACF/TCAM, ACF/VTAM, ACF/VTAME.

ACK Control code or designation for a positive acknowledgment; sent from a receiver to a transmitter to indicate that a transmission, or sequence of transmissions, has been received correctly.

Acoustic coupler A device that allows a telephone handset to be used for access to the switched telephone network for data transmission; digital signals are modulated as sound waves; data rates are typically limited to about 300 bit/s, some up to 1.2 kbit/s.

ACS Asynchronous Connection Server; a gateway device that facilitates start/stop connections for synchronous devices.

ACSE Association Control Service Element (OSI); a control point for the establishment, control, and termination of application relationships in an OSI network.

A/D Analog-to-Digital (conversion); the process of converting analog information such as waveforms into binary digital information.

ADCCP Advanced Data Communications Control Procedure (ANSI); the ANSI implementation of the HDLC communications protocol. *See* HDLC.

Address A sequence of bits, a character, or a group of characters that identifies a network station, user, or application; used mainly for routing purposes; in telephony, the number entered by the caller that identifies the party called.

ADMD Administration Management Domain (MHS/X.400); the set of the MTS (Message Transfer System) directly controlled and operated by PTT (Postal, Telephone, and Telegraph authority in Italy) or by common carriers.

ADPCM Adaptive Differential Pulse Code Modulation; encoding technique, standardized by the CCITT, that allows an analog voice conversation to be carried within a 32-kbit/s digital channel; 3 or 4 bits are used to describe each sample, which represents the difference between two adjacent samples; sampling is done 8,000 times a second.

AIX Advanced Interactive eXecutive (IBM); IBM's implementation of the UNIX operating system.

ALERTs Error messages regarding the condition of the network generated by network nodes and forwarded to a central control point.

AM *See* Amplitude Modulation

Amplifier Any electronic component that boosts the strength or amplitude of a transmitted — usually analog — signal; functionally equivalent to a repeater in digital transmissions.

Amplitude Modulation (AM) Transmission method in which variations in the voltage or current waveform of a carrier signal determine encoded information.

Analog In communications, transmission employing variable and continuous waveforms to represent information values, where interpretation by the receiver is an approximation of the encoded value; compare with digital.

ANSI American National Standards Institute; a non-profit, non-governmental standards body that is the United States' representation to ISO.

Answerback The response of a terminal or other communications device to remotely transmitted control signals; typically part of handshaking between devices.

API *See* Application Program Interface

APPC Advanced Program-to-Program Communications; also called Logical Unit 6.2, an IBM definition for high-level program interaction capabilities on a peer-to-peer basis.

Application layer A logical entity of the OSI model; the top of the seven-layer structure, generally regarded as offering an interface to, and largely defined by, the network user; in IBM's SNA, the end-user layer.

Application Program Interface (API) A set of formalized software calls and routines that can be referenced by an application program to access underlying network services.

APPN Advanced Peer-to-Peer Networking; an SNA version for IBM midrange systems, based on a peer-to-peer relationship and adaptive algorithms, allowing any-to-any communications in a meshed network.

ARM Asynchronous Response Mode (HDLC); a mode of operation that allows a secondary system to transmit without receiving permission from the primary system.

ARP Address Resolution Protocol; a protocol associated with TCP/IP that handles the translation of Internet addresses into actual hardware addresses.

ARPA Advanced Research Projects Agency; operates within the U.S. Department of Defense.

ARPAnet ARPA network; the network organized and maintained by ARPA for communications between government and non-government agencies.

ARQ Automatic request for repeat or retransmission; communications feature whereby the receiver asks the transmitter to resend a block or frame, generally because of errors detected by the receiver.

ASC Abbreviation for asynchronous communications frequently used in the AS/400 environment. *See* asynchronous.

ASCII American National Standard Code for Information Interchange; the standard, and predominant, seven-bit (eight bits, with parity) character code used for data communications and data processing.

Asynchronous Transmission that is not related to a specific frequency, or to the timing, of the transmission facility; describing transmission characterized by individual characters, or bytes, encapsulated with start and stop bits, from which a receiver derives the necessary timing for sampling bits; also, start/stop transmission.

Asynchronous Balanced Mode (ABM) ABM allows systems to establish connection-oriented links with one another without prior permission.

ATM Asynchronous Transfer Mode; a "fast" packet-switching mode that breaks information down into 53-byte cells for transmission over high-speed switched networks or local area network links; also, an acronym used for automated teller machine.

Attenuation Reduction or loss of signal strength, measured in decibels; opposite of gain.

AU Access Unit; a device or unit that permits the connection of a system to a network.

Audiotex A service that allows a database host to pass data to a voice-mail computer, where it is interpreted and delivered over the telephone as a natural, spoken-voice message.

Authentication In security, ensuring that the message is genuine, that it has arrived exactly as it was sent, and that it comes from the stated source.

Auto-answer Automatic answering; capability of a terminal, modem, computer, or similar device to respond to an incoming call on a dial-up telephone line and to establish a data connection with a remote device without operator intervention; unattended operation for incoming dial-up calls.

Autodial Automatic dialing; capability of a terminal, modem, computer, or similar device to place a call over the switched telephone network and establish a connection without operator intervention; also, autocall.

Automatic fallback A modem's ability to negotiate an appropriate data rate with the modem on the other end of the link, depending on line quality; for example, if two 1.2-kbit/s modems could not pass data at 1.2 kbit/s, each might "fall back" to 300 bit/s automatically to transmit data without excessive errors.

Automatic Route Selection (ARS) The capability of a switch, typically a private branch exchange (PBX), to automatically determine an optimal route establishing a circuit; also called least-cost routing (LCR).

B

Backbone network A transmission facility designed to interconnect lower-speed distribution channels or clusters of dispersed user devices.

Balanced-to-ground With a two-wire circuit, where the impedance-to-ground on one wire equals the impedance-to-ground on the other wire; compare with unbalanced-to-ground, which in most cases is a preferable condition for data transmission.

Balun Balanced/unbalanced, in the IBM cabling system, refers to an impedance-matching device used to connect balanced twisted-pair cabling with unbalanced coaxial cable.

Bandwidth The difference, expressed in Hertz (Hz), between the highest and lowest frequencies of a transmission channel.

Baseband Describing a signal frequency that is below the point that the signal is modulated as an analog carrier frequency; in modulation, the frequency band occupied by the aggregate of the transmitted signals when first used to modulate the carrier (IBM).

Basic rate In ISDN, two 64-kbit/s information-carrying B channels and one 16-kbit/s signaling D channel (2B+D).

Baud A measurement of the signaling speed of a data-transmission device; equivalent to the maximum number of signaling elements, or symbols, per second that are generated; may be different from bit/s rate, however, especially at higher speeds, as several bits may be encoded per symbol, or baud, with advanced encoding techniques such as phase-shift keying.

Baudot code An aging data transmission code using five bits for character representation, usually with one start and one or two stop bits added.

BCC Block Check Character, a control character appended to blocks in some protocols used for determining whether the block was received in error; used in longitudinal and cyclic redundancy checking.

BCD Binary-Coded Decimal; aging, numeric-based character code set, where numbers zero through nine have a unique 4-bit binary representation.

B channel In Integrated Services Digital Network (ISDN), a 64-kbit/s information-carrying channel.

Bipolar The predominant signaling method used for digital transmission services, such as DDS and T1, in which the signal carrying the binary value successively alternates between positive and negative polarities; zero and one values are represented by the signal amplitude at either polarity, while no-value "spaces" are at zero amplitude; also, a type of Integrated Circuit (IC, or semiconductor) that uses both positively and negatively charged currents, characterized by high operational speed and cost.

B-ISDN Broadband ISDN; an implementation of ISDN that uses extremely high-speed wide-area optical links in place of the digital links used in a conventional ISDN network.

Bisync Binary Synchronous Communications (BSC); character-oriented data-communications protocol developed by IBM; oriented toward half-duplex link operation; still widely employed, though replaced in current IBM data communications products by the bit-oriented Synchronous Data Link Control (SDLC).

Bit duration The time it takes one encoded bit to pass a point on the transmission medium; in serial communications, a relative unit of time measurement.

Bit error The case where the value of an encoded bit is changed in transmission and interpreted incorrectly by the receiver.

Bit Error Rate (BER) The ratio of received bits that are in error (relative to a specific number of bits received); usually expressed as a number referenced to a power of 10; e.g., 1 error in 105 bits — also referred to as a BER of 10.-5

Bit-oriented Describing a communications protocol or transmission procedure where control information is encoded in fields of one or more bits; oriented toward full-duplex link operation; uses less overhead — and is therefore more efficient — than character- or byte-oriented protocols.

Bit/s Bits per second; basic unit of measure for serial data transmission capacity; kbit/s, or kilobit/s, for thousands of bits per second; Mbit/s, or megabit/s, for millions of bits per second; Gbit/s, or gigabit/s, for billions of bits per second.

Bit stuffing Process, in bit-oriented data communications protocols, where for example, string of "one" bits is broken by an inserted zero, added by the sender and removed by the receiver; adding of zero bits is done to prevent user data containing a series of one bits from being interpreted as a flag control character.

Block A quantity of transmitted information regarded as a discrete entity by size; more commonly, a discrete entity by its own starting-and-ending control delimiters, usually with its own self-contained control, routing, and error-checking information; in (primarily) Bisync, that portion of a message terminated by an EOB or ETB line-control character or, if the last block in a message, by an EOT or ETX line-control character; a block may contain one or more records, or a record one or more blocks.

BOC Bell Operating Company; one of 22 local telephone companies spun off from AT&T as a result of divestiture, reorganized into seven regional Bell holding companies.

Boundary node In IBM's SNA, a sub-area node that can provide certain protocol support for adjacent sub-area nodes, including transforming network addresses to local addresses, and vice versa, and performing session-level sequencing and flow control for less intelligent peripheral nodes.

BPS Bit per second; a measurement applied to serial communications lines.

Bridge A device that connects local-area networks at the data link layer.

Bridge tap An undetermined length of wire attached between the normal endpoints of a circuit that introduces unwanted impedance imbalances for data transmission; compare with terminated line; also, bridging tap, bridged tap.

Broadband Describing transmission equipment and media that can support a wide range of electromagnetic frequencies; typically, the technology of CATV transmission, as applied to data communications, that employs coaxial cable as the transmission medium and radio-frequency carrier signals in the 50-to-500-MHz range; any communications channel having a bandwidth greater than a voice-grade telecommunications channel, sometimes used synonymously with wideband.

Broadcast Delivery of a transmission to two or more stations at the same time, such as over a bus-type local-area network or by satellite; protocol mechanism whereby group and universal addressing is supported.

BSC Abbreviation for synchronous communications frequently used in the AS/400 environment. *See* Bisync.

BTAM Basic Telecommunications Access Method (IBM); IBM mainframe software responsible for managing application access; precursor of VTAM.

Buffering Process of temporarily storing data in a register or in RAM, which allows transmission devices to accommodate differences in data rates and to perform error checking and retransmission of data received in error.

Bus A transmission path or channel; typically, an electrical connection, with one or more conductors, wherein all attached devices receive all transmissions at the same time; a local-area network topology, such as used in Ethernet and the token bus, where all network nodes "listen" to all transmissions, selecting certain ones based on address identification; involves some sort of contention-control mechanism for accessing the bus transmission medium.

C

CAD Computer-Aided Design; design processes aided by the use of computer equipment.

CAE Computer-Aided Engineering; engineering processes aided by the use of computer equipment.

CAI Computer-Aided Instruction; instructional processes aided by the use of computer equipment.

Callback modem A modem that must be password-activated by the caller. It will then typically hang up and call back the caller's predefined telephone number to establish a communications session.

Call-detail recording (CDR) A feature of Private Branch Exchanges (PBXs) where each telephone call is logged, typically by time and charges, and retrievable by the network operator for cost charging by department; also called station message detail recording (SMDR).

Call forwarding A PBX feature that lets a user direct calls to another extension.

Call pickup A PBX feature that lets a user answer an incoming call from any station other than the called destination.

Call waiting A PBX feature that informs a station user of an incoming call when another call is already in progress.

CAM Computer-Aided Manufacturing; manufacturing processes aided by the use of computer equipment.

Carrier A continuous frequency capable of being modulated or impressed with a second data-carrying signal.

Carrier band A band of continuous frequencies that can be modulated with a signal.

CATV Community Antenna Television (formal) or Cable Television (colloquial); data communications based on Radio Frequency (RF) transmission, generally using 75-ohm coaxial cable where multiple frequency-divided channels allow mixed transmissions to be carried simultaneously; broadband.

CBX Computerized Branch eXchange; local phone switching equipment augmented by computerization.

CC Communication Controller; a front-end processor on an IBM mainframe responsible for managing all or a portion of the data communications network; any device used to control an aspect of a data communications network.

CCITT International Telegraph and Telephone Consultative Committee (from the French, *Comite Consultatif International Telegraphique et Telephonique*); *see* CCITT V.XX and X.XX specifications under appropriate alphabetical listings.

CDRM *See* Cross Domain Resource Manager

Cell The geographic area served by a single transmitter in a cellular radio network.

Cellular radio Technology employing low-power radio transmission as an alternative to local loops for accessing the switched telephone network; users may be stationary or mobile — in the latter case, they are passed, under control of a central site, from one cell's transmitter to an adjoining one's with minimal switchover delay.

CEPT Conference of European Postal and Telecommunications Administrations (Conference Europeenne des administrations des Postes et des Telecommunications).

Channel In communications, a physical or logical path allowing the transmission of information; the path connecting a data source and a data receiver.

Channel-attached Describing the attachment of devices directly to the input/output channels of a (mainframe) computer; devices attached to a controlling unit by cables, rather than by telecommunications circuits; same as locally attached 3270 displays (IBM).

Channel bank Equipment, typically in a telephone central office, that performs multiplexing of lower-speed, generally digital, channels into a higher-speed composite channel; the channel bank also detects and transmits signaling information for each channel and transmits framing information so that time slots allocated to each channel can be identified by the receiver.

Character Standard bit representation of a symbol, letter, number, or punctuation mark; generally means the same as byte.

Character code One of several standard sets of binary representations for the alphabet, numerals, and common symbols, such as ASCII or EBCDIC.

Characteristic impedance The impedance termination of an electrically uniform (approximately) transmission line that minimizes reflections from the end of the line.

Character-oriented Describing a communications protocol or transmission procedure that carries control information encoded in fields of one or more bytes; compare with bit-oriented; also, byte-oriented.

Checksum The sum of a group of data items, associated with the group, for checking purposes.

CICS Customer Information Control System; an IBM program product and mainframe operating environment, designed to enable transactions entered at remote terminals to be processed concurrently by user-written application programs; includes facilities for building and maintaining databases; now also available on the AS/400.

CIM Computer-Integrated Manufacturing; a manufacturing environment that includes one or more computers closely integrated with the manufacturing and administrative processes.

Circuit Generally, a transmission medium interconnecting two or more electronic devices.

Circuit switching The process of establishing and maintaining a circuit between two or more users on demand and giving them exclusive use of the circuit until the connection is released.

Class of service The way in APPN to specify for a given user session the transmission priority and the route to be selected.

Clear channel Characteristic of a transmission path wherein the full bandwidth is available to the user; said primarily of telephone-company digital circuits that do not require that some portion of the channel be reserved for carrier framing or control bits.

Clock An oscillator-generated signal that provides a timing reference for a transmission link; used to control the timing of functions such as sampling interval, signaling rate, and duration of signal elements; an "enclosed" digital network typically has only one "master" clock.

Closed user group In communications, a subgroup of users assigned to a network facility that restricts communications from any member of that subgroup to members of other subgroups; typically, however, a Data Terminal Equipment (DTE) device may be accessed by more than one closed user group.

Cluster controller A device that handles the remote communications processing for multiple (usually dumb) terminals or workstations; generally considered to be an IBM 3270-family controller, such as the IBM 3274 or a compatible device.

CMIP Central Management Information Protocol; a low-level protocol used in the OSI network management scheme.

CMIS Central Management Information Service; a high-level collection point in the OSI network management scheme.

CNN Composite Network Node. The pair formed by an IBM host such as an AS/400 and a 37XX communications controller, able to operate as a network node in an APPN network.

Coaxial cable A popular transmission medium consisting of, usually, one central wire conductor (two in the case of twinaxial cable) surrounded by a dielectric insulator and encased in either a wire mesh or an extruded metal sheathing; coaxial cable exists in many varieties, depending on the degree of EMI shielding afforded and voltages and frequencies accommodated; common Community Antenna Television (CATV) transmission cable, typically supporting RF frequencies from 50 to about 500 MHz; also called coax.

Codec Coder/decoder; an Integrated Circuit (IC), or series of ICs, that performs a specific analog-to-digital conversion (e.g., conversion of an analog voice signal to a 64-kbit/s digital bit stream, or an analog television signal to a digital format).

Code conversion The process of changing the bit grouping for a character in one code into the corresponding bit grouping for the character in another.

Combined station In the High-level Data Link Control (HDLC) protocol, a data station capable of assuming either the role of a primary or a secondary station; also, a balanced station.

Common carrier In the United States, any supplier of transmission facilities or services to the general public that is authorized to provide such facilities or services by the appropriate regulatory authority and bound to adhere to the applicable operating rules, such as making services available at a common price (tariff) and on a nondiscriminatory basis.

Communications server   An intelligent device providing communications functions; usually, an intelligent, specially configured node on a local network designed to enable remote communications access to, and egress from, LAN users.

Compaction   *See* Compression

Companding   Compressing/expanding; the process of reducing the bandwidth required for representation of an analog waveform for transmission and then reconstructing (most of) the original waveform at the receiving end; performed by electronic circuitry that applies a compression algorithm; generally, the compression/expansion of analog voice or video signals.

Compression   Any of several techniques that reduce the number of bits required to represent information in data transmission or storage, therefore conserving bandwidth and/or memory, wherein the original form of the information can be reconstructed; also called compaction.

Computer Inquiry II (CI II)   Formally known as the Second Computer Inquiry, FCC Docket No. 20828. The final decision, in 1980, articulated a policy toward competition and deregulation for all participants in the telecommunications industry, including major long-distance carriers.

Computer Inquiry III (CI III)   Adopted by the Federal Communications Commission (FCC) in May 1986, Computer Inquiry III removed the structural separation requirement between basic and enhanced services, for the Bell operating companies (BOCs) and for AT&T; CI III replaced that requirement with "nonstructural safeguards"; this action resulted in the imposition of such concepts as "comparably efficient interconnection (CEI)" and Open Network Architecture (ONA).

Concentrator   Any communications device that allows a shared transmission medium to accommodate more data sources than there are channels currently available within the transmission medium.

Contention   In communications, the situation when multiple users vie for access to a transmission channel, whether a PBX circuit, a computer port, or a time slot, within a multiplexed digital facility.

Control characters   In communications, any extra transmitted characters used to control or facilitate data transmission between Data Terminal Equipment (DTE) devices; characters transmitted over a circuit that are not message or user data but cause certain control functions to be performed when encountered; also, extra characters associated with addressing, polling, message delimiting and blocking, framing, synchronization, error checking and other control functions.

Conversational Time-dependent data transmissions, during which an operator, upon initiating a transmission, waits for a response from a destination before continuing; also, interactive.

Corporation for Open Systems (COS) A nonprofit organization of networking vendors and users designed to promote OSI and ISDN standards in the United States and to advance interoperability certification.

COS Class Of Service; an IBM network variable that helps determine the priority and route a given message will take; also Corporation for Open Systems.

CP Central Processor; the core processing service of a computer or computer network.

CPE Customer Premises Equipment; in telephony, equipment that interfaces to the telephone network and physically resides at the user's location; includes most, but not all, gear referred to as Network Channel Terminating Equipment (NCTE).

CPI-C Common Programming Interface for Communications; an interface specification with the IBM SAA scheme that defines how programs access communications services.

CRC Cyclic Redundancy Check; a basic error-checking mechanism for link-level data transmissions; a characteristic link-level feature of (typically) bit-oriented data communications protocols, wherein the data integrity of a received frame, or a packet, is checked by the use of a polynomial algorithm based on the content of the frame and then matched with the result that is performed by the sender and included in a (most often 16-bit) field appended to the frame.

Cross-Domain Resource Manager (CDRM) An IBM SNA function that, together with another CDRM, manages communications between two applications across domains by exchanging handshaking messages, determining the validity of the session request, determining if the requested resources are available, and binding the session users together.

CSMA/CD Carrier-Sense Multiple Access with Collision Detection; a leading local-area network access-control technique, by which all devices attached to the network "listen" for transmissions in progress before attempting to transmit and, if two or more begin transmitting at the same time, each backs off (defers) for a variable period of time (determined by a preset algorithm) before again attempting to transmit.

CSU Channel Service Unit; a component of Customer Premises Equipment (CPE) used to terminate a digital circuit, such as DDS or T1, at the customer site; performs certain line-conditioning functions, ensures network compliance per FCC rules, and responds to loopback commands from the central office; also ensures proper ones density in transmitted bit stream and performs bipolar-violation correction; *see also* DSU.

CTS Clear to Send; a modem control signal supported by several electrical interfaces, such as RS-232-C and V.24.

CVSD Continuous Variable-Slope Delta modulation; speech encoding and digitizing technique that uses a one-bit sample to encode the difference between two successive signal levels; sampling usually done at 32,000 times a second, though some implementations employ lower sampling rates.

Cyclic Redundancy Check   *See* CRC

D

Data Encryption Standard (DES)   Cryptographic algorithm designed by the National Bureau of Standards to encipher and decipher data using a 64-bit key; specified in Federal Information Processing Standard Publication 46, dated January 15, 1977.

Data link   Any serial data communications transmission path, generally between two adjacent nodes or devices and without any intermediate switching nodes.

Data-link layer   Layer 2 in the OSI model; the network processing entity that establishes, maintains, and releases data-link connections between (adjacent) elements in a network.

Data PBX   A switch that allows a user on an attached circuit to select from among other circuits, usually one at a time and on a contention basis, for the purpose of establishing a through connection; distinguished from a PBX in that only data transmission, and not analog voice, is supported.

Data transfer rate   The average number of bits, characters, or blocks per unit of time transferred from a data source to a data sink.

DB/DC   Database/Data Communications. Another term to indicate an Online Transaction Processor (OLTP) monitor on IBM mainframes.

DCA   *See* DIA/DCA

DCE   Data Circuit-terminating Equipment (also, incorrectly, data communications equipment); in a communications link, equipment that is either part of the network, an access point to the network, a network node, or equipment at which a network circuit terminates; in the case of an RS-232-C connection, the modem is usually regarded as DCE, while the user device is DTE, or data terminal equipment; in a CCITT X.25 connection, the network access and packet-switching node is viewed as the DCE.

DCE   Distributed Computer Environment; DCE is a product of the Open Software Foundation (OSF) that implements distributed computing services such as network file access, shared printer services, and program-to-program services.

D channel   In Integrated Services Digital Network (ISDN), a 16-kbit/s signaling channel for basic-rate access, or a 64-kbit/s signaling channel within primary-rate access.

DCM   Digital Circuit Multiplication; a means of increasing the effective capacity of primary-rate, and higher-level, PCM hierarchies, based upon speech coding at 64 kbit/s.

DDCMP   Digital Data Communications Message Protocol (Digital Equipment Corporation); DDCMP is a byte-oriented protocol used for system-to-system communications under DECnet.

DDD Direct Distance Dialing; referring to the conventional long-distance-switched telephone network, dial-up calls placed over the network, or dial-up long-distance circuits; *see* MTS.

DDM Distributed Data Management; an APPN function allowing an application to transparently access files on another system.

DDN Defense Data Network. The data network used by the U.S. Department of Defense.

DDP *See* Distributed Data Processing

DDS Dataphone Digital Service (AT&T); private-line digital service offered intraLATA by BOCs and interLATA by AT&T Communications, with data rates typically at 2.4, 4.8, 9.6, and 56 kbit/s; now part of the services listed by AT&T under the Accunet family of offerings.

DDS-SC Dataphone Digital Service with Secondary Channel (also often referred to as DDS II); a tariffed private-line service offered by AT&T and certain BOCs that allows 64-kbit/s clear-channel data with a secondar

DEC Digital Equipment Corporation; major manufacturer of mainframe, midrange, and micro computers.

DECnet Digital Equipment Corporation NETwork; DEC's proprietary network architecture that works across all of the company's machines; endowed with a peer-to-peer methodology.

Dedicated line A dedicated circuit, a nonswitched channel; also called a private line; *see* Leased line.

Delay In communications, the wait time between two events, such as from when a signal is sent until it is received; *see* Propagation delay, Response time.

Demodulation The extraction of transmitted information from a modulated carrier signal.

DES *See* Data Encryption Standard

Destination field A field in a message header that contains the address of the station to which a message is being directed.

D4 framing T1 12-frame format in which the 193rd bit is used for framing and signaling information; ESF is an equivalent but newer 24-frame technology.

DHCF Distributed Host Command Facility (IBM/SNA); DHCF is the remote system counterpart to the mainframe Host Command Facility (HCF) and enables mainframe 3270 terminals to access the remote system as a native terminal.

DIA/DCA Document Interchange Architecture/Document Content Architecture; IBM-promulgated architectures, part of SNA, for transmission and storage of documents over networks, whether text, data, voice, or video; becoming industry standards by default.

Dial backup A network scheme using two dial-up lines to effect data transmission as a temporary replacement for a failed dedicated line; in this configuration, one dial-up link is used to transmit data and the other to receive data.

Dial-up Describing the process of, or the equipment or facilities involved in, establishing a temporary connection via the switched telephone network.

Digital Referring to communications procedures, techniques, and equipment by which information is encoded as either a binary "1" or "0".

Digital Speech Interpolation (DSI) A voice-compression technique that takes advantage of the pauses inherent in human speech to multiplex other voice conversations onto the same transmission link.

Digital switching The process of establishing and maintaining a connection, under stored program control, by which binary-encoded information is routed between an input and an output port; generally, a "virtual" through circuit is derived from a series of time slots (time-division multiplexing), which is more efficient than requiring dedicated circuits for the period of time that connections are set up.

DISOSS Distributed Office Support System (IBM/SNA); IBM mainframe software that manages the transfer of documents, files, and messages in an SNA network.

Distributed Data Processing (DDP) Describing a network of geographically dispersed, though logically interconnected, data processing nodes; generally configured so that nodes can share common resources, such as a file server, a print server, host applications, or a database; communications between DDP nodes may be sporadic or intensive, interactive or batch; also, distributed processing.

DLC Data-Link Control; the protocols and control routines that manage the transmission operations of the physical network interface; also, data-line card.

DMA Direct Memory Access; a memory access technique that enables a peripheral device to access the main computer memory without the services of the Central Processing Unit (CPU).

DNA Digital Network Architecture (Digital Equipment Corporation); Digital's architecture of the interconnection and networking of Digital and non-Digital systems; logically analogous to IBM's SNA.

DoD Department of Defense (United States); the United States government department responsible for the research, development, and possible deployment of defense technology.

Domain In IBM's Systems Network Architecture (SNA), a host-based Systems Services Control Point (SSCP) and the physical units (PUs), logical units (LUs), links, link stations, and all the associated resources that the host (SSCP) has the ability to control.

DOS Disk Operating System; used to describe both PC operating systems (PC-DOS, MS-DOS) and the DOS/VSE mainframe operating system.

DOS/VSE Disk Operating System/Virtual Storage Extended; an IBM mainframe operating system commonly used in smaller mainframes; also known as just "VSE."

DOV Data Over Voice; technology used primarily with local Centrex services or special customer-premises PBXs for transmitting data and voice simultaneously over twisted-pair copper wiring; typical data rates for DOV applications with Centrex are 19.2 kbit/s, although speeds of up to 1 Mbit/s have been achieved with certain PBX-based networks.

Draft proposal An ISO standards document that has been registered and numbered but not yet given final approval.

DRDA Distributed Relational Database Access (IBM/SNA); an IBM product that enables one or more databases to be implemented in a distributed fashion among different types of IBM systems (e.g., AS/400s, RS/6000s, and mainframes).

Driver Usually a software module that, under control of the processor, manages an I/O port to an external device, such as a serial RS-232-C port to a modem.

Drop-and-insert A term applied to a multiplexer that can add data (insert) to a T1 data stream, or act as a terminating node (drop) to other multiplexers connected to it.

Drop cable In local-area networks, a cable that connects perpendicularly to the main network cable, or bus, and attaches to Data Terminal Equipment (DTE).

DS-0 Digital Signal Level 0; telephony term for a 64-kbit/s standard digital telecommunications signal or channel.

DS-1 Digital Signal Level 1; telephony term describing the 1.544-Mbit/s digital signal carried on a T1 facility.

DS-1C Digital Signal Level 1C; telephony term describing a 3.152-Mbit/s digital signal.

DS-3 Equivalent of 28 T1 channels, communications access operating at 44.736 Mbit/s; effectively synonymous with T3.

DSA Distributed System Architecture. The name of Bull's architecture for distributed applications, roughly comparable to IBM's SNA and DEC's DNA.

DSE Data Switching Equipment; a node in a circuit-switching or packet-switching network.

DSNX Distributed System Node eXecutive; the software counterpart in a distributed system of Netview/Distribution Manager (N/DM) in an IBM mainframe. The pair allows the interchange of files and programs.

DSPT Display Station Pass-Through, a 3X/400 communications function allowing a workstation of a computer in APPN to access the applications of another system.

DSU Data Service Unit; component of customer premises equipment (CPE) used to interface to a digital circuit (say, DDS or T1), combined with a channel service unit (CSU); performs conversion of customer's data stream to bipolar format for transmission.

DSX-1 Digital Signal cross-connect Level 1; telephony term for the set of parameters used where DS-1 digital signal paths are cross-connected.

DTE Data and Terminal Equipment; generally, user devices, such as terminals and computers, that connect to Data Circuit-terminating Equipment (DCE); they either generate or receive the data carried by the network; in RS-232-C connections, designation as either DTE or DCE determines the signaling role in handshaking.

Dynamic bandwidth allocation A feature available on certain high-end T1 multiplexers that allows the total bit rate of the multiplexer's tail circuits to exceed the bandwidth of the network trunk; this is allowable since the multiplexer only assigns channels on the network trunk to tail circuits that are transmitting.

E

EBCDIC Extended Binary Coded Decimal Interchange Code; 8-bit character code set developed and promulgated by IBM.

Echo In communications, the reflection back to the sender of transmitted signal energy; length of delay in an echo depends on the distance from the transmitter to the point of reflection.

Echo cancellation Technique used in higher-speed modems that allows for the isolation and filtering out of unwanted signal energy caused by echoes from the main transmitted signal.

ECMA European Computer Manufacturers Association; ECMA is a standards organization composed of European computer manufacturers.

EDI Electronic Data Interchange; an intercompany communications application for the exchange of records, with a structure standardized and equivalent to business documents; a set of services for information and document exchange.

EDIFACT EDI For Administration, Commerce and Transport. A set of standardized record formats for commercial transactions, such as invoices or orders, exchanged between companies in EDI applications. Also, the specific committee, formed under ISO and EEC control, responsible for these standards.

EFT Electronic funds transfer; a set of protocols and services to facilitate the transfer of funds from one bank location to another.

EIA Electronic Industries Association; *see* EIA RS-XX specifications under appropriate alphabetical listings.

E-mail Electronic mail; the transfer of documents or files between specific users in a network.

EMI Electromagnetic Interference; a device's radiation leakage that is coupled onto a transmission medium, resulting (mainly) from the use of high-frequency wave energy and signal modulation; reduced by shielding; minimum acceptable levels are detailed by the FCC, based on type of device and operating frequency.

Emulation The imitation of all or part of one device, terminal, or computer by another, so that the imitating device accepts the same data, performs the same functions, and appears to other network devices as the imitated device.

Emulation Program (EP) An IBM control program that permits functions written for one system or device to be run on another system or device. In IBM networks, the program that allows a 37X5 communications controller to emulate the previous controllers of the 270X series.

EN End Node IBM/SNA-APPN; an APPN network node that is not capable of routing requests to or from other APPN nodes; term also used in DECnet.

Encoding/decoding The process of reforming information into a format suitable for transmission, and then reconverting it after transmission.

Encryption In security, the ciphering of data by applying an algorithm to plaintext in order to convert it to ciphertext.

EP *See* Emulation Program

Equalization In the telephone network, the spacing and operation of amplifiers so that the gain provided by the amplifier, per transmission frequency, coincides with the signal loss at the same frequency; within communications devices, equalization is achieved by circuitry that compensates for the differences in attenuation at different frequencies, usually a combination of adjustable coils, capacitors, and resistors.

Error burst A sequence of transmitted signals containing one or more errors but regarded as a unit in error in accordance with a predefined measure; enough consecutive transmitted bits that are in error to cause a loss of synchronization between sending and receiving stations, and to necessitate resynchronization.

Error-correction code In computers, rules of code construction that facilitate reconstruction of part or all of a message received with errors.

ESF Extended Superframe Format; an AT&T-proposed T1-framing standard that provides frame synchronization, cyclic redundancy checking, and data link bits; frames consist of 24 bits instead of the previous standard 12 bits; the standard allows control information to be stored and retrieved easily, facilitating network performance monitoring and maintenance.

Ethernet A popular local-area network design and the trademarked product of Xerox Corp. and of Digital Equipment Corp., characterized by 10-Mbit/s baseband transmission over a shielded coaxial cable and employing CSMA/CD as the access-control mechanism; standardized by the IEEE as specification IEEE 802.3; referring to the Ethernet design or compatible with Ethernet.

F

Facsimile The communications process in which graphics and text documents are scanned, transmitted via a (typically dial-up) telephone line, and reconstructed by a receiver; facsimile-device operation typically follows one of the CCITT standards for information representation and transmission (Group 1 analog, with page transmission in four or six minutes; Group 2 analog, with page transmission in two or three minutes; Group 3 digital, with page transmission in less than one minute; and Group 4 digital, with page transmission in less than 10 seconds); also, often called fax.

Fading A phenomenon, generally of microwave or radio transmission, whereby atmospheric, electromagnetic, or gravitational influences cause a signal to be attenuated, deflected, or diverted away from the target receiver.

Fast packet switching New packet-switching technique such as frame relay.

Fax *See* Facsimile

FBSS Financial Branch System Services; PC software to facilitate and manage the connection of banking devices.

FCC Federal Communications Commission; board of commissioners appointed by the President under the Communications Act of 1934, with the authority to regulate all interstate telecommunications originating in the United States.

FCS *See* Frame Check Sequence (SDLC/HDLC)

FDDI Fiber Distributed Data Interface; a 100-Mbps local-area network based on fiber optic links that is modeled on the Token-Ring architecture, plus enhancements.

FDM *See* Frequency-Division Multiplexing

FDX *See* Full duplex; sometimes called duplex or "dux."

FED-STD-1001 Synchronous high-speed data signaling rate between data terminal equipment and data circuit-terminating equipment.

FED-STD-1002 Time and frequency reference information in telecommunications "systems."

FED-STD-1003-A Synchronous bit-oriented data-link control procedures (Advanced Data Communications Control Procedures).

FED-STD-1005 Coding and modulation requirements for nondiversity 2.4-kbit/s modems.

FED-STD-1006 Coding and modulation requirements for 4.8-kbit/s modems.

FED-STD-1007 Coding and modulation requirements for duplex 9.6-kbit/s modems.

FED-STD-1008 Coding and modulation requirements for duplex 600-bit/s and 1.2-kbit/s modems.

FEP Front-End Processor; a dedicated computer linked to one or more host computers or multiuser minicomputers that performs data communications functions and serves to offload the attached computers of network processing; in IBM SNA networks, an IBM 3704, 3705, 3725, or 3745 communications controller.

Fiber Distributed Data Interface (FDDI) An American National Standards Institute (ANSI)-specified standard for fiber-optic links with data rates up to 100 Mbit/s. The standard specifies multimode fiber; 50/125, 62.5/125, or 85/125 core-cladding specification; an LED or laser light source; and 2 kilometers for unrepeated data transmission at 100 Mbit/s.

Fiber optics Transmission technology by which modulated lightwave signals, generated by a laser or LED, are propagated along a (typically) glass or plastic medium, and then typically demodulated back into electrical signals by a light-sensitive receiver.

File Transfer, Access, and Management (FTAM) An ISO application- layer standard for network file transfer and remote file access.

Filter Electronic circuitry that removes energy in unwanted frequencies from a transmission channel; may be analog or digital in operation; used mainly on broadcast lines with FDM (Frequency Division Multiplexing).

Final-form document An electronic document that is only suitable for printing or displaying but not for modifying.

FIPS Federal Information Processing Standard; specifications produced by the United States government and mandated for use by the government and its agencies.

FIPS PUB 1-1 Code for information interchange.

FIPS PUB 7 Implementation of the code for information interchange and related standards.

FIPS PUB 15 Subsets of the standard code for information interchange.

FIPS PUB 16-1 Bit sequencing of the code for information interchange in serial-by-bit data transmission.

FIPS PUB 17-1 Character structure and character parity sense for serial-by-bit data communications in the code for information interchange.

FIPS PUB 22-1 Specifies synchronous signaling rates between data terminal equipment (DTE) and data circuit-terminating equipment (DCE).

FIPS PUB 37 Synchronous high-speed data signaling rates between data-terminal equipment and data circuit-terminating equipment.

FIPS PUB 46 *See* Data Encryption Standard

FIPS PUB 71 Advanced Data Communications Control Procedures (ADCCP).

FIPS PUB 78 Guideline for implementing Advanced Data Communication Control Procedures (ADCCP).

Flag In communications, a bit pattern of six consecutive "1" bits (character representation is 01111110) used in many bit-oriented protocols to mark the beginning (and often also the end) of a frame.

Flow control Capability of network nodes to manage buffering schemes while handling devices operating at different data rates, enabling them to talk with each other.

FM *See* Frequency Modulation

FNC Abbreviation for financial communications links frequently used in the AS/400 environment.

Four-wire Refers to a transmission path that allows for physically separate transmit and receive channels; at one time, four-wire was the only method for implementing full-duplex transmission.

Frame A group of bits sent serially over a communications channel; generally, a logical transmission unit sent between data-link layer entities that contains its own control information for addressing and error checking; the basic data-transmission unit employed with bit-oriented protocols, similar to blocks; also, in video transmission, a set of electron scan lines (usually 525 in the United States) that comprise a television picture.

Frame-Check Sequence (FCS) In bit-oriented protocols, a 16-bit field that contains transmission error-checking information, usually appended at the end of a frame.

Framing A control procedure used with multiplexed digital channels, such as T1 carriers, whereby bits are inserted so that the receiver can identify the time slots that are allocated to each subchannel; framing bits may also carry alarm signals indicating specific alarm conditions.

Frequency The number of repetitions per time unit of a complete waveform; typically, the number of complete cycles per second, usually expressed in Hertz (Hz).

Frequency band Portion of the electromagnetic spectrum within a specified upper- and lower-frequency limit; also, frequency range.

Frequency-Division Multiplexing (FDM) Technique for sharing a transmission channel wherein carrier signals of different frequencies are transmitted simultaneously.

Frequency Modulation (FM) Method of encoding a carrier wave by varying the frequency of the transmitted signal.

FTAM File Transfer, Access, and Management; specifications that define the services used to accommodate transfer of files within an OSI network.

FTP File Transfer Protocol; part of the TCP/IP protocol suite, FTP provides application and end-user services to permit the transfer of a file from one system to another.

FTS File Transfer Support (IBM/SNA-APPN); general-purpose utility for transferring files between IBM midrange systems; also Federal Telecommunications System.

Full Duplex (FDX) Operation of a data-communications link where transmissions are possible in both directions at the same time between devices at both ends.

G

Gateway A conceptual or logical network station that serves to interconnect two otherwise incompatible networks, network nodes, subnetworks, or devices; performs a protocol-conversion operation across numerous communications layers.

GOSIP Government OSI PROfile; the sets of requirements independently issued by the United States and United Kingdom governments to dictate the use of OSI-compliant products.

Group addressing In transmission, the use of an address that is common to two or more stations; on a multipoint line, where all stations recognize addressing characters, but only one station responds.

H

HDX *See* Half duplex

Half duplex Operational mode of a communications line whereby transmission occurs in both directions but only in one direction at a time; transmission directions may be alternately switched to accommodate two-way data flow.

Handshake protocol A predefined exchange of signals or control characters between two devices or nodes that sets up the conditions for data transfer; also, handshaking.

HCF Host Command Facility; an IBM host function allowing a 3270 terminal connected to it to access a remote midrange system.

HDLC *See* High-Level Data Link Control

Head end A passive component in a broadband LAN that translates one range of frequencies (transmit) to a different frequency band (receive); allows devices on a single-cable network to send and receive without the signals interfering with each other.

Header Control information and codes that are appended to the front of a block of user data for control, synchronization, routing, and sequencing of a transmitted data frame or packet.

Hz Hertz; measurement that distinguishes electromagnetic waveform energy; number of cycles, or complete waves, that pass a reference point per second; measurement of frequency by which one Hertz equals one cycle per second.

High-level Data Link Control (HDLC) CCITT-specified, bit-oriented, data-link control protocol; the model on which most other bit-oriented protocols are based; similar to IBM SDLC.

I

IBCN Integrated Broadband Communication Network. Another term for B-ISDN, the integrated digital network that will ultimately replace ISDN. IBCN will offer higher bandwidth (100 Mpbs or more).

ICF Intersystem Communications Function; conversational software on IBM systems 3X/400 allowing two applications on remote systems to interact in conversational mode; also, Interactive Communications Facility.

IEEE Institute of Electrical and Electronics Engineers; a professional society that researches and recommends interface standards to ANSI.

IFIPS *See* International Federation of Information Processing Societies

Impedance The effect on a transmitted signal, which varies at different frequencies, or resistance, inductance, and capacitance.

IMS/VS Information Management System/Virtual Storage; a common IBM host operating environment, usually under the MVS operating system, oriented toward batch processing and telecommunications-based transaction processing.

Intelligent terminal A programmable terminal.

Interactive Describing time-dependent (real-time) data communications, typically one in which a user enters data and then awaits a response message from the destination before continuing; also conversational; contrast with batch (processing).

Interface A shared boundary; a physical point of demarcation between two devices, where the electrical signals, connectors, timing, and handshaking are defined; the procedures, codes, and protocols that enable two entities to interact for a meaningful exchange of information.

International Federation of Information Processing Societies (IFIPS) Organization whose Working Group 6.5 originally developed the functional model and the layered model for electronic mail systems. The functional model provides logical abstractions that clarify the operation of electronic mail systems and define when responsibility for a message changes hands. The layered model shows how electronic mail systems protocols fit in the seven-layered Basic Reference Model for Open Systems Interconnection (the OSI reference model). (Both models were further enhanced by the CCITT working group that developed the X.400 series of recommendations for electronic mail systems.)

International standard An ISO standards document that has been approved in final balloting.

IP Internet Protocol; used in TCP/IP to connect networks (at OSI network Level 3).

IPL Initial Program Load; the process a computer goes through during power-on to load its operating system from magnetic media (disk or tape).

IPX The LAN protocol used in Novell NetWare networks.

ISDN Integrated Services Digital Network; ISDN allows a variety of mixed digital transmission services to be accommodated; access channels under definition include basic rate (144 kbit/s) and primary rate (nominally, 1.544 or 2.048 Mbit/s, depending upon the country).

I-series recommendations A group of CCITT recommendations concerning digital networks in general and ISDN in particular.

ISO International Standards Organization; a voluntary, independent organization chartered to define international standards for all types of communications.

ISO 646 7-bit character set for information processing interchange.

ISO 2022 Code-extension techniques for use with ISO 7-bit coded-character set.

ISO 2110 25-pin DTE/DCE interface connector and pin assignments.

ISO 2593 Connector pin allocations for use with high-speed data terminal equipment.

ISO 3309 High-level data-link procedures; frame structure.

ISO 4902 HDLC unbalanced classes of procedures.

ISO 4903 15-pin DTE/DCE interface connector and pin assignments.

ITU International Telecommunications Union; a United Nations agency responsible for international telecommunications standards.

J

Jamming The intentional interference of (typically) open-air radio-frequency transmission to prevent communications between a transmitter and a receiver.

JCL Job Control Language; an IBM term for the commands and directives that control execution within an operating system; equivalent to CL in the AS/400 environment.

JES Job Entry Subsystem; control protocol and procedure for directing host processing of a task in an IBM host environment; the specific IBM software that allows local or remote job input.

Jitter The slight movement of a transmission signal in time or phase that can introduce errors and loss of synchronization in high-speed synchronous communications; *see* Phase jitter.

Job A large file, typically transmitted in batch mode; specifically, a set of data, including programs, files, and instructions to a computer, that collectively constitutes a unit of work to be done by a computer.

K

kbit/s Kilobits per second; standard measure of data rate and transmission capacity.

Kermit An asynchronous file-transfer protocol designed for academic computing at Columbia University and named after a famous puppet frog.

Keying Modulation of a carrier signal, usually by frequency or phase, to encode binary information; also, interruption of a DC circuit for the purpose of signaling information.

Key management The management of the cryptographic keys or algorithms used to cipher data.

L

LAN *See* Local-Area Network

LANACS LAN Asynchronous Communications Support. A software package running on an IBM PC LAN attached to and allowing other PCs of the LAN to access remote hosts via asynchronous connection.

LAP Link Access Procedure (HFDLC subset); the data-link-level protocol specified in the CCITT X.25 interface standard; original LAP has been supplemented with LAPB (LAP-Balanced) and LAPD.

LAPB Link Access Procedure Balanced (X.25); a revised version of the original LAP implementation that allows any systems to interact with an X.25 node in a balanced mode.

LAPD Link Access Procedure D; link-level protocol devised for ISDN connections, differing from LAPB (LAP-Balanced) in its framing sequence. Likely to be used as the basis for LAPM, the proposed CCITT modem error-control standard.

LAPX Link Access Procedure X. A subset of HDLC defined by CCITT as the standard data link protocol for Teletex applications.

Laser Light amplification through the stimulated emission of radiation; a major light-signal source for optical-fiber transmission; produces a generally more coherent single-wavelength light signal than an LED and is also, typically, more expensive and shorter-lived; used mainly with single-mode optical fiber.

LAT Local Area Transport; a Digital Equipment Corporation protocol used on Ethernet LANs to carry traffic between terminal servers and systems.

Latency The time interval between when a network station seeks access to a transmission channel and when access is granted or received; equivalent to waiting time.

Layer In the OSI reference model (seven basic layers), referring to a collection of related network-processing functions that comprises one level of a hierarchy of functions.

LDM *See* Limited-Distance Modem

Leased line A dedicated circuit, typically supplied by the telephone company, that permanently interconnects two or more user locations; generally voice-grade in capacity and in range of frequencies supported; typically analog, though sometimes it refers to DDS subrate digital channels (2.4 to 9.6 kbit/s); used for voice (2000 Series leased line) or data (3002-type); could be point-to-point or multipoint; may be enhanced with line conditioning; also, private line.

Least-cost routing *See* Automatic Route Selection

LED Light-Emitting Diode; device that accepts electrical signals and converts the energy to a light signal; with lasers, the main light source for optical-fiber transmission; used mainly with multimode fiber.

LEN *See* Low-Entry Networking

LENN Low-End Network Node; *see* Low-Entry Networking.

Lightwave Referring to electromagnetic wavelengths in the region of visible light; wavelengths of approximately 0.8 to 1.6 microns; referring to the technology of fiber-optic transmission.

Limited-Distance Modem (LDM) A comparatively low-cost modem used on customer premises for transmitting data within or between buildings to a maximum distance of a few miles.

Line of sight Characteristic of some open-air transmission technologies where the area between a transmitter and a receiver must be clear and unobstructed; said of microwave, infrared, and open-air, laser-type transmissions; a clear, open-air, direct transmission path free of obstructions such as buildings but in some cases impeded by adverse weather or environmental conditions.

Line turnaround The action in a (typically half-duplex) communications link that, for example, a device takes after receiving a block of data to prepare sending its own block; in RS-232-C connections, the delay after request-to-send has been signaled and a clear-to-send indication is received; *see* Turnaround time.

Link-attached Describing devices that are connected to a network, a communications data link, or telecommunications circuit; compare with channel-attached.

Link Problem Determination Aid (LPDA) In SNA, a set of commands used to operate a modem and to diagnose problems.

LLC *See* Logical Link Control

Loading Adding inductance to a transmission line to minimize amplitude distortion; generally accomplished with loading coils; also, ("loading") adding a program to a computer.

Local-Area Network (LAN) A type of high-speed (typically in the Mbit/s range) data communications arrangement wherein all segments of the transmission medium (typically coaxial cable, twisted-pair wire, or optical fiber) are in an office or campus environment under the control of the network operator.

Logical Link Control (LLC) A protocol developed by the IEEE 802 committee, common to all of its LAN standards, for data-link-level transmission control; the upper sublayer of the IEEE Layer 2 (OSI) protocol that complements the MAC protocol; IEEE standard 802.2; includes end-system addressing and error checking; in more general terms, a logical interface that adapts physical layer protocols (such as Token-Ring or Ethernet) to higher level services (such as SNA).

Long-haul Long distance, describing (primarily) telephone circuits that cross out of the local exchange, or serving, area; now generally applied to any interLATA circuits, whether intrastate or interstate; said of a modem to distinguish it from an LDM.

Loopback Diagnostic procedure used for transmission devices; a test message is sent to a device being tested, which is then sent back to the originator and compared with the original transmission; loopback testing may be within a locally attached device or conducted remotely over a communications circuit.

Low Entry Networking (LEN)   An aspect of APPN networks that allows systems with no inherent routing ability to use adjacent systems for routing. Systems of this type are sometimes referred to as Low-Entry Network Nodes (LENN) or just (LEN).

LPDA   *See* Link Problem Determination Aid

LU   Logical Unit; in IBM's SNA-APPN, a port through which a user gains access to the services of a network; some LUs can support two types of sessions: with the host-based System Services Control Point (SSCP) and with other LUs.

LU 6.2   In Systems Network Architecture (SNA), a set of protocols that provides peer-to-peer communications between applications.

LWS   Local Workstation; abbreviation frequently used in the AS/400 environment for 5250 workstations.

M

MAC   Media Access Control; media-specific access control protocol with IEEE 802 specifications; currently includes variations for Token-Ring, token bus, and CSMA/CD, the lower sublayer of the IEEE's link layer (OSI), which complements the Logical Link Control (LLC).

Main network address   In IBM's SNA, the Logical Unit (LU) network address, within ACF/VTAM, that is used for SSCP-to-LU sessions and for certain LU-to-LU sessions.

Maintenance services   In IBM's SNA, network services performed between a host SSCP and remote physical units (PUs) that test links and collect and record error information; related facilities include configuration services, management services, and session services.

MAN   Metropolitan Area Network; network that extends to 50-kilometer range, operates at speeds from 1 Mbit/s to 200 Mbit/s, and provides an integrated set of services for real-time data, voice, and image transmission; two standards bodies are involved with work on MANs: IEEE 802.3 and ANSI X3T9.5.

Management services   In IBM's SNA, network services performed between a host SSCP and remote physical units (PUs) that include the request and retrieval of network statistics.

Manchester encoding   Digital encoding technique (specified for the IEEE 802.3 Ethernet baseband network standard and also used in Token-Ring) in which each bit period is divided into two complementary halves: a negative-to-positive (voltage) transition in the middle of the bit period designates a binary "1," while a positive-to-negative transition represents a "0"; the encoding technique also allows the receiving device to recover the transmitted clock from the incoming data stream (self-clocking).

Manufacturing Automation Protocol (MAP)   A General Motors-originated suite of networking protocols, services, and application interfaces put forth as a suggested standard for the manufacturing environment, the implementation of which tracks the seven layers of the OSI model.

MAP *See* Manufacturing Automation Protocol

Mapping In network operations, the logical association of one set of values, such as addresses on one network, with quantities or values of another set, such as devices on another network (e.g., name-address mapping, internetwork-route mapping, protocol-to-protocol mapping).

Master clock The source of timing signals — or the signals themselves — that all network stations use for synchronization.

Master station A station that controls slave stations; *see* Primary station.

Matrix In switch technology, that portion of the switch architecture where input leads and output leads meet, any pair of which may be connected to establish a through circuit.

Matrix switch Device that allows a number of channels, connected via serial interfaces (typically RS-232-C), to connect, under operator control, to designated remote or local analog circuits, as well as to other serial interfaces.

MAU Multistation Access Unit; wiring concentrator used in Token-Ring local-area networks.

Medium Any material substance that can be, or is, used for the propagation of signals, usually in the form of electrons or modulated radio, light, or acoustic waves, from one point to another, such as optical fiber, cable, wire, dielectric slab, water, air, or free space (ISO).

Megabyte (Mbyte or M) 1,048,576 bytes, equal to 1,024 Kilobytes; basic unit of measurement of mass storage; also used in describing (primarily parallel) data-transfer rates as a function of time (e.g., Mbyte/s).

Message Any information-containing data unit, in an ordered format, sent by means of a communications process to a named network entity or interface; in Bisync, the data between two ETX control characters.

Message-Handling System (MHS) The standard defined by CCITT as X.400 and by ISO as Message-Oriented Text Interchange Standard (MOTIS).

Message switching Transmission method by which messages are transmitted to an intermediate point, where they are temporarily stored, and then transmitted later to a final destination in their original form (*see* Store-and-forward); the destination of the message is typically indicated in an internal address field of the message itself.

Message-switching network A public data communications network over which subscribers send primarily textual messages to one another (e.g., TWX, Telex).

MHS *See* Message-Handling System

Microwave Portion of the electromagnetic spectrum above about 890 megahertz (Mhz); describing high-frequency transmission signals and equipment that employ microwave frequencies, including line-of-sight, open-air microwave transmission and, increasingly, satellite communications.

MNP Microcom Networking Protocol; proprietary error-correcting protocol for modems operating at speeds from 2.4 kbit/s to 9.6 kbit/s or higher; commercially licensed to more than 50 vendors, the protocol has been proposed as an adjunct to the CCITT LAP (link-access procedure) family; operates only point-to-point and does not have easy connections to X.25 and ISDN technology.

Modem Modulator/demodulator; electronic device that enables digital data to be sent over analog transmission facilities; the most prevalent modem types include the following Bell models:

- 103/113 Series: 300 bit/s, full-duplex, dial-up, asynchronous; originate-only (113C), answer-only (113D), or originate-and-answer (103J).
- 201 Series: 2.4 kbit/s, synchronous; dial-up (201-L1C) or via 3002-type, unconditioned, two- or four-wire circuits (201C-L1D).
- 208 Series: 4.8 kbit/s, synchronous; full duplex over 3002-type leased line (208A) or dial-up (208B).
- 212A: 0-300 bit/s or 1.2 kbit/s, dial-up, full duplex.

Mode (AS/400) Defines the characteristics of APPC sessions used by an application such as the maximum number of parallel sessions allowed and the number of sessions to be pre-established. The mode is an object created via the CRTMODD command and it is associated with the APPC device when the session is activated. The mode in an APPN network also specifies the class of service (COS) to be used for the choice of the route for the session.

MQI Message Queue Interface; an asynchronous program-to-program communications interface offered by IBM as an alternative to the synchronized APPC interface.

MS Message Store; a component within an X.400 electronic mail network that is capable of storing incoming messages for subsequent access by an authorized User Agent.

MSNF *See* MultiSystem Networking Facility

MTA (Message Transfer Agent) One of the major entities in an X.400 (OSI) application for electronic mail. It is responsible for message transfer across the network.

MTS Message Transfer System; a set of Message Transfer Agents within an X.400 electronic mail network.

Multiplexer Network components used at the two ends of a transmission line, with the purpose of sharing the line bandwidth among two or more information flows. The different flows can be data only or data and voice mixed. The most-used techniques are Time Division Multiplexing (TDM) and Frequency Division Multiplexing (FDM). The first technique divides the total bandwidth into a series of fixed time slots, with one slot allocated to each data stream. The second technique assigns different ranges of frequencies (subchannels) to the various data streams, allowing them to transmit concurrently.

Multisystem Networking Facility (MSNF)   One possible implementation of SNA, this IBM facility permits the interconnection of many single-host SNAs and their respective domains into a larger multiple-host network. MSNF provides an extensive distributed processing framework with the ability to share resources across sites. MSNF is established with tables that are part of the System Services Control Point (SSCP) and the Cross-Domain Resource Manager (CDRM). These tables contain the resources that are owned by domains and shared by other domains.

MVS   Multiple Virtual Storage (IBM); an IBM mainframe operating system frequently used in large, commercial mainframe environments.

N

NAU   Network Addressable Units (SNA); the entities that in SNA can be addressed. The major entities are SSCP (System Services Control Points), CP (Control Point, APPN), PU (Physical Unit, or Controller in APPN terms), LU (Logical Unit, or devices in APPN terms).

NCP   *See* Network Control Program

N/DM-DSNX   NetView Distribution Manager - Distributed System Node eXecutive; software on remote systems (such as an AS/400) that works in conjunction with a mainframe NetView application (DM) to distribute information from the central host to the remote system(s).

Network Control Program (NCP)   In IBM SNA networks, a host-generated program that controls the operation of a communications controller (such as an IBM 3705 or 3725).

Network layer   Layer 3 in the OSI model; the logical network entity that services the transport layer; responsible for ensuring that data passed to it from the transport layer is routed and delivered through the network.

Network services   In IBM's SNA, the services within network-addressable units (NAUs) that control network operations via sessions to and from the host SSCP.

NetView   An IBM mainframe network-management product that integrated the functions of several earlier IBM network-management products.

Network   An interconnected group of nodes (ISO TC97); a series of points, nodes, or stations connected by communications channels; the assembly of equipment through which connections are made between data stations (IBM).

Network Addressable Unit (NAU)   In IBM's SNA, a host-based logical unit (LU), physical unit (PU), or System Services Control Point (SSCP) that is the origin or destination of information transmitted by the path-control portion of an SNA network.

Network architecture   A set of design principles, including the organization of functions and the description of data formats and procedures, used as the basis for the design and implementation of a network (ISO).

Network Terminal Option (NTO) An IBM program product that enables an SNA network to accommodate a select group of non-SNA asynchronous and bisynchronous devices via the NCP-driven communications controller.

Network topology The physical and logical relationship of nodes in a network; the schematic arrangement of the links and nodes of a network (IBM); networks are typically of either a star, ring, tree, or bus topology, or some hybrid combination thereof.

Network virtual terminal A communications concept wherein a variety of DTEs, with different data rates, protocols, codes, and formats, are accommodated in the same network; this is done as a result of network processing, whereby each device's data is converted into a network standard format and then converted into the format of the receiving device at the destination end.

NFS Network File System; a distributed file system designed by Sun Microsystems that allows systems on a LAN to share access to sets of files.

NFTP NetView File Transfer Protocol. A software package that runs on IBM mainframes to allow file transfer among them.

NLDM Network Logical Data Manager (IBM/SNA); a NetView module that monitors the information being collected from NetView agent software.

NN Network Node (IBM/SNA-APPN); an SNA-APPN network node that is capable of routing requests to or from other SNA nodes.

Node A point where one or more functional units interconnect transmission lines (ISO); a physical device that allows for the transmission of data within a network; an endpoint of a link or a junction common to two or more links in a network (IBM SNA); typically includes host processors, communications controllers, cluster controllers, and terminals.

Node type In IBM's SNA, the classification of a network device based on the protocols it supports and the Network-Addressable Units (NAUs) it can contain; Type 1 and Type 2 nodes are peripheral nodes; Type 4 and Type 5 nodes are subarea nodes.

Noise Any extraneous and unwanted signal disturbances in a link (electromagnetic interference, or EMI); usually, random variations in signal voltage or current, or interfering signals.

NPDA Network Problem Determination Aid (IBM/SNA); a NetView module that presents the current status of the network.

NPM Network Performance Monitor. A complementary NetView product used to collect network performance data.

NPSI Network Packet Switching Interface (IBM/SNA); optional software for a communications controller that allows it to interface with an X.25 network.

NRM Normal Response Mode (SDLC/HDLC); a data-link-protocol-related mode of operation where a primary system controls the operation of one or more secondary systems.

NRZ Nonreturn to zero; a binary encoding and transmission scheme in which "ones" and "zeros" are represented by opposite, and alternating, high and low voltages; wherein there is no return to a reference (zero) voltage between encoded bits.

NRZI Nonreturn to zero inverted code; a binary encoding scheme that inverts the signal on a "one" and leaves the signal unchanged for a "zero"; wherein a change in the voltage state signals a "one" bit, and the absence of a change denotes a "zero" bit value; also, transition coding.

NTO *See* Network Terminal Option

Null characters Control characters that can be inserted into, or removed from, a data stream without affecting the meaning of a sequence; typically added to fill in time slots or unused fields.

Nyquist theorem In communications theory, a formula stating that two samples per cycle are sufficient to characterize a bandlimited analog signal; in other words, the sampling rate must be twice the highest frequency component of the signal (e.g., sampling at 8 kHz for a 4-kHz analog signal).

O

ODF Object Distribution Facility (IBM/SNA-APPN); a network-oriented facility that enables the transfer of programs, files, and other objects in an SNA-APPN network.

OEM Original Equipment Manufacturer; the maker of equipment that is marketed by another vendor, usually under the name of the reseller; the OEM may manufacture certain components, or complete devices, which are then often configured with software and/or other hardware by the reseller.

Off-line Condition in which a user, terminal, or other device is not connected to a computer or is not actively transmitting via a network; operation of a functional unit without the continual control of a computer; compare with on-line.

Ones density The requirement for digital transmission lines in the public switched telephone network that eight consecutive zeros cannot be in a digital data stream; exists because repeaters and clocking devices within the network will lose timing after receiving eight zeros in a row; any number of techniques or algorithms used to insert a one after every seventh consecutive zero; *see* Bit stuffing.

ONDS Open Network Distribution Service. IBM mainframe software for electronic mail based on OSI-X.400 standards.

Online Condition in which a user, terminal, or other device is actively connected with the facilities of a communications network or computer; pertains to the operation of a functional unit under the continual control of a computer; opposite of off-line.

Optical fiber Any filament or fiber, made of dielectric materials, that is used to transmit laser- or LED-generated light signals; optical fiber usually consists of a core, which carries the signal, and cladding, a substance with a slightly higher refractive index than the core, which surrounds the core and serves to reflect the light signal; *see also* Fiber optics.

OSF Open Software Foundation; an entity formed by a consortium of computer manufacturers to address the distributed processing issues.

OSI Open Systems Interconnection; referring to the OSI reference model, a logical structure for network operations standardized within the ISO; a seven-layer network architecture being used for the definition of network protocol standards to enable any OSI-compliant computer or device to communicate with any other OSI-compliant computer or device for a meaningful exchange of information; the layers are named (refer to each one for its specific definition) Physical, Data link, Network, Transport, Session, Presentation, and Application.

OSICS OSI Communication Subsystem (OSI/IBM); IBM's implementation underlying OSI services; OSICS is a prerequisite for all other OSI products (OSIFS and OSIMS).

OSIFS OSI File Services (OSI/IBM); IBM's implementation of OSI FTAM.

OSIMS OSI Message Services (OSI/IBM); IBM's implementation of OSI X.400.

Overhead In communications, all information, such as control, routing, and error-checking characters, that is in addition to user-transmitted data; includes information that carries network-status or operational instructions, network routing information, as well as retransmissions of user-data messages that are received in error.

Overrun Loss of data because a receiving device is unable to accept data at the rate it is transmitted.

P

PABX Private Automated Branch eXchange; *see* PBX.

Pacing group In IBM's SNA, the number of data units (path information units, or PIUs) that can be sent before a response is received; IBM term for window.

Packet A sequence of data, with associated control information, that is switched and transmitted as a whole; refers mainly to the field structure and format defined within the CCITT X.25 recommendation.

Packetized voice Digitized voice technology that lends itself to T1 and ISDN applications.

Packet switching A data transmission technique whereby user information is segmented and routed in discrete data envelopes called packets, each with its own appended control information for routing, sequencing, and error checking; allows a communications channel to be shared by many users, each using the circuit only for the time required to transmit a single packet; describing a network that operates in this manner.

PAD Packet Assembler/Disassembler; network interface device that allows multiple asynchronous terminals or host-computer ports to interface to a packet-switching network; a protocol conversion device that allows user terminals not equipped for packet switching to communicate over an X.25-based channel; PAD operations and functions are fully delineated in CCITT recommendations.

Pad characters In (primarily) byte-synchronous transmission, characters that are inserted to ensure that the first and last characters of a packet or block are received correctly; inserted characters that aid in clock synchronization at the receiving end of a synchronous transmission link; also, fill characters.

PAM *See* Pulse-Amplitude Modulation

Parallel sessions In IBM's SNA, two or more concurrently active sessions between the same two logical units (LUs) using different network addresses; each session can have different transmission parameters.

Parallel transmission A type of data transfer in which all bits of a character, or multiple-bit data blocks, are sent simultaneously, either over separate communications lines or circuits, over a single channel using multiple frequencies, or over a multiple-conductor cable.

Parity bit An additional noninformation bit appended to a group of bits, typically to a 7- or 8-bit byte, to make the number of ones in the group of bits either an odd or even number; a basic and elementary mechanism for error checking.

Parity check Process of error checking using a parity method; varied methods include longitudinal parity check and transverse parity check; *see* Parity bit.

Pass-through Describing the ability to gain access to one network element through another.

Path-control layer In IBM's SNA, the network processing layer that handles, primarily, the routing of data units as they travel through the network and manages shared link resources.

PBX Private Branch eXchange; telephone switch located on a customer's premises that primarily establishes circuits over tie-lines between individual users and the switched telephone network; typically also provides switching within a customer's premises and usually offers numerous other enhanced features such as least-cost routing and call-detail recording; also, PABX, for private automatic branch exchange.

PCM Pulse Code Modulation; digital transmission technique that involves sampling of an analog information signal at regular time intervals and coding the measured amplitude value into a series of binary values, which are transmitted by modulation of a pulsed, or intermittent, carrier; a common method of speech digitizing using 8-bit code words, or samples, and a sampling rate of (typically) 8 kHz.

PCNE Protocol Converter for Non-SNA Equipment (SNA/X.25). A complementary software product running on IBM's 37XX communications controller to support, via X.25 networks, remotely asynchronous terminals connected via PAD.

PDMD Private Management Domain. The set of MTS (X.400) controlled and operated by private organizations or enterprises.

PDN Public Data Network; typically, a tariffed packet-switching data carrier.

PDU Protocol Data Unit; ISO term referring to a packet of information exchanged between two network-layer entities.

PEP Partitioned Emulation Program (IBM). A software package for IBM 37XX communications controllers enabling simultaneous running of NCP and EP on the same unit.

Peripheral device With respect to a particular processing unit, any equipment that provides the processor with outside communications (ISO); any device that is peripheral to the major function of its attached processor or other controlling device.

Permanent Virtual Circuit (PVC) A virtual circuit in a pocket-switching network resembling a leased line in that invariant logical channel numbers allow it to be dedicated to a single user; a contracted arrangement within a switched network where a link between two locations is maintained at all times.

Phase jitter In telephony, the measurement, in degrees out of phase, that an analog signal deviates from the referenced phase of the main data-carrying signal; often caused by alternating-current components in a telecommunications network.

Phaselock loop In electronics, a circuit that acts as a phase detector by comparing the frequency of a known oscillator with an incoming signal and then feeds back the output of the detector to keep the oscillator in phase with the incoming frequency.

Phase modulation A data-transmission encoding method by which the phase angle of the carrier wave is varied, usually by 90 or 180 degrees, to represent a different bit value to the receiver; the encoding technique used in phase-shift keying.

Phase shift A change in the time that a signal is delayed with respect to a reference signal.

Phase-Shift Keying (PSK) The phase-modulation encoding technique employed by many modems; *see* Phase modulation.

Physical layer Within the OSI model, the lowest level (1) of network processing, below the link layer, that is concerned with the electrical, mechanical, and handshaking procedures over the interface that connects a device to a transmission medium; referring to an electrical interface, such as RS-232-C.

Physical Unit (PU) In IBM's SNA, the component that manages and monitors the resources of a node, such as attached links and adjacent link stations; PU types follow the same classification as node types; *see* Node type.

Picosecond One-trillionth of a second; one-millionth of a micro-second.

PIN Positive, Intrinsic, Negative; type of photodetector used to sense lightwave energy and then to convert it into electrical signals; also, personal identification number.

PIU Path Information Unit; *see* Pacing group.

Pixel Picture element; smallest unit of a graphics or video display, the light characteristics of which (color and intensity) can be coded into an electrical signal for transmission.

Polling Communications control procedure by which a master station or computer systematically invites tributary stations on a multipoint circuit to transmit data; contrast with selection.

Polling delay The specified interval at which a tributary device is polled by a master station; often a user-specified parameter.

Port A point of access into a computer, a network, or other electronic device; the physical or electrical interface through which one gains access; the interface between a process and a communications or transmission facility.

Presentation layer In the OSI model, Layer 6, which provides processing services to the application layer (7), allowing it to interpret the data exchanged, as well as to structure data messages to be transmitted in a specific display and control format.

Primary rate In North American ISDN, 23 64-kbit/s, information-carrying B channels and one 64-Kbit/s D channel used for signaling (23B+D) (in Europe, 30 B channels and one D channel).

Primary station A network node that controls the flow of information on a link; the station that, for some period of time, has control of information flow on a communications link (in this case, primary status is temporary).

Prioritization The process of assigning different values to (network) users, so that a user with a higher priority value will be offered access or service before (or more often than) a user with a lower priority value; increasingly available as an added option with network operation; any procedure with different levels of precedence.

Private line A leased line; a nonswitched circuit.

Private network A network established and operated by a private organization or corporation for users within that organization or corporation; compare with public network.

Programmable terminal A user terminal that has computational capability; also, intelligent terminal.

PROFS Professional Office System; PROFS is an IBM office automation and electronic mail package for mainframes.

PROM Programmable Read-Only Memory; a memory circuit that can be pre-programmed with information for subsequent retrieval.

Propagation delay The time it takes a signal, composed of electromagnetic energy, to travel from one point to another over a transmission channel; usually most noticeable in communicating with satellites; normally, the speed-of-light delay. This delay is noticeable in every network with very high speeds (for example, LAN FDDI).

Protocol Formal set of rules governing the format, timing, sequencing, and error control of exchanged messages on a data network; may be oriented toward data transfer over an interface, between two logical units directly connected, or on an end-to-end basis between two users over a large and complex network.

PSDN Public Switched Data Network (X.25); a packet-switching network managed by a public carrier.

PSDS Public Switched Digital Service; a BOC service; AT&T's Circuit-Switched Digital Capability (CSDC), also known commercially as AT&T's Accunet Switched 56 service; allows full-duplex, dial-up, 56-kbit/s digital circuits on an end-to-end basis.

PSTN Public Switched Telephone Network; acronym for the dial-up telephone network.

PTT Postal, Telegraph, and Telephone; government authority or agency that typically operates the public telecommunications network, sets standards and policy, and negotiates communications issues internationally for a particular country; not found in the United States; compare with common carrier.

PU *See* Physical Unit

Public network Generically, a network operated by common carriers or telecommunications administrations for the provision of circuit-switched, packet-switched, and leased-line circuits to the public; compare with private network.

Pulse-Amplitude Modulation (PAM) A method of adding information to an electronic carrier where the height (amplitude) of the carrier wave and the pulses of the data transmission are both changed to convey the added information. In PAM, the pulse coincides with different voltages along the wave form.

PVC *See* Permanent Virtual Circuit

Q

Quality of service (QOS) In network operation, a parameter specifying certain performance characteristics of a service, session, connection, or link.

Queue Any group of items, such as computer jobs or messages, waiting for service.

R

RAR Routing Addition Resistance; a variable used in SNA-APPN networks to determine a routing node's "willingness" to route traffic for other nodes; higher values mean less "willingness."

RARP Reverse ARP; a protocol associated with TCP/IP that handles the translation of actual hardware addresses into Internet addresses.

Real time A transmission or data processing operating mode by which data is entered in an interactive session; pertaining to an application whereby response to input is fast enough to affect subsequent input, such as a process-control "system" or a computer-aided design "system" (IBM); describing processing in which the results are used to influence an ongoing process.

Receive Only (RO) Describing operation of a device, usually a page printer, that can receive transmissions but cannot transmit.

Redundancy In data transmission, that portion of the gross information content of a message that can be eliminated without losing essential information; also, duplicate facilities.

Remote Job Entry (RJE) The submission of data processing jobs via a data link.

Remote station Any device that is attached to a controlling unit by a data link; also, a tributary station on a multipoint link.

Repeater In digital transmission, equipment that receives a pulse train, amplifies it, retimes it, and then reconstructs the signal for retransmission; in fiber optics, a device that decodes a low-power light signal, converts it to electrical energy, and then retransmits it via an LED or laser light source; also, regenerative repeater.

Response An answer to an inquiry; in IBM's SNA, the control information sent from a secondary station to the primary station under SDLC.

Response time For interactive sessions, the elapsed time between the end of an inquiry and the beginning of the response; the interval between a user data entry and the reply from a CPU or destination device.

Retry In the Bisync protocol, the process of resending the current block of data a prescribed number of times or until it is accepted.

Return to Zero (RZ) Method of transmitting binary information in such a way that after each encoded bit, voltage returns to the zero level.

RH Request Header (IBM/SNA); a control header added to data units transported through SNA networks.

Ring network A network topology in which the transmission medium is closed on itself.

RISC Reduced Instruction Set Computing; internal computing architecture where processor instructions are pared down so that most can be performed in a single processor cycle, theoretically improving computing efficiency.

RJE *See* Remote Job Entry

Routing The process of selecting the correct circuit path for a message.

RPC Remote Procedure Call (TCP/IP); a set of routines that enables a program on one system to activate (and possibly communicate with) a program on another system.

RS-232-C An EIA-specified physical interface, with associated electrical signaling, between Data Circuit-terminating Equipment (DCE) and data terminal equipment (DTE); the most commonly employed interface between computer devices and modems.

RS-422-A Electrical characteristics of balanced-voltage digital interface circuits (EIA).

RS-423-A Electrical characteristics of unbalanced-voltage digital interface circuits (EIA).

RS-449 General-purpose 37-position and 9-position interface for data terminal equipment and data circuit-terminating equipment employing serial binary data interchange (EIA).

RSCS Remote Spooling Communications Subsystem (IBM); RSCS is the standard job entry subsystem for the VM operating system.

RTS Request to send; part of modem handshaking.

RWS Remote workstation; abbreviation frequently used in the AS/400 environment.

S

SAA System Application Architecture (IBM); a global architecture to facilitate the development and implementation of cross-platform applications. SAA strives to provide consistent user and program interfaces across all IBM systems.

Satellite communications The use of geostationary orbiting satellites to relay transmissions from one earth station to one or more other earth stations.

SCS SNA Character String; type of transmission data format for IBM devices, consisting of EBCDIC control characters optionally mixed with user data, that is carried within an SNA request/response unit.

SDLC Synchronous Data Link Control; bit-oriented IBM version of the HDLC protocol; the mainstay of SNA communications.

Secondary station A station or node selected to receive transmission from a primary station; the secondary-station designation is usually temporary and only for the duration of the session or transaction; *see* Primary station.

Selection The process by which a computer contacts a station to send the station a message (IBM); *see* Polling.

Sequencing The process of dividing a user data message into smaller frames, blocks, or packets for transmission, in which each has an integral sequence number for reassembly of the complete message at the destination end.

Serial interface Usually, as pertains to computers or terminals, the mechanical and electrical components that allow data to be sent sequentially-by-bit over a transmission medium; in contrast to a parallel interface.

Serial transmission The sequential transmission of the bits constituting an entity of data over a data circuit (ISO).

Session A connection between two stations that allows them to communicate (ISO); the time period that a user engages in a dialogue with an interactive computer; in IBM's SNA, the logical connection between two network addressable units (NAUs).

Session layer in the OSI model, the network-processing layer (5) responsible for binding and unbinding logical links between users and maintaining an orderly dialogue between them; also, serves the presentation layer (6).

Shielding Protective enclosure surrounding a transmission medium, such as coaxial cable, designed to minimize electromagnetic leakage and interference.

Short-haul modem Generally, a limited-distance modem with transmission distances of less than a mile; *see* Limited-distance modem.

Signal converter An electronic device that takes input signal information and outputs it in another form.

Signal-to-Noise Ratio (SNR) Relationship of the magnitude of a transmission signal to the noise of its channel; measurement of signal strength compared to error-inducing circuit noise; given in decibels.

SMTP Simple Message Transfer Protocol; the protocol in the TCP/IP suite of protocols that handles the delivery of electronic mail.

SNA *See* Systems Network Architecture

SNADS SNA Distribution Service (IBM/SNA); a general distribution mechanism that permits the movement of files and objects between peer SNA systems.

SNBU *See* Switched Network Back-Up

SNMP Simple Network Management Protocol; a protocol originating from the TCP/IP environment that collects and reports information on network errors and configuration settings.

SNUF SNA Upline facility (IBM/SNA); a distribution mechanism used to facilitate the movement of files between IBM midrange and mainframe systems.

SSCP *See* System Services Control Point

Starlan A local-area network design and specification within the IEEE 802.3 standards subcommittee, characterized by 1-Mbit/s baseband data transmission over two-pair twisted-pair wiring.

Start bit In asynchronous transmission, the first element in each character that prepares the receiving device to recognize the incoming information elements.

Star topology The point-to-point wiring of network elements to a central node.

Start/stop transmission Asynchronous transmission characterized by each byte containing its own start and stop bits of data elements that are preceded by a start and followed by a stop signal; reference employed to designate asynchronous transmission.

Station Any DTE that receives or transmits messages on a data link, including network nodes and user devices.

Stop bit In asynchronous transmission, the last transmitted element in each character, which informs the receiver to come to an idle condition before accepting another character.

Store-and-forward Describing operation of a data network where packets, messages, or frames are temporarily stored within a network node before being transmitted to the destination.

SVC Switched Virtual Call (X.25); a temporary link within a packet-switching network.

Swift Society for Worldwide Interbank Financial Telecommunications.

Switched line Communications link for which the physical path, established by dialing, may vary with each use (e.g., a dial-up telephone circuit).

Switched network backup An option in certain communications links, and with certain communications devices such as modems, by which a switched, or dial-up, line is used as an alternate path if the primary, typically leased-line, path is unavailable.

Sync bits Synchronizing bits in synchronous transmission; maintains synchronism between transmitter and receiver.

Synchronous transmission Data communications in which characters or bits are sent at a fixed rate, with the transmitting and receiving devices synchronized; eliminates the need for start and stop bits basic to asynchronous transmission and significantly increases data throughput rates.

Sysgen System generation (or generator); loading of an operating system or its components in a CPU.

System A logical collection of computers, peripherals, software, service routines, accounting and control procedures, terminals, and end users; a collection of men, machines, and methods organized to accomplish a set of specific functions (*American National Dictionary for Information Processing*); an assembly of components united by some form of regulated interaction to form an organized whole (IBM); generally, systems may include networks, but only to the limited degree that those networks connect users directly to system resources; *see* Network.

System Services Control Point (SSCP) In IBM's SNA, a host-based network entity that manages the network configuration, coordinates network operator and problem-determination requests, maintains network address-mapping tables, and provides directory support and session services.

System Network Architecture (SNA) In IBM networks, the layered logical structure, formats, protocols, and procedures that govern information transmission; somewhat analogous to the OSI reference model.

T

TA Terminal Adaptor; in ISDN, a device that provides conversion between a non-ISDN terminal device and the ISDN user/network interface.

Tariff The formal process whereby services and rates are established by and for communications common carriers; submitted by carriers for government regulatory approval, reviewed, often amended, and then (usually) approved; the published rate for a specific communications service, equipment, or facility that constitutes a contract between the user and the communications supplier or carrier.

TCP/IP Transmission Control Protocol/Internet Protocol; internetworking software suite originated on the Department of Defense's Arpanet network; IP corresponds to OSI network Level 3, TCP to OSI Layers 4 and 5.

T1 AT&T term for a digital carrier facility used to transmit a DS-1 formatted digital signal at 1.544 Mbit/s.

T3 AT&T term for a digital carrier facility with an aggregate rate of 44.736 Mbit/s.

TDM *See* Time-Division Multiplexing

TDMA Time-division multiple access; a satellite transmission technique in which several earth stations have use of total available transponder power and bandwidth, with each station in sequence transmitting in short bursts.

Technical and Office Protocols (TOP) A Boeing version of the MAP protocol suite aimed at office and engineering applications.

Telecommunications A term encompassing both voice and data communications in the form of coded signals over media.

Teleprocessing Remote-access data processing (ISO); the use of data-link communications to accomplish a computer-based task; distinguished from distributed data processing (DDP), in which remote communications is not a prerequisite to all processing.

Teletex Akin to a higher-speed version of ASCII Telex, intended eventually to replace Telex.

Teletext Generically, one-way data transmission designed for widespread broadcasting of graphics and textual information, for display on subscriber television sets or (typically) low-cost video terminals; a data communications technique akin to, but more limited than, two-way videotex, by which users can select from among many pages of information for viewing.

Teletypewriter Generic term for a teleprinter terminal; Teletype is a trademark of the former Teletype Corp.

Telex Teleprinter exchange; a worldwide switched message-exchange service, characterized by Baudot-coded data (though numerous conversion facilities are now available).

Terminal A point in a network at which data can either enter or leave; a device, usually equipped with a keyboard, often with a display, capable of sending and receiving data over a communications link (IBM); generically the same as data terminal equipment (DTE).

Text In communications, transmitted characters forming the part of a message that carries information to be conveyed; in some protocols, the character sequence between start-of-text (STX) and end-of-text (ETX) control characters; information for human, as opposed to computer, comprehension that is intended for presentation in a two-dimensional form (ISO).

TH Transmission Header (IBM/SNA); a routing header added to data units transported through SNA networks.

Tie line A leased or private dedicated telephone circuit provided by common carriers that links two points together without using the switched telephone network.

Time-Division Multiplexing (TDM) Interleaving digital data from many users onto one or two serial communications links by dividing channel capacity into time slices; two common techniques are bit interleaving and byte (by character) interleaving.

Time-out Expiration of predefined time period, at which time some specified action occurs; in communications, timeouts are employed to avoid unnecessary delays and improve traffic flow; used, for example, to specify maximum response times to polling and addressing before a procedure is automatically reinitiated.

Timesharing Describing the interleaved use of time on a computer that enables two or more users to execute computer programs concurrently (IBM); any concurrent use of the same processing resource by multiple users.

Token bus A local-area network access mechanism and topology in which all stations actively attached to the bus listen for a broadcast token or supervisory frame; stations wishing to transmit must receive the token before doing so; however, the next logical station to receive the token is not necessarily the next physical station on the bus; bus access is controlled by preassigned priority algorithms.

Token-Ring A local-area network access mechanism and topology in which a supervisory frame or token is passed from station to adjacent station sequentially; stations wishing to gain access to the network must wait for the token to arrive before transmitting data; in a Token-Ring, the next logical station receiving the token is also the next physical station on the ring; compare with token bus.

TP Transaction Processing; term used to describe a style of application processing that breaks up the overall application task into a series of transactions.

Transaction In communications, a message destined for an application program; a computer-processed task that accomplishes a particular action or result; in interactive communications, an exchange between two devices, one of which is usually a computer; in batch or remote job entry, a job or job step.

Transceiver Generic term describing a device that can both transmit and receive.

Transmission The dispatching of a signal, message, or other form of intelligence by wire, radio, telegraphy, telephony, facsimile, or other means (ISO); a series of characters, messages, or blocks including control information and user data; the signaling of data over communications channels.

Transparent mode (Typically) binary synchronous communications data transmission in which the recognition of control characters is suppressed; the operation of a (usually) digital transmission facility during which the user has complete and free use of the available bandwidth and is unaware of any intermediate processing.

Transponder In satellite communications, the circuitry that receives an up-link signal, translates it to another, usually higher, frequency, amplifies it, and retransmits it as the down-link signal.

Transport layer In the OSI model, Layer 4; the network processing entity responsible, in conjunction with the underlying network, data link, and physical layers, for the end-to-end control of transmitted data and the optimized use of network resources; also serves the session layer (5).

Tree A network topology, characterized by the existence of only one route between any two network nodes; describing a network that resembles a branching tree, such as most CATV distribution networks.

Trellis coding A method of forward-error correction used in certain high-speed modems whereby each signal element (baud) is assigned a coded binary value, which represents that element's phase and amplitude; allows the receiving modem to determine — based on the value of the preceding signal elements — whether a given signal element is received in error.

Trunk A dedicated aggregate telephone circuit connecting two switching centers, central offices, or data concentration devices.

Trunk group Multiple trunk circuits between the same two switching centers that can be accessed by dialing a single trunk number and can use the same multiplexing equipment at each end.

TSO Time Sharing Option; an IBM mainframe subsystem that permits interactive terminal access to file, print, and batch job facilities.

TTY transmission Teletypewriter communications; generally, basic asynchronous ASCII-coded or Baudot-coded data communications.

Turnaround time In communications, the time, measured at either the send or receive end, required to reverse the direction of transmission, from send to receive or vice versa, over a half-duplex channel; also, the elapsed time between submission of a transaction, or job, and the return of processed output; typically, the combined time required for line propagation, modem timing, and computer processing; *see* Response time.

Twinaxial cable A shielded coaxial cable with two central conductors.

Twisted pair A pair of insulated copper conductors that are twisted around each other, mainly to cancel the effects of electrical noise; typical of standard telephone wiring; unshielded twisted pair contains no outside wraparound conductor.

Two-way alternate Synonym for half-duplex communications.

Two-way simultaneous Synonym for full-duplex communications.

Two-wire Applies to the local-loop transmission path from the customer's premises to the central-office switch of a Local Exchange Carrier (LEC); on a two-wire circuit, data is received and transmitted over the same wire loop; also applies to connections between Data Terminal Equipment (DTE) and a Private Branch Exchange (PBX).

TWX Teletypewriter exchange; a switched message service serving Canada and the United States provided by Western Union; employs ASCII-coded equipment.

U

UA User Agent (X.400/OSI); the element of an X.400 electronic mail network that is responsible for interfacing with the user.

UDP User Datagram Protocol (TCP/IP); a protocol in the TCP/IP suite of protocols that provides transport services similar to TCP, but without the overhead of error detection and correction.

Unattended mode Describing the operation of any device, such as an auto-answer modem, designed to operate without the manual intervention of an operator.

Up-link Describing the earth-station transmission and the carrier signal used to transmit information to a geosynchronous satellite; complement of down-link.

Uptime Colloquial expression for the period of time when network or computer resources are accessible and available to a user; the length of time between failures or periods of nonavailability.

V

VAN Value Added Network; a network that provides services that go beyond the pure switching function.

VAX Virtual Address eXtension; the product name assigned to Digital Equipment Corporation's line of midrange and mainframe commercial systems.

Vertical Redundancy Check (VRC) An odd-parity check performed on each character of an ASCII block as the block is received.

Video teleconferencing The real-time, and usually two-way, transmission of digitized video images between two or more locations; requires a wideband transmission facility, for which satellite communications has become a popular choice; transmitted images may be freeze-frame (where a television screen is "repainted" every few seconds) or full-motion; bandwidth requirements for two-way videoconferencing range from 56 kbit/s (freeze-frame) to T1 rates (1.544 Mbit/s).

Videotex An interactive data communications application designed to allow unsophisticated users to converse with a remote database, enter data for transactions, and retrieve textual and graphics information for display on subscriber television sets or (typically) low-cost video terminals.

Virtual circuit In packet switching, network facilities that give the appearance to the user of an actual end-to-end circuit; in contrast to a physical circuit, a dynamically variable network connection where sequential user data packets may be routed differently during the course of a "virtual connection"; virtual circuits enable transmission facilities to be shared by many users simultaneously.

Virtual private network A carrier-provided service in which the public switched network provides capabilities similar to those of private lines, such as conditioning, error testing, and higher-speed, full-duplex, four-wire transmission with a line quality adequate for data.

VM Virtual Machine; an IBM mainframe operating system frequently used in commercial mainframe environments.

VMS Virtual Management System; one of Digital Equipment Corporation's operating systems for the VAX line of computers.

Voice digitization The conversion of an analog voice into digital symbols for storage or transmission.

Voice Frequency (VF) Describing an analog signal within the range of transmitted speech, typically from 300 to 3,400 Hz; any transmission supported by an analog telecommunications circuit.

Voice-grade channel A telecommunications circuit used primarily for speech transmission but suitable for the transmission of analog or digital data or facsimile; typically supporting a frequency range of 300 to 3,400 Hz; also, voice band.

VRC *See* Vertical Redundancy Check.

VSAT Very Small Aperture Terminal; in satellite communications, small-diameter receiver stations typically operated in the ku band.

VT Virtual Terminal; an OSI upper-layer service that allows any type of terminal to access any OSI-based application.

VTAM Virtual Telecommunications Access Method; IBM mainframe communications-software product, oriented toward managing SNA/SDLC communications and links.

V-series recommendations CCITT-specified standards dealing mainly with modem operation over an interface with the telephone network, including:

V.21 300-bit/s duplex modem standardized for use in the general switched telephone network.

V.22 1.2-kbit/s duplex modem standardized for use in the general switched telephone network and on leased circuits.

V.22bis 2.4-kbit/s duplex dial-up modem standard.

V.23 600-bit/s and 1.2-kbit/s modem standardized for use in the general switched telephone network.

V.24 List of definitions for interchange circuits between data terminal equipment and data circuit-terminating equipment.

V.25 Automatic calling and/or answering equipment in the general switched telephone network, including disabling of echo suppressors on manually established calls.

V.26 2.4-kbit/s modem standardized for use on four-wire leased circuits.

V.26bis 1.2/2.4-kbit/s modem standardized for use in the general switched telephone network.

V.26ter A standard for the 2.4-kbit/s full-duplex modem that uses echo-cancellation techniques suitable for application to the public.

V.27 4.8-kbit/s modem with manual equalizer standardized for use on leased telephone-type circuits.

V.27bis 2.4/4.8-kbit/s modem with automatic equalizer standardized for use on leased telephone-type circuits.

V.27ter 2.4/4.8-kbit/s modem standardized for use in the general switched telephone network.

V.29 9.6-kbit/s modem standardized for use on point-to-point leased telephone-type circuits.

V.32 9.6-kbit/s two-wire duplex modem standard.

W

WAN Wide-Area Network; a network spanning a wide geographical area.

Wideband Generally, a communications channel offering a transmission bandwidth greater than a voice-grade channel; data transmission speeds on wideband facilities are typically in excess of 9.6 kbit/s and often at rates such as 56 kbit/s and 1.544 Mbit/s.

Window A flow-control mechanism in data communications, the size of which is equal to the number of frames, packets, or messages that can be sent from a transmitter to a receiver before any reverse acknowledgment is required; called a pacing group in IBM's SNA.

Wire center A spatial midpoint at the confluence of several cables.

Wiring closet Termination point for customer premises wiring, offering access to service personnel; generally serves a specific area, with multiple wiring closets that are cross-connected.

Working draft In ISO, the initial stage of a standards document describing the standard as envisioned by a working group of a standards committee or subcommittee.

Workstation Input/output equipment at which an operator works; a station at which a user can send data to, or receive data from, a computer or other workstation for the purpose of performing a job.

X

X The designation assigned to International Telegraph and Telephone Consultative Committee (CCITT, from the French *Comite Consultatif International Telegraphique et Telephonique*) recommendations related to data transmission over public data networks, most notably:

X.3 Packet assembly/disassembly facility in a public data network.

X.20 Interface between Data Terminal Equipment (DTE) and Data Circuit-terminating Equipment (DCE) for start/stop transmission services on public data networks.

X.20bis Used on public data networks of data terminal equipment (DTE) that is designed for interfacing to asynchronous duplex V-series modems.

X.21 Interface between data terminal equipment (DTE) and data circuit-terminating equipment (DCE) for synchronous operation on public circuit-switched data networks.

X.21bis Used on public data networks of data terminal equipment (DTE) that is designed for interfacing to synchronous V-series modems.

X.24 List of definitions for interchange circuits between data terminal equipment (DTE) and data circuit-terminating equipment (DCE) on public data networks.

X.25 A CCITT recommendation that specifies the interface between user data terminal equipment (DTE) and packet-switching data circuit-terminating equipment (DCE).

X.28 DTE/DCE interface for start/stop-mode data terminal equipment accessing the packet assembly/disassembly facility (PAD) in a public data network situated in the same country.

X.29 Procedures for the exchange of control information and user data between a packet assembly/disassembly facility (PAD) and a packet-mode DTE or another PAD.

X.32 Interface between data terminal equipment and data circuit-terminating equipment for terminals operating in the packet mode and accessing a packet-switched public data network through a public-switched telephone network or a circuit-switched public data network.

X.75 Terminal and transit call-control procedures and data-transfer mechanisms on (typically) international circuits between packet-switched data networks.

X.121 The CCITT's international numbering plan for public data networks.

X.400 A series of protocol standards for international electronic-mail interexchange.

X3 Sequence of data communications standards promulgated by the American National Standards Institute (ANSI).

X3.15 Bit sequencing of ASCII in serial-by-bit data transmission.

X3.16 Character structure and character parity sense for serial-by-bit data communications in ASCII.

X3.36 Synchronous high-speed data signaling rates between data terminal equipment and data circuit-terminating equipment.

X3.79 Determination of the performance of data communications devices that use bit-oriented control procedures.

X3.92 Data encryption algorithm.

XI X.25 SNA Interconnection (IBM/SNA). A software package for IBM 37XX communications controller that allows any system, IBM or not, using X.25 to pass through a SNA network for communications with another system using X.25.

XID eXchange IDentification (IBM/SNA); an SNA link command used to verify the identity of two systems when they first establish communication with one another.

XNS Xerox Network Systems; local-area network protocol suite operating at ISO Network and Transport layers.

X-off/X-on Transmitter off/transmitter on; a commonly used peripheral-device flow-control protocol, used extensively for modem control by an attached terminal or processor.

XRF eXtended Recovery Facility. Software for IBM mainframes running under the MVS operating system. XRF allows automatic switch-over of the network and on-line applications from one mainframe to another.

Z

ZBTSI Zero Byte Time Slot Interchange; a technique used with the T-carrier Extended Superframe Format (ESF) in which an area in the ESF frame carries information about the location of all-zero bytes (eight consecutive zeroes) within the data stream.

Zero code suppression The insertion of a "one" bit to prevent the transmission of eight or more consecutive "zero" bits; used primarily with T1 and related digital telephone company facilities, which require a minimum "ones density" in order to keep the individual subchannels of a multiplexed, high-speed facility active; several different schemes are currently employed and are being evaluated to accomplish this; *see also* Bit stuffing, Ones density.

Index

3174 controllers, 70, 88
3270 terminals, 62, 70
    API, 88
    BSC operations, 87
    emulation, 87, 88
    keyboard modification, 91
    See also Terminals
3274 controllers, 70, 88
3477 display terminal, 69
3780 RJE workstations, 90
5250 terminals, 62, 69–70
    model line, 69
    remote connections for, 70
    See also Terminals
5494 controllers, 70
6611 routers, 55–56

A

Access Units (AUs), 99
Address Resolution Protocol (ARP), 115
Advanced Peer-to-Peer Network. *See* APPN
Advanced Program-to-Program Communications (APPC), 46
AIX AS/400 Connection Program/6000, 118–119
AIX SNA Services/6000, 119
Analog transmission, 5–7
Andrew Corporation, 120
AnyNet, 117–118
Apertus software products, 124
Application layer (OSI), 31, 33–34, 106, 108
Application program Interface (APIs)
    3270, 88
    level 7, 35
Applications
    asynchronous, 136–137
    host session functions, 88
    Internet, 117
    LU 6. interaction via, 43
    synchronization of, 135–137
    TCP/IP functions, 116–117
APPN, 46–49
    advantages of, 51
    communications in, 77–85
    communications software, 65
    connection services, 49
    defined, 47
    directory services, 49
    ease-of-use of, 52
    electronic mail distribution, 85
    End Node (EN), 48, 77
    functions
        DDM, 79
        DRDA, 80
        DSPT, 77–78
        FTS, 80
        ICF, 80–84
        list of, 77
        SNADS/ODF, 84
    future direction, 52–57
    hierarchical SNA vs., 53
    illustrated, 48
    Low-Entry Network Node (LEN), 48–49, 77
    Network Node (NN), 48, 77
    PU 2.1 vs., 51
    remote commands, 77
    routing services, 49–50
    SNA relationships, 51–52
APPN networks
    AS/400 end users in, 77
    device definitions and, 128
    interconnected with SNA network, 65
    navigation in, 77
    network definitions for, 133
    planning, 65
    with two end nodes/one network node, 132
    See also APPN; Network(s)
AS/400
    AnyNet, 117–118
    banking terminal support, 71–72
    CICS on, 89
    communications
        capabilities, 60
        function implementation, 61
        software, 59–61
    Communications Utilities product, 85
    DEC connection
        DEC tools, 123
        IBM tools, 123

third-party solutions, 124–125
in DECnet network, 67
distributed, 64
as host and server, 62, 69–75
as host in small-to medium-sized bank, 72
host sessions application functions, 88
in large/mixed SNA network, 63
to mainframe connection, 87
in medium-sized networks, 62–63
network entities, 127–134
networking roles, 59–67
in OSI network, 65–66
OSI product support, 96–97
peer-to-peer network, 63
POS terminal support, 71
RS/6000 communications, 118–120
TCP/IP implementation on, 66, 115–117
X.25-PC DOS connection, 74–75
ASCII terminals, 62, 70
    ASCII controller and, 62
    support for, 70
Asynchronous communications, 136–137
Asynchronous Transfer Mode (ATM), 53
Asynchronous transmission, 14, 135
Autodial, 6

B

Banking Monitor, 91
Banking terminal support, 71–72
Bell 801 ACU, 6
Bridge MVS/VM function, 90–91
Broadband ISDN (B-ISDN), 53–54
BSC line protocol, 18–19
    3270, 87
    use of, 19
    See also Line protocols
Bus network, 4, 5

C

Call-back devices, 11
Carrier sense multiple-access with collision
   detection (CSMA/CD), 26
Checksum method, 15
Class of Service (COS), 130
    defined, 127
    definition, 130
    See also APPN networks
Client Access for OS/400 (CA/400), 72–74
    flexibility, 73–74
    user functions, 73

Cluster controllers, 10
Codecs (coder-decoders), 9
Commands
    CHGNETA, 132, 133
    CRTCOSD, 130
    CRTCTL, 129
    CRTCTLAPPC, 131, 133
    CRTDEV, 129
    CRTDEVAPPC, 132
    CRTLIN, 128
    CRTLINASC, 128
    CRTLINSDLC, 128, 131, 133
    CRTMODD, 129
Common Programming Interface-
   Communications (CPI-C), 54
Communications
    in APPN, 77–85
    AS/400-RS/6000, 118–120
    asynchronous, 136
    software, 59–61
Communications Utilities product, 85, 90
Composite Network Node (CNN), 56–57
    APPN network integration, 57
    defined, 56
"Connectionless" transfer mode, 113
Controllers
    3174, 70, 88
    3274, 70, 88
    4704, 71
    4720, 71
    5394, 70
    ASCII, 62
    cluster, 10
    defined, 127
    definitions of, 128, 129
    front-end, 10
Copper Distributed Data Interface (CDDI), 27
Customer Information Control System (CICS), 89
Cyclic Redundancy Check (CRC), 15

D

Data Communications Equipment (DCE), 1–2
Data Service Unit (DSU), 2
Data Switching Equipment (DSE), 10
Data Terminal Equipment (DTE), 1–2
Data-link control layer (OSI), 33, 34, 107, 108
DDM facility, 46
DECnet, 121–123
    architectural characteristics, 122
    networks, AS/400 in, 67

Device definitions, 127, 129
Digital Equipment Corporation (DEC), 121
    AS/400 connection
        DEC tools, 123
        IBM tools, 123
        third-party solutions, 124–125
    DNA, 121–122
    VTXXX terminals, 123
    See also DECnet
Digital Network Architecture (DNA), 121–122
    defined, 121
    goals, 121–122
    See also DECnet
Digital transmission, 8–9
Display Station Pass-Through (DSPT), 46, 77–78
    defined, 77
    illustrated pass-through environment, 78
    target system, 78
Distributed Computing Environment (DCE), 117
Distributed Data Management (DDM), 79
    defined, 79
    illustrated environment, 79
    SNA networks and, 89
    uses, 79
Distributed Relational Database Architecture (DRDA), 80

E

EHLLC protocol, 21
Electrical and Electronics Engineers (IEEE), 23
Electronic Data Interchange (EDI), 95
    implementations, 101
    standards, 101
Electronic Industries Association (EIA), 23
Electronic mail distribution, 85
Electronic messaging systems, 97–98
End Node (EN), 48, 77
    routing and, 49
    See also APPN
Ethernet LANs, 26

F

Fax services, 75
FDDI LANs, 26, 27
File System I/O Processor (FSIOP), 74
File transfer, 125–126
File Transfer Protocol (FTP), 116
File Transfer Support (FTS), 80
Forest Computer, 119, 124
Frame Check Sequence (FCS), 15, 30

Front-end controllers, 10
FTAM standard, 34, 35, 96
Full-duplex, 3

G

Gateways, 113
    Forest Computer, 124
    OpenConnect System, 124

H

Half-duplex, 3
Hayes "smart modem" call procedure, 6
HDLC line protocol, 37
Hierarchical structure, 29–30
High-Level Data Link Control. *See* HDLC line protocol
Host and server (AS400), 62, 69–75
    3270 terminals, 70
    5250 terminals and printers, 69–70
    ASCII terminals, 70
    banking terminal support, 71–72
    fax services, 75
    PC workstations, 72–74
    POS terminal support, 71
    services, 69
    See also AS/400
Host Command Facility/DHCF (HCF/DHCF), 91–92
    defined, 91
    uses, 92

I

IBM
    network interfaces, 54–55
    OSI products, 96–97
    protocol strategy, 55
    See also AS/400
IDEAssociates, 124
IDLC protocol, 21
IEEE 803 protocols, 34
Integrated Services Digital Network. *See* ISDN
International Standards Organization (ISO), 29
    hierarchical structure, 29–30
    modularity, 30
    symmetry, 29
International Telegraph and Telephone Consultative Committee (CCITT), 23, 33
Internet applications, 117
Internet Protocol (IP), 112–113
    function of, 113

See also TCP/IP
Interpel, 126
Intersystem Communications Function (ICF), 80–84
    APPN functions, 81
    defined, 80
    ICFFILE file, 80
    interactions, operations in source system, 82
    interactions, operations in target system, 83
    process steps, 81–83
    program interface through, 84
    SNA networks and, 89
ISDN, 24
    Broadband (B-ISDN), 53–54
    defined, 24

L

LAN Asynchronous Communications Support (LANACS), 123
LANs
    Ethernet, 26
    FDDI, 26, 27
    Token-Ring, 26
    wireless, 26–27
    See also Network(s)
Leased lines, 6–7
Line
    adapters, 2
    definition, 127, 128–129
    point-to-point, 2
    speeds, 9–10
    See also Line protocols
Line Print Remote/Line Print Daemon (LPR/LPD), 116
Line protocols, 18–19
    asynchronous transmission and, 14
    BSC, 18–19
    general objectives of, 13
    HDLC, 37
    SDLC, 19–22
    stop/start-oriented, 15
    summary of, 19
    synchronous transmission and, 14–15
    See also Protocols
Link Access Procedure B (LAPB), 19
Link Access Procedure D (LAPD), 19
Link Access Procedure (LAP), 19
Link Access Procedure X (LAPX), 19
Logical Link Control (LLC), 19
Logical Units (LUs), 41–43

    defined, 41
    dialogue functions, 41
    LU 2, 41
    LU 3, 41–42
    LU 6, 42
    LU 6.2. *See* LU 6.2
    LU 7, 42
    services, 41
    servicing two end users in session, 42
    support of, 42
    See also SNA
Low-Entry Network Node (LEN), 48–49, 77
    routing and, 49
    See also APPN
LU 6.2, 42–43, 46
    application interaction via, 43
    defined, 46
    session activation, 42
    supported by control point component, 46
    using, 42
    See also Logical Units (LUs); PU 2.1

M

Master-slave relationships
    defined, 16
    SDLC for, 19
Mesh networks, 4, 5
    illustrated, 39
    See also Network(s)
Message Queue Interface (MQI), 54–55, 123
Message Transfer Agent (MTA), 99
    defined, 99
    See also User Agent (UA); X.400 standard
Modems, 7–8
    internal clock, 8
    modulation, 7
    switched mode and, 6
    wave forms and, 7–8
Modes, 130
    defined, 127
    definitions of, 129
    See also APPN networks
Modularity, 30
Multiplexers, 10
Multiprotocol network, 105
Multivendor support, 53–54

N

NetView/Distribution Manager-Distributed System Node Executive (N/DM-DSNX), 90, 92–93

defined, 93
  at host level, 93
  uses, 93
Network Data Mover (NDM), 125–126
  file transfers with, 126
  support, 126
Network entities, 127–134
  Class of Service (COS), 127, 130
  controller, 127, 129
  creating, 128–130
  definitions, 128–130
    for APPN network, 133
    examples of, 130–134
    for two systems not using APPN, 131
  device, 127, 129
  line, 127, 128–129
  modes, 127, 129
  See also Network(s)
Network File System (NFS), 117
Network layer (OSI), 34, 107, 108
Network management (SNA), 93
Network Nodes (NNs), 10, 48, 77
  Composite (CNNs), 56–57
  extension to mainframe environment, 52
  NN1, 59
  PU 2.1 as, 52
  search task, 50
  topology database, 49
  weight assignment, 50
  See also APPN
Network(s)
  APPN, 65, 77, 128, 132–133
  bus, 5
  call-back devices, 11
  cluster controllers, 10
  components, 1–3
  compression equipment, 11
  data enciphering equipment, 11
  DECnet, 67, 121–123
  defined, 1
  DSE, 10
  front-end controllers, 10
  full-duplex, 3
  half-duplex, 3
  illustrated, 2
  interfaces, 23, 54–55
  master and, 3
  medium-sized, 62–63
  mesh, 4, 5
  multidomain, 39

multiplexers, 10
multiprotocol, 105
multivendor, 109
OSI, 65–66, 95–109
peer-to-peer, 63
private, 25–26
public, 23–25
ring, 4, 5
roles, 59–67
simplex, 3
single-domain, 39
slave and, 3
SNA, 87–93
star, 4–5
switched mode transmission, 6
TCP/IP, 66, 111–120
topology, 3–5
transmission flow, 3
tree, 4
two computer, 1, 2
types, 23–27
See also LANs; Network entities

O

Office Facsimile Application (OFA), 75
OfficeVision/400, 98
Open Software Foundation (OSF), 66
Open Systems Interconnection (OSI) standards.
  See OSI; OSI model; OSI products
OpenConnect Systems, 119
  gateway functions, 119
  gateways, 124
OSI, 95–109
  advantages, 101
  AS/400 in, 65–66
  future of, 109
  SNA vs., 37, 105–108
  software, 101
  solution for SNA-DSA network interaction, 102
  virtual terminal concept, 103
OSI Message Service/400, 101
OSI model, 30–35
  AS/400 support, 66
  characteristics, 30–31
  functions, 96
  future of, 35
  HDLC, 37
  illustrated, 31
  layers, 32–35
    application, 31, 33–34, 106, 108

data-link control, 33, 34, 107, 108
   illustrated, 31, 32
   network, 34, 107, 108
   physical, 34, 107
   presentation, 33, 34, 106, 108
   session, 33, 34, 106, 108
   standards, 34–35
   summary, 34
   transport, 32–33, 34, 107, 108
measuring, 35
messages, 31
standards, 34–35
translation of, 35
   See also OSI; SNA
OSI products, 96–97
   OSICS, 96
   OSIFS, 96
   OSIMS, 97

P

Parity checking, 15
PC DOS connection, 74–75
PC Support, 72
Peer relationship, 15
Peer-to-peer networks, 63
Physical Units (PUs)
   remote system with multiple users, 43
   type 1 (PU 1), 40
   type 2 (PU 2), 40–41
   type 4 (PU 4), 40
   type 5 (PU 5), 38, 40
   See also PU 2.1; SNA
Point-of-sale (POS) terminal support, 71
Point-to-point lines, 2
Polling
   defined, 16
   illustrated, 17
   pace of, 17
Presentation layer (OSI), 33, 34, 106, 108
Printers, support for, 69
Private networks, 25–26
   direct connections, 25–26
   LAN links, 26
   twinaxial links, 25
   See also Network(s)
Protocols
   conversion, 104
   defined, 2
   levels of, 2
   line, 13–15, 18–22

   peer-to-peer, 16
   X.400, 100
PU 2.1
   APPN vs., 51
   configurations, 46–47
   control point and, 45
   defined, 45
   as NN of APPN, 52
   structure elements, 45
   See also LU 6.2; Physical Units (PUs)
Public networks, 23–25
   defined, 23
   ISDN and, 24
   X.25, 24
   See also Network(s)

Q

QLLC protocol, 21

R

Remote commands (APPN), 77
Remote Job Entry (RJE), 90
Remote Logical Unit of Work (Remote LUW), 80
Remote procedure Call (RPC), 54
Reverse ARP (RARP), 115
Ring network, 4, 5
RS/6000
   AS/400 communications, 118–120
   software products, 118–119

S

SDLC line protocol, 19–22
   defined, 19, 37
   frame structure, 20
   for master-slave relationships, 19
   transmission sequences, 20–21
   variations, 21
   See also Line protocols
Session layer (OSI), 33, 34, 106, 108
Shielded Distributed Data Interface (SDDI), 27
Simple Mail Transfer Protocol (SMTP), 116
Simple Network Management Protocol (SNMP), 116
Simplex, 3
SNA, 37–43
   APPN relationships, 51–52
   AS/400 implementation of, 61
   backbone function, 54
   characteristics, 51–52
   data flow control, 106

data link control, 107
development phases, 39
future direction, 52–57
hierarchical vs. APPN, 53
large, 63–65
layers, 37
LUs, 41–43
mixed, 63–65
multidomain, 56
OSI vs., 37, 105–108
path control, 107
physical interface, 107
presentation services, 106
PUs, 38, 40–41
SDLC. *See* SDLC line protocol
session, 41
structure, 37
TCP/IP vs., 115
transaction, 106
transaction control, 107
VTAM functions, 38–41
See also OSI model
SNA Distribution Services/Object Distribution Facility (SNADS/ODF), 84, 98
   defined, 84
   uses, 84
SNA networks, 87–93
   access, 41
   APPN networks interconnected with, 65
   AS/400 in, 63–65
   Banking Monitor, 91
   Bridge MS/VM function and, 90–91
   centralized host-based, 64
   CICS and, 89
   communications between programs, 89
   DDM and, 89
   HCF/DHCF and, 91–92
   ICF and, 89
   N/DM-DSNX and, 92–93
   network management, 93
   Physical Units (PUs) and, 40
   RJE and, 90
   VTAM and, 87
   See also Network(s); SNA
SNA-DSA network interaction
   asymmetrical solution for, 103
   gateway solution for, 103
   OSI solution for, 102
Sockets, 116
Spazio, 126

Star network, 4–5
Switched mode, 6
Symmetry, 29
Synchronous applications, 135–137
Synchronous transmission, 14–15, 135
   bit-oriented, 15
   byte-oriented, 14
   defined, 14
   See also Transmission
System Network Application Distribution Services (SNADS), 51
System Services Control Point (SSCP). *See* VTAM
Systems Application Architecture (SAA), 46
Systems Network Architecture. *See* SNA

T

TCP/IP, 111–120
   address format, 113
   addresses, 114–115
   application functions, 116–117
   AS/400 implementation, 115–117
   "connectionless" mode, 113
   core functions, 66
   defined, 111
   error handling, 113
   frame headers, 114
   frames, transporting/routing with, 55
   functions, 111–112
   gateways, 113
   hosts, 111, 114
   importance of, 111
   Internet Protocol (IP), 112
   for multivendor networking, 109
   SNA vs., 115
   stack usage, 55
   structure, 112
   support, 53
   Transmission Control Protocol (TCP), 112
   User Datagram Protocol (UDP), 112, 114
TCP/IP networks
   AS/400 in, 66
   illustrated, 112
   interoperability, 66
   See also Network(s); TCP/IP
TDLC protocol, 21
TELNET, 116
Terminals
   3270, 62, 70
   3477, 69
   5250, 62, 69–70

ASCII, 62, 70
banking support, 71–72
DEC VTXXX, 123
point-of-sale (POS) support, 71
WORKSTATION files for, 69
Time Division Multiplexers (TDM), 104
Token-Ring LANs, 26
Topologies, 3–5
   bus, 4, 5
   defined, 3
   illustrated, 4
   mesh, 4, 5
   ring, 4, 5
   star, 4–5
   tree, 4
   See also Networks
Transmission
   analog, 5–7
   asynchronous, 14
   blocks, managing, 18
   characteristics, 7
   digital, 8–9
   errors, controlling, 15
   leased lines and, 6–7
   message, illustrated, 14
   performance, 9
   speed, 9–10
   switched mode, 6
   synchronous, 14–15
   techniques, 13–15
   turnarounds, 17
Transmission Control Protocol (TCP), 112
   error handling, 113
   functions, 113
   See also TCP/IP
Transport layer (OSI), 32–33, 34, 107, 108
Tree network, 4

U

User Agent (UA), 99
   defined, 99
   See also Message Transfer Agent (MTA); X.400 standard
User Datagram Protocol (UDP), 112, 114
   functions, 114
   See also TCP/IP

V

VTAM, 38–41
   component support, 38
   functions, 38
   output mode, 40
   PU 5, 38
   SNA networks and, 87

W

Wave forms, 7–8
Wingra Technologies, 124
Wireless LANs, 26–27
WORKSTATION files, 69

X

X.25
   AS/400-PC DOS connection and, 74–75
   links, 66
   packet switching, 24, 96
   software, 96
X.121 standard, 100
X.400 standard, 34, 35, 96, 98–99
   defined, 98
   e-mail software, 98
   illustrated, 97
   main entities, 99
   message, sending, 99–100
   message handling system, 97
   Message Transfer Agent (MTA), 99
   P1, 100
   P2, 100
   P3, 100
   P7, 100
   probes and, 100
   protocols, 100
   store-and-forward technique, 98
   summary, 101
   User Agent (UA), 99
   versions of, 98–99
X.500 standard, 34, 100–101
   defined, 34, 100
   using, 100
XCOM 6.2, 125–126
   file transfers with, 126
   support, 126

VISIT OUR WEB SITE AT **WWW.DUKEPRESS.COM** FOR A MORE DETAILED LISTING OF ALL DUKE PRESS BOOKS

New Books in the Duke Press Library

BUILDING AS/400 CLIENT/SERVER APPLICATIONS
Put ODBC and Client Access APIs to Work
By Mike Otey
Mike Otey gives you the why, what, and how-to of AS/400 client/server computing, which matches the strengths of the AS/400 with the PC GUIs that users want. Mike covers APPC and TCP/IP communications, as well as the underlying architectures for each of the major AS/400 client/server APIs. CD with complete source code for several working applications included. 505 pages.

CONTROL LANGUAGE PROGRAMMING FOR THE AS/400, SECOND EDITION
By Bryan Meyers and Dan Riehl, NEWS/400 *technical editors*
This comprehensive CL programming textbook offers students up-to-the-minute knowledge of the skills they will need in today's MIS environment. Chapters progress methodically from CL basics to more complex processes and concepts, guiding students toward a professional grasp of CL programming techniques and style. 522 pages.

DATA WAREHOUSING AND THE AS/400
By Scott Steinacher
Scott Steinacher takes an in-depth look at data-warehousing components, concepts, and terminology. After laying this foundation, Scott presents a compelling case for implementing a data warehouse on the AS/400. Included on an accompanying CD are demos of AS/400 data-warehousing software from several independent software vendors. 342 pages.

DEVELOPING YOUR AS/400 INTERNET STRATEGY
By Alan Arnold
This book addresses the issues unique to deploying your AS/400 on the Internet. It includes procedures for configuring AS/400 TCP/IP and information about which client and server technologies the AS/400 supports natively. This enterprise-class tutorial evaluates the AS/400 as an Internet server and teaches you how to design, program, and manage your Web home page. 248 pages.

INSIDE THE AS/400, SECOND EDITION
Featuring the AS/400e series
By Frank G. Soltis
Learn from the architect of the AS/400 about the new generation of AS/400e systems and servers, and about the latest system features and capabilities introduced in Version 4 of OS/400. Dr. Frank Soltis demystifies the system, shedding light on how it came to be, how it can do the things it does, and what its future may hold. 402 pages.

THE ADMINISTRATOR'S GUIDE TO MICROSOFT SQL SERVER 6.5
By Kevin Cox and William Jones
This book guides database managers and administrators into a thorough understanding of the client/server aspects of the SQL Server 6.5 product, and includes many useful tips for managing security, troubleshooting, and improving performance. 469 pages.

THE MICROSOFT OUTLOOK E-MAIL AND FAX GUIDE
By Sue Mosher
Here's a book for Microsoft Outlook 97 end users and the administrators who support them. This easy to read volume will expand your knowledge of Outlook's e-mail functions and explain the real world tasks that you are likely to encounter. Users at all levels will learn from this comprehensive introduction to Microsoft's next generation of messaging software. 500 pages

RAPID REVIEW STUDY GUIDES

Series Editor: Mike Pastore

Seeking the MCSE certification isn't a goal for the faint of heart. Our *Rapid Review Study Guides* give you pre- and post-assessments to measure your progress, exam preparation tips, an overview of exam material, vocabulary drills, hands-on activities, and sample quiz questions on CD and in the book. Current titles include

WINDOWS 95

WINDOWS NT 4.0 WORKSTATION

NETWORKING ESSENTIALS

TCP/IP FOR MICROSOFT WINDOWS NT 4.0

Also Published by Duke Press

CLIENT ACCESS TOKEN-RING CONNECTIVITY
By Chris Patterson

Client Access Token-Ring Connectivity details all that is required to successfully maintain and troubleshoot a Token-Ring network. 122 pages.

THE ESSENTIAL GUIDE TO CLIENT ACCESS FOR DOS EXTENDED
By John Enck, Robert E. Anderson, and Michael Otey

The Essential Guide to Client Access for DOS Extended contains key insights and need-to-know technical information about Client Access for DOS Extended, IBM's strategic AS/400 product for DOS and Windows client/server connectivity. Written by industry experts based on their personal and professional experiences with Client Access, this book can help you avoid time-consuming pitfalls that litter the path of AS/400 client/ server computing. 447 pages.

THE MICROSOFT EXCHANGE SERVER INTERNET MAIL CONNECTOR
By Spyros Sakellariadis

Achieve Internet connectivity using Exchange Server 4.0 and 5.0. This book presents four Internet connectivity models, shows how to set up the Internet Mail Connector with an Internet Service Provider, and illustrates how to monitor Internet traffic. It also includes troubleshooting and reference guides. 234 pages.

POWERING YOUR WEB SITE WITH WINDOWS NT SERVER
By Nik Simpson

Powering Your Web Site with Windows NT Server explores the tools necessary to establish a presence on the Internet or on an intranet using Web technology and Windows NT Server. The author helps readers navigate the process of creating a new information infrastructure, from the basics of justifying the decision through the implementation cycle. 640 pages. CD included.

USING VISUAL BASIC WITH CLIENT ACCESS APIs
By Ron Jones

This book is for programmers who want to develop client/server solutions on the AS/400 and the personal computer. It provides a thorough overview of the principles and requirements for programming in Windows using VB. Companion diskettes contain source code for all the book's programming projects as well as for numerous other utilities and programs. All the projects are compatible with Windows 95 and VB 4.0. 654 pages.

FOR A COMPLETE CATALOG OR TO PLACE AN ORDER, CONTACT

Duke Press
Duke Communications International
221 E. 29th Street • Loveland, CO 80538-2727
(800) 621-1544 • (970) 663-4700 • Fax: (970) 203-2756